Mac OS® X Panther™

QuickSteps

Mac OS® X Panther™
QuickSteps

GUY HART-DAVIS

McGraw-Hill/Osborne

New York Chicago San Francisco
Lisbon London Madrid Mexico City
Milan New Delhi San Juan
Seoul Singapore Sydney Toronto

McGraw-Hill/Osborne

2100 Powell Street, 10th Floor
Emeryville, California 94608
U.S.A.

To arrange bulk purchase discounts for sales promotions, premiums, or fund-raisers, please contact McGraw-Hill/Osborne at the above address. For information on translations or book distributors outside the U.S.A., please see the International Contact Information page inside the back cover of this book.

This book was composed with Adobe® InDesign

MAC OS® X PANTHER™ QUICKSTEPS

234567890 WCK WCK 0198765

ISBN 0-07-225505-6

PUBLISHER / Brandon A. Nordin

VICE PRESIDENT & ASSOCIATE PUBLISHER / Scott Rogers

ACQUISITIONS EDITOR / Roger Stewart

ACQUISITIONS COORDINATOR / Agatha Kim

TECHNICAL EDITOR / Marty Matthews

COPY EDITOR / Chara Curtis

PROOFREADER / Lisa McCoy

INDEXER / Kellen Diamanti

LAYOUT ARTIST / Bailey Cunningham

ILLUSTRATORS / Kathleen Edwards, Pattie Lee, Bruce Hopkins

SERIES DESIGN / Bailey Cunningham

COVER DESIGN / Pattie Lee

To Rhonda and Teddy

About the Author

Guy Hart-Davis:

Guy is the author of *How to Do Everything with iLife '04*, *How to Do Everything with Your iPod & iPod mini*, *Mac OS X and Office v.X Keyboard Shortcuts*, *Adobe Creative Suite Keyboard Shortcuts*, and thirty other computer books.

Contents at a Glance

Contents

1

2

Acknowledgments

My thanks go to the following people, who put in a huge amount of work on this book:

Marty Matthews, series editor and technical editor, developed the book, checked it for technical accuracy, and made countless suggestions for improvements throughout.

Chara Curtis, editor, edited the book deftly and with good humor.

Bailey Cunningham, series designer and layout artist, laid out the book with great skill, turning the raw manuscript and graphics into a highly polished book.

Lisa McCoy, proofreader, caught widely varied inconsistencies and suggested improvements to the text.

Roger Stewart, Editorial Director at Osborne, helped create the series and pulled strings in the background throughout the process.

Introduction

QuickSteps books are recipe books for computer users. They answer the question "How do I...?" by providing quick sets of steps to accomplish the most common tasks in a particular operating system or application.

The sets of steps are the central focus of the book. QuickSteps sidebars show how to quickly perform many small functions or tasks that support primary functions. Notes, Tips, and Cautions augment the steps, presented in a separate column so as not to interrupt the flow of the steps. Introductions are minimal rather than narrative, and numerous illustrations and figures, many with callouts, support the steps.

QuickSteps books are organized by function and the tasks needed to perform that function. Each function is a chapter. Each task, or "How To," contains the steps needed for accomplishing the function with the relevant Notes, Tips, Cautions, and screenshots. You can easily find the tasks you need through:

- The Table of Contents, which lists the functional areas (chapters) and tasks in the order they are presented

- A How To list of tasks on the opening page of each chapter

- The index, which provides an alphabetical list of the terms that are used to describe the functions and tasks

- Color-coded tabs for each chapter or functional area with an index to the tabs in the Contents at a Glance (just before the Table of Contents)

Conventions Used in this Book

Mac OS X Panther QuickSteps uses several conventions designed to make the book easier for you to follow. Among these are

- A ⊙ in the table of contents and in the How To list in each chapter references a QuickSteps sidebar in a chapter.

- The symbol represents the Apple menu at the left end of the menu bar. The ⌘ symbol represents the Command key on the keyboard.

- **Bold type** is used for words or objects on the screen that you are to do something with—for example, open the menu and click **System Preferences**.

- *Italic type* is used for a word or phrase that is being defined or otherwise deserves special emphasis.

- <u>Underlined type</u> is used for text that you are to type from the keyboard.

- **BOLD SMALL CAPITAL LETTERS** are used for keys on the keyboard such as **RETURN** and **SHIFT**.

- When you are expected to enter a command, you are told to press the key(s). If you are to enter text or numbers, you are told to type them.

How to...

Chapter 1
Stepping into Mac OS X

Mac OS X is an *operating system*. Operating systems perform *the* central role in managing what a computer does and how it is done. An operating system provides the interface between you and the computer hardware: it lets you store a file, print a document, connect to the Internet, or transfer information over a local area network without knowing anything about how the hardware works.

This chapter explains how to start Mac OS X and how to log on; how to use its screens, windows, menus, and dialog boxes; how to shut it down, and how to get help.

Start Mac OS X

To start Mac OS X, turn on your Mac by pressing the Power button. Sometimes that is all you need to do. If, when you turn on your Mac, you get a screen similar to Figure 1-1, then you have started Mac OS X. You may also need to log on, as explained later in this chapter.

NOTE

The desktop on your Mac may look different from the one shown in Figure 1-1. As you'll see later in this book, you can configure many aspects of the desktop to give it the look and the functionality you need.

Register Mac OS X and Perform Initial Setup

If you buy a new Mac with Mac OS X already installed, or if you upgrade to Mac OS X from an older version of Mac OS, you will need to register your copy of Mac OS X. The registration process requires a name, address, phone number, occupation, and a description of where you will primarily use this Mac (for example, at home); it also requests your e-mail address (if you have one).

The registration process helps you create an Apple ID if you want one, but you can easily create one later if you prefer.

If you don't want to receive Apple news, software updates, special offers, and information, be sure to select the **No** option button on the A Few More Questions screen of the registration process before clicking **Continue**.

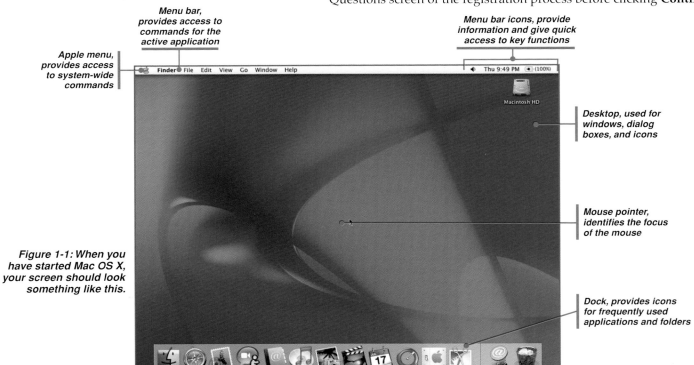

Menu bar, provides access to commands for the active application

Menu bar icons, provide information and give quick access to key functions

Apple menu, provides access to system-wide commands

Desktop, used for windows, dialog boxes, and icons

Mouse pointer, identifies the focus of the mouse

Figure 1-1: When you have started Mac OS X, your screen should look something like this.

Dock, provides icons for frequently used applications and folders

SET UP YOUR USER ACCOUNT

If you've bought a new Mac or installed a fresh copy of Mac OS X (rather than migrating an existing installation to Mac OS X), you must also create your user account:

1. Type your name in the Name box in your preferred format—for example, <u>Chris Smith</u>.

2. Mac OS X enters a default version of what you typed in the Short Name box. This "short name" uses only lowercase letters and no spaces or punctuation: for example, chrissmith. Change the name to a lowercase short name you want to use: for example, <u>chris</u>.

3. Type a password in the Password box and the Verify box. It appears as dots rather than as the letters you typed.

4. If you want, type a reminder for the password in the Password Hint box.

5. Scroll the **Your Picture** list to find an icon you like, and click it.

6. Click **Continue**. Mac OS X creates your account.

SET UP YOUR INTERNET CONNECTION

After you create your user account, Mac OS X displays the Get Internet Ready screen. Choose the option button that describes how your Mac will connect to the Internet—for example, I'll Use My Existing Internet Service, or I'm Not Ready To Connect To The Internet. Click **Continue**, and follow through the resulting screens.

If you chose I'll Use My Existing Internet Service, specify how to connect on the How Do You Connect? screen and the Your Internet Connection screen. On the Get .Mac screen, choose whether to create a trial membership with Apple's .Mac online service, use your existing .Mac membership on this Mac, or set up a .Mac membership later.

Mac OS X then connects to the Internet (if you specified a means of connection) and sends your registration information.

NOTE

If you don't want to use a password, leave the Password box and the Verify box blank. Anybody who can access your Mac will then be able to log on using your user account without entering a password.

SET UP MAIL

After registration, Mac OS X displays the Set Up Mail screen, on which you can quickly set up an account with the Mac OS X e-mail application, which is simply called Mail. If you have an e-mail account and know its details, this screen is an easy way to enter the information. You'll need to know the following:

- Your e-mail address (for example, csmith6446@example.com)
- Your account name with the e-mail provider (for example, csmith)
- Your password
- The incoming mail server's name (for example, pop3.example.com) and its type (POP or IMAP)
- The outgoing mail server's name (for example, smtp.example.com)

If you don't know this information, leave this screen blank. You can set up an account later. See "Establish an E-mail Account" in Chapter 4.

SELECT YOUR TIME ZONE

On the Select Time Zone screen, specify your time zone by choosing the nearest major city, either by clicking where that city is on the map or by selecting that city in the Closest City drop-down list box.

On the Thank You screen, click the **Go** button to start using Mac OS X.

Log On to Mac OS X

If, when you start Mac OS X, you see the Mac OS X screen displayed in Figure 1-2, click your name, enter your password if prompted for it (as shown here), and click **Log In**.

TIP

For security, it's a good idea to create a separate user account for each person who will use a particular Mac and to assign a password to each user account. That way, each user can have his or her preferred settings. Also, when you use separate accounts for users, Mac OS X's security features help you to keep each user's files secure from all other users, allowing each user privacy and preventing damage to other user's files (accidentally or otherwise). If you want to share files with other users, Mac OS X enables you to do that easily too.

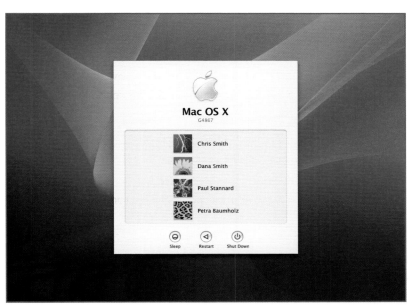

Figure 1-2: If Mac OS X displays this login screen, click your user name. If Mac OS X prompts you for your password, type it and click Log In.

If you see the screen displayed in Figure 1-3, which doesn't list user names, type your user name and password, and click **Log In**. Mac OS X will open. If a systems administrator installed your Mac, he or she should have given you your user name and password. If you installed your Mac, you will have created the user name and set the password (if there is one). See "Control Who Is a User" in Chapter 8 for instructions on setting up users.

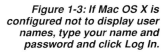

NOTE

There are two usual reasons for configuring Mac OS X to display the login screen that doesn't list user names: security and convenience. Having each user demonstrate that they know a login name and password, rather than attempting to guess the password of a user name that's displayed, increases security. Second, having to navigate a long list of users on the login screen can be even less convenient than typing your user name.

Figure 1-3: If Mac OS X is configured not to display user names, type your name and password and click Log In.

NOTE

In some cases, the entire mouse is its single button, and you press the mouse itself to activate this button.

NOTE

Apple uses both "control" and "ctrl" on desktop keyboards and uses "ctrl" on PowerBook and iBook keyboards, all for the **CONTROL** key. This book uses **CONTROL** to represent that key.

Use the Mouse in Mac OS X

A *mouse* is any pointing device—including trackballs, pointing sticks, and graphic tablets—with one or more buttons. This book assumes you'll be using a standard Apple mouse, which has only one button, or the touchpad on a PowerBook or iBook. However, you may have chosen to add a mouse with two or more buttons to make right-clicking easier.

Moving the mouse moves the pointer on the screen. You *select* an object on the screen by moving the pointer so that it is on top of the object and then pressing the button on the mouse. (If your mouse has two buttons, press the left button.)

If your mouse has two buttons, press the left button to click. Press the right button to right-click. You can use either your left or right hand to control the mouse. (To control a trackpad, you can use either hand or even both hands together.)

If your mouse has only one button, hold down **CONTROL** and click to right-click.

Use the Screen

The Mac OS X screen can hold windows and other objects. In its simplest form, shown in Figure 1-1, you see a background scene, a menu bar at the top, a bar containing icons at the bottom, and an icon for the hard disk from which your Mac starts. You may also see icons for your Mac's CD drive (or DVD drive) and any network drives that your Mac is connected to.

The parts of the screen are: the *desktop*, which takes most of the screen; the *menu bar* across the top; the *Dock* across the bottom; *desktop icons*, which can be anywhere on the desktop; and the *mouse pointer*, which can be anywhere on the screen.

QUICKSTEPS

USING THE MOUSE

HIGHLIGHT AN OBJECT ON THE SCREEN

Highlight an *object* (a button, an icon, a border) on the screen by pointing to it. *Point* at an object on the screen by moving the mouse until the tip of the pointer is on top of the object.

SELECT AN OBJECT ON THE SCREEN

Select an object on the screen by clicking it. *Click* means to point at an object you want to select and quickly press and release the mouse button.

OPEN OR START AN OBJECT

Open an object or start an application by double-clicking it. *Double-click* means to point at an object you want to select and then press and release the mouse button twice in rapid succession.

OPEN A CONTEXT MENU FOR AN OBJECT

Open a context menu, which allows you to do things to an object, by **CONTROL**+clicking it. **CONTROL**+*click* means to point at an object you want to select, hold down **CONTROL**, and quickly press and release the mouse button. If your mouse has two buttons, you right-click by quickly pressing and releasing the right mouse button.

MOVE AN OBJECT ON THE SCREEN

Move an object on the screen by dragging it. *Drag* means to point at an object you want to move, then press and hold the mouse button while moving the mouse. You will drag the object as you move the mouse. When the object is where you want it, release the mouse button.

USE THE DESKTOP

The *desktop* is the entire screen except for the Dock and the menu bar. Windows, dialog boxes, and icons (such as the icon for your Mac's startup disk) are displayed on the desktop. You can store *aliases*, which are icons for your favorite applications and documents, on the desktop (see Chapter 2). You can drag windows, dialog boxes, and icons around the desktop. Double-click an icon on the desktop to open it.

USE THE MENU BAR

The menu bar gives you access to the commands in the active application. Only one application can be active at a time; the active application is said to have the *focus*.

At the left end of the menu bar is the menu. This menu is referred to as the "Apple menu" and provides access to system-wide commands, such as configuring your Mac, logging out, or shutting down your Mac.

At the right end of the menu bar are information icons and small menus called *menulets*.

NOTE

Throughout this book you'll see phrases such as "open **File**" or "choose **Go**." These tell you to click a menu in the menu bar (File or Go in this case) in order to open it.

USE THE DOCK

The Dock, which appears at the bottom of the screen by default, contains icons for frequently used applications, documents, and folders. "Use the Dock," later in this chapter, shows you how to understand the icons on the Dock and work with them.

USE A DESKTOP ICON

A *desktop icon* represents an application or folder that can be started or opened and moved about. Double-click a desktop icon to open or activate it.

USE THE MOUSE POINTER

The *mouse pointer*, or simply the *pointer*, shows where the mouse is pointing. Move the mouse to move the pointer.

Use the Dock

The Dock is divided into two by a narrow vertical divider bar. Shortcuts to applications appear to the left of the divider bar. Shortcuts to folders and documents appear to the right of the divider bar, together with an icon for each open window you've minimized (reduced to an icon). The Trash appears at the right end of the Dock.

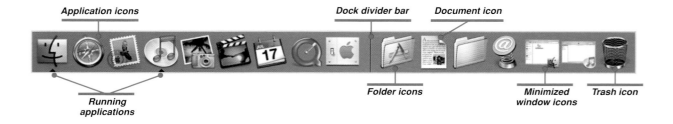

Application icons   *Dock divider bar*   *Document icon*

Running applications   *Folder icons*   *Minimized window icons*   *Trash icon*

QUICKSTEPS

STARTING AN APPLICATION

The method for starting an application depends on where the application icon is located. The alternatives are:

ON THE DESKTOP

Double-click the application icon, or "alias," on the desktop. Alternatively, double-click the icon for a document to open it in the application associated with it.

ON THE DOCK

Click the application icon on the Dock. Alternatively, click the icon for a document on the Dock to open it in the associated application.

ON THE RECENT ITEMS SUBMENU

1. Open .
2. Highlight (move the mouse pointer over) **Recent Items** to display the submenu.
3. Click the item for the application or document you want to open (see Figure 1-4).

If you choose a document on the menu, Mac OS X opens the document in the application associated with it.

IN YOUR APPLICATIONS FOLDER

1. Click the desktop to activate the Finder.
2. Open **Go** in the menu bar.
3. Click **Applications**. A Finder window opens showing your Applications folder.
4. Double-click the application icon.

To identify an icon, hover the mouse pointer over it for a moment, and Mac OS X will display its name.

Click an icon to open an application, folder, or document, or to restore a minimized window to its previous size.

Use the Apple Menu

The menu provides instant access to system-wide commands for Mac OS X. These are the key items on the menu:

- **Software Update** runs the Software Update application, which checks automatically for updates to Mac OS X and major applications.

- **System Preferences** displays the System Preferences window, which contains icons for configuring most aspects of Mac OS X.

- The **Dock** submenu contains commands for quickly configuring the Dock's position and behavior.

- The **Location** submenu lets you switch quickly between sets of settings for different network locations. For example, you might switch between settings for your office and settings for home.

- The **Recent Items** submenu (see Figure 1-4) contains entries for the last ten applications and the last ten documents you've used.

- **Force Quit** displays the Force Quit Applications window, which you can use to close an application that has stopped responding. See "Quit an Application When It Goes Wrong" in Chapter 5 for instructions on using Force Quit.

- **Sleep**, **Restart**, **Shut Down**, and **Log Out** provide you with ways to leave your Mac. See "Leave Mac OS X," later in this chapter, for details.

Figure 1-4: The Recent Items submenu on the menu lets you quickly open any of the last ten applications or the last ten documents you've worked with.

Use a Window

When you start an application or open a folder, the application or folder appears in a "window" on your screen, as does the Applications window in Figure 1-5.

Each window has a number of features that are shown in Figure 1-5 and are referred to in the balance of this book.

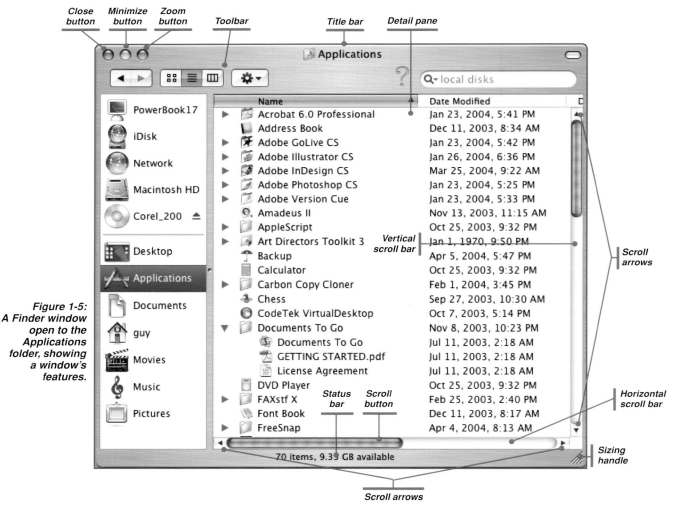

Figure 1-5:
A Finder window
open to the
Applications
folder, showing
a window's
features.

- The **title bar** contains the name of the application or folder in the window and is used to drag the window around the screen.

- The **toolbar** contains tools related to the contents of the window. Click a tool to use it. The toolbar is optional.

- The **detail pane** displays the principal object of the window, such as files, folders, applications, documents, or images.

- The **status bar** provides messages and information about what is displayed or selected in the window. The status bar is optional.

- The **sizing handle** allows the window to be sized diagonally, increasing or decreasing its height and width as you drag.

- The **vertical scroll bar** lets you move the contents of the pane vertically within the window so that you can see information, further up or further down the window, that wasn't displayed.

- The **horizontal scroll bar** lets you move the contents of the pane horizontally within the window so that you can see information, further across to the left or the right, that wasn't displayed.

- The **scroll bar** moves the contents in large increments vertically or horizontally by clicking within it.

- The **scroll button** on a scroll bar can be dragged in either direction to move the contents in that direction.

- The **Close button** closes the window but usually leaves the application running.

- The **minimize button** collapses the window down to an icon on the Dock. Click the window's icon on the Dock to restore the window to its previous size.

- The **zoom** button toggles the window between its current size and the largest size at which it will fit on the screen and usefully display its contents. Zooming some windows makes them take up the whole screen, whereas zooming other windows makes them take up only the full height or width of the screen. Click the zoom button again to restore the window to its former size.

Use a Menu

A menu provides a way of selecting an action, such as Find, on an object, such as a folder. To use a menu:

File	Edit	Format	Wii
New			⌘N
Open...			⌘O
Open Recent			▶
Close			⌘W
Save			⌘S
Save As...			⇧⌘S
Save All			
Revert to Saved			
Page Setup...			⇧⌘P
Print...			⌘P

1. Click an application window to make it active. Mac OS X will display the menu bar for the application.

2. Click the menu name in the menu bar.

3. Move the pointer to the desired item.

4. Click the desired item.

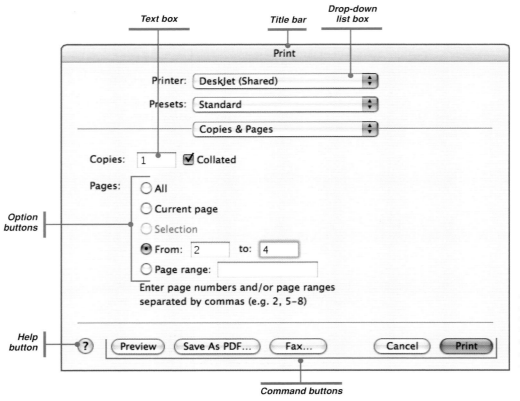

Use a Dialog Box, Sheet, or Window

Dialog boxes present choices to enable you to take actions. A *dialog box* uses a common set of features called *controls* to accomplish its purpose. For example, a typical Print dialog box (see Figure 1-6) presents choices such as the various printers available, the range of pages to print, and how many copies to print.

Figure 1-6: A typical Print dialog box enables you to make choices and take actions. This dialog box uses many of the standard controls.

Unlike some other operating systems (such as Windows), Mac OS X doesn't draw a very distinct line between dialog boxes and small windows. As you work with Mac OS X, you'll find that many features use windows not only to present information but also to allow you to make configuration choices. There are two main differences between a dialog box and a window in this type of usage:

- You can leave the window displayed and return to the application to continue work. (By contrast, you usually must close a dialog box before you can return to the application that displayed it.)

- Most windows of this type are for setting preferences or choosing configurations rather than executing a command. You close a window by clicking its close button (the red button in its title bar) rather than by clicking a command button.

Figure 1-7 shows the General sheet of the Preferences window for Safari, Mac OS X's default web browser.

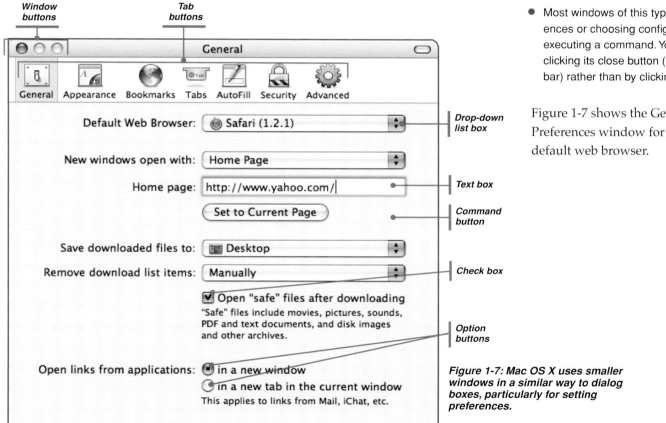

Window buttons

Tab buttons

Drop-down list box

Text box

Command button

Check box

Option buttons

Figure 1-7: Mac OS X uses smaller windows in a similar way to dialog boxes, particularly for setting preferences.

A *sheet* is a special type of dialog box that's attached to a particular document rather than floating free on the screen. A sheet prevents you from working further in that document until you close it, but you can work in other documents in the same application. Most sheets don't have a title bar and remain attached to their documents, but otherwise they behave like dialog boxes. For simplicity, this book refers to this type of sheet as "dialog box" after this chapter, to distinguish it from the other type of sheet: one of the major sets of controls in a dialog box or window.

Figure 1-8 shows an example of a Save sheet for a workbook file in Microsoft Excel.

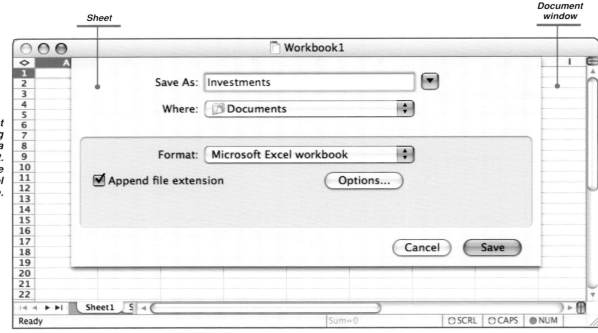

Figure 1-8: A sheet is a type of dialog box attached to a particular document. This is the Save sheet for an Excel workbook file.

The common controls in dialog boxes, windows, and sheets are used in these ways:

- The **title bar** usually contains the name of the dialog box or window and is used to drag the dialog box or window around the desktop. On Mac OS X, some dialog boxes and windows do not have names—instead, they simply have a title bar. Most sheets don't have a title bar.

- **Tab buttons** let you select from among several sheets or tabs in a dialog box.

- A **drop-down list box** opens a list from which you can choose one item that will be displayed when the list is closed.

- A **list box** lets you select one or more items from a list; it may include a scroll bar if the list contains many items.

- **Option buttons**, also called *radio buttons*, let you select one among mutually exclusive options.

- A **text box** lets you enter and edit text.

- **Command buttons** perform functions such as closing the dialog box and accepting the changes (the OK button) or closing the dialog box and ignoring the changes (the Cancel button).

- A **spinner** lets you select from a sequential series of numbers.

- A **slider** lets you select from several values.

- **Check boxes** let you turn features on or off.

- The **Help button** displays the Help Viewer and makes it show a topic appropriate to the dialog box.

You will have many opportunities to use dialog boxes, windows, and sheets. For the most part, you can try the controls in these interface elements and see what happens. If you don't like the outcome, you can return and change the setting back to what it was before you changed it.

TIP

Instead of using the mouse to click a command button in a dialog box or sheet, you can sometimes "click" it from the keyboard. Press **RETURN** to click the default button—the button that has the blue highlight. Press **ESC** to click the Cancel button. In a dialog box that provides only Yes, No, and Cancel buttons, press **Y** to click Yes, **N** to click No, or **C** to click Cancel.

LEAVING MAC OS X QUICKLY

If you have a PowerBook or iBook, you can press the **Power button** to display the Shut Down dialog box (shown here). You can also display this dialog box by pressing the **POWER** key (if your keyboard has one) or by pressing **CONTROL+EJECT** or **CONTROL+F12** (depending on your Mac).

Click **Sleep** to put your Mac to sleep, or click **Shut Down** to shut your Mac down. Alternatively, press **S** for sleep or **RETURN** for shut down.

Leave Mac OS X

You can leave Mac OS X in five ways depending on what you want to do:

SLEEP

Putting your Mac to sleep suspends Mac OS X and all applications you had open. Putting your Mac to sleep is much faster than shutting it down, and waking it is much faster than starting again.

To put your Mac to sleep, open and click **Sleep**. Your Mac's display will go dark and the hard drive will stop running.

To reawaken your Mac, press any key or click the mouse.

LOG OUT

Log out means to close the active applications and network connections and to close your user account but leave your Mac running. To log out:

1. Open and click **Log Out** *Your Name*, where *Your Name* is your user name (for example, **Log Out Lisa**). Mac OS X will display this confirmation message box:

2. Click **Log Out**. Your Mac will display the Login screen, from which you or another user can log in.

NOTE

Instead of clicking **Log Out**, you can wait 120 seconds, and then Mac OS X will log you out automatically. This automatic logout helps ensure that you don't stay logged in even if you forget to click **Log Out** in the confirmation dialog box.

SWITCH USERS

Switch users means to leave the active applications and network connections active and keep your user account active while you let another user use the Mac. To switch users:

1. Click your user name at the right end of the menu bar.

2. Click the name of the desired user.

3. If Mac OS X prompts you for the user's password, enter it and click **Log In**, as shown here:

Mac OS X will hide your desktop and will display the desktop for the user you selected. Your user session and applications continue to run, but they are hidden until you switch users back to your account.

RESTART

The Restart command is another way of leaving Mac OS X—and coming back immediately. Restart shuts down Mac OS X so that no information is lost, and it then restarts Mac OS X. Restarting is usually done when there is a problem that restarting Mac OS X will fix. You may also need to restart Mac OS X after installing or updating system software or applications. To restart:

1. Open and click **Restart**. Mac OS X will display the confirmation dialog box shown here:

2. Click **Restart**. Mac OS X will close all running applications, restart itself, and then display the login screen.

SHUT DOWN

Shutting down means to log off all users and shut down your Mac. To shut down:

1. Open and click **Shut Down**. Mac OS X will display the confirmation dialog box shown here:

2. Click **Shut Down**. Mac OS X will close all running applications, close itself, and then turn off your Mac.

Get Help

Mac OS X Help provides both built-in documentation and online assistance that you can use to learn how to work with Mac OS X. To use Help to get started with Mac OS X:

1. If the menu bar is displaying the menus for any application except the Finder, click the desktop to activate the Finder menus.

Figure 1-9: The Mac Help home page opens in the Help Viewer application.

2. Open **Help** and click **Mac Help**. The Help Viewer window will open, like the one in Figure 1-9, displaying the home page of the Mac Help topic.

3. Click the **New To Mac OS X?** link. A list of topics for new Mac OS X users will be displayed.

4. Click **For New Computer Users**. Notes for new computer users starting with Mac OS X will be displayed.

5. Click links, such as Browse Mac OS Help, as required to explore the information available.

6. Open **Help Viewer** and click **Quit Help Viewer** to close Help Viewer.

How to...

Chapter 2

Customizing Mac OS X

Mac OS X has many features that can be customized. You can keep the default Mac OS X setup; or you can change the display, Dock, and sounds, rearrange the desktop, and enable accessibility options.

Change the Look of Mac OS X

A flexible and important area is how Mac OS X looks. Here you'll see how to change the screen's look, including the desktop background and the Dock.

Open System Preferences

Much of what you see on the Mac OS X screen is controlled by the settings in System Preferences. You'll need to open System Preferences to make many of the changes in this chapter.

1. With Mac OS X running and displayed on your computer, click ⌘ at the left end of the menu bar. Mac OS X will display the ⌘ menu.

NOTE

The selection of icons available in the System Preferences window depends on the configuration of your Mac. The items shown in the Other category in Figure 2-1, M-Audio MobilePre USB and TinkerTool, are third-party software unlikely to be installed on your Mac.

2. Click **System Preferences**. The System Preferences window will open, as shown in Figure 2-1.

Figure 2-1: The System Preferences window contains most of the graphical configuration tools for Mac OS X, including those for configuring the display and appearance.

UICKSTEPS

You'll probably need to open System Preferences frequently to configure Mac OS X as you find out which settings work best for you. Mac OS X provides several ways to open System Preferences.

USE THE DOCK ICON

If you have a System Preferences icon on the Dock, you can open System Preferences by clicking it.

USE THE MENU

Open and click **System Preferences**.

USE THE APPLICATIONS FOLDER

1. Open **Go** and click **Applications** to display the Applications folder.

2. Double-click the **System Preferences** icon.

CUSTOMIZE SYSTEM PREFERENCES

Regardless of which sheet of System Preferences you display, the toolbar remains available, giving you instant access to key preference sheets. You can customize the toolbar so that it shows the icons you need most.

1. Open and click **System Preferences**. The System Preferences window will be displayed. (If System Preferences is already open to a preference sheet, click **Show All** on the left of the toolbar to display all categories.)

2. To add an icon, drag it to the toolbar.

3. To move an icon, drag it along the toolbar to where you want it.

4. To remove an icon, drag it off the toolbar to the detail area. (You can't move or remove the Show All button.)

Change the Desktop Background

Because the desktop background covers almost the entire desktop (until you cover it with windows), it contributes greatly to the look of your Mac. By changing the desktop background, you can make your Mac look substantially different from its default settings. Mac OS X lets you put either a single picture or a changing sequence of pictures on your desktop.

CHANGE THE DESKTOP FROM SYSTEM PREFERENCES

1. **CONTROL**+click (hold down **CONTROL** and click) or right-click the desktop. The context menu appears.

2. Choose **Change Desktop Background**. The Desktop & Screen Saver sheet of System Preferences is displayed.

3. If the Screen Saver tab is displayed, click the **Desktop** tab button (see Figure 2-2). The preview at the top displays your current background and its name.

Figure 2-2: The Desktop tab of the Desktop & Screen Saver sheet in System Preferences lets you change your desktop background.

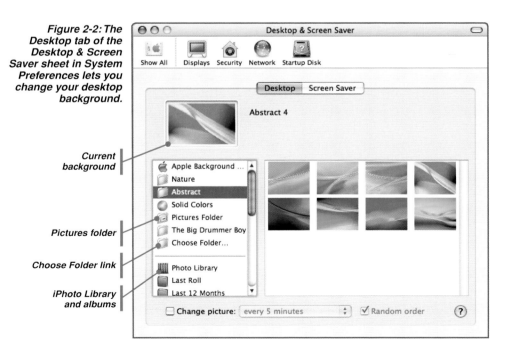

4. In the list box, select the category or folder. Its contents are displayed in the box on the right.

- Mac OS X includes several folders of backgrounds, including Apple Backgrounds, Nature, Abstract, and Solid Colors.

- You can access pictures stored in your Pictures folder by clicking **Pictures Folder**.

- To access any folder, click **Choose Folder** and use the resulting sheet to specify the folder.

- To use a picture from your iPhoto Photo Library, select **Photo Library**.

- To use a photo album from iPhoto, select it from the list under the Photo Library item.

5. To use a single picture, select it in the box on the right. To use all the pictures in the folder or category, don't make a selection in the box on the right.

6. If you're using multiple pictures:

- Select the **Change Picture** check box.

- Specify the frequency in the drop-down list box: When Logging In, When Waking From Sleep, Every 5 Seconds, Every Minute, Every 5 Minutes, Every 15 Minutes, Every 30 Minutes, Every Hour, or Every Day.

- You can also select the **Random Order** check box to display the pictures in random order.

7. If a picture doesn't fit the screen, use the drop-down list box in the preview area to specify how to treat it: Fill Screen, Stretch To Fill Screen, Center, or Tile.

8. Click **System Preferences | Quit System Preferences** to close System Preferences.

CHANGE THE DESKTOP FROM IPHOTO

You can also change the desktop background quickly from iPhoto, the photographic application that Apple includes with Mac OS X. (See "View Pictures with iPhoto" in Chapter 6 for more information on iPhoto.)

To use a single picture as a desktop background:

1. Click the **iPhoto** icon in the Dock.

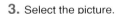

2. In iPhoto, crop the picture to the aspect ratio of the screen if necessary. (See the QuickSteps "Cropping Pictures to Fit Your Desktop" in Chapter 6.)

3. Select the picture.

4. Click **Desktop** in the toolbar at the bottom of the window to put the picture on the desktop immediately.

To put an album or a group of pictures on your desktop:

1. In iPhoto, crop the pictures to the aspect ratio of your screen if necessary. (See the QuickSteps "Cropping Pictures to Fit Your Desktop" in Chapter 6.)

2. Select the album or the pictures:

   - To use an entire album, select it in the Source list and make sure no pictures are selected in the viewing area.

   - To use just some pictures from an album, select the album in the Source list, then select the pictures in the viewing area. To select multiple contiguous pictures, click the first, and then **SHIFT**+click the last. To select noncontiguous pictures, select the first, and then ⌘+click the other pictures.

3. Click **Desktop**. iPhoto applies the first picture to your desktop. iPhoto then displays the Desktop tab of the Desktop & Screen Saver sheet in System Preferences, selecting iPhoto Selection in the left list box and selecting the Change Picture check box.

4. Choose the frequency in the Change Picture drop-down list box, and select or clear the Random Order check box as appropriate.

5. Click **System Preferences** | **Quit System Preferences** to close System Preferences. Mac OS X returns the focus to iPhoto.

NOTE

These instructions are for iPhoto 4. iPhoto 2 and iPhoto 3 work a little differently. When you click **Desktop** with multiple pictures selected, iPhoto displays the Screen Effects dialog box. Make sure **Current Selection** is selected in the drop-down list box, and then click **Screen Effects Preferences** to display the Screen Effects sheet of System Preferences. System Preferences lists the pictures as "Screen Effects" rather as "iPhoto Selection." Follow steps 4 and 5 in the list to complete the procedure, close **System Preferences**, and then click **OK** in the Screen Effects dialog box to close it.

Pick a New Screen Saver

Until a few years ago, if you left your computer on but didn't use it, the unchanging image on the screen could become burned into the face of the cathode-ray tube (CRT) monitor, where it would remain displayed as a ghostly image superimposed on what the screen was supposed to be displaying. To avoid burn-in occurring, software engineers developed *screen savers*, applications that constantly change the image on screen when the computer is left unused.

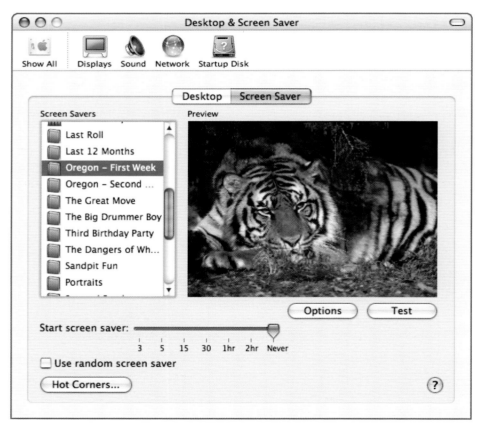

Burn-in seldom occurs on graphical operating systems (such as Mac OS X) and modern CRT monitors, and liquid crystal display (LCD) monitors are largely immune to burn-in. Nevertheless, screen savers have become popular for both entertainment and security (hiding your work while you're away from your computer). Mac OS X provides several alternative screen savers you can use.

1. **CONTROL**+click or right-click the **desktop** to display the *context menu*.

2. Click **Change Desktop Background**. The Desktop & Screen Saver sheet of System Preferences will appear.

3. If the Desktop tab button is selected, click the **Screen Saver** tab button to display the Screen Saver tab (see Figure 2-3).

Figure 2-3: You can use your own pictures as a screen saver.

TIP

You can also set another hot corner to prevent the screen saver from activating by selecting **Disable Screen Saver** in that corner's drop-down list box. Being able to disable the screen saver is useful when you leave your Mac while performing a demanding operation, such as burning a DVD, that you don't want the screen saver to interrupt.

CAUTION

You can find many screen savers on the Internet, some free and others for sale. While many free screen savers are fully functional and entertaining (or educational), others have been created or adapted deliberately to spread malicious code. Others yet are so poorly programmed as to cause Mac OS X problems. So, before installing a free screen saver on your Mac, it's a good idea to check for feedback from other users.

4. Select a screen saver in the Screen Savers list to see it previewed in the Preview box. Click **Test** to see it previewed full screen. Move the mouse to cancel the test.

5. Click **Options** to display the Display Options sheet, on which you can choose options for the screen saver. (Which options are available depends on the type of screen saver you chose. See the two examples here.) When you've made your choices, click **OK** to close the Display Options sheet.

 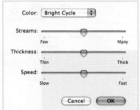

6. Drag the **Start Screen Saver** slider to specify how long your Mac remains inactive before the screen saver starts.

7. Select the **Random Screen Saver** check box if you want Mac OS X to pick a screen saver for you at random.

8. If you want to be able to start your screen saver by moving your mouse to a particular corner of the screen, click **Hot Corners**. The Hot Corners sheet will appear. Select **Start Screen Saver** in the drop-down list box that corresponds to the corner you want to use, and then click **OK** to close the sheet.

9. Click **System Preferences** | **Quit System Preferences** to close System Preferences.

Alter the Appearance of Objects

You can alter some aspects of the appearance of windows and text by working on the Appearance sheet in System Preferences.

1. Open and click **System Preferences**. The System Preferences window will be displayed.

2. Click **Appearance**. The Appearance sheet will be displayed (see Figure 2-4).

3. In the Appearance drop-down list box, select **Blue** (the default) or **Graphite** to change the overall look of windows, menus, and buttons. This change has a surprisingly large effect: applying Graphite makes your Mac look subdued and sober.

4. In the Highlight Color drop-down list box, select the color you want to use for selected text and lists. Again, the default is Blue.

5. In the Place Scroll Arrows area, specify how to place the scroll arrows on the scroll bars by selecting the **At Top And Bottom** option button or the **Together** option button. Together places the scroll arrows together at the bottom of a vertical scroll bar and the right end of a horizontal scroll bar.

6. In the Click In The Scroll Bar To area, select the **Jump To The Next Page** option button or the **Scroll To Here** option button to specify what you want to happen when you click in an empty space in the scroll bar: move to the previous or next page of information, or move to the location in the document that corresponds to the place you click in the scroll bar.

7. Select the **Use Smooth Scrolling** check box if you want Mac OS X to make scrolling as smooth as possible. This may slow down scrolling.

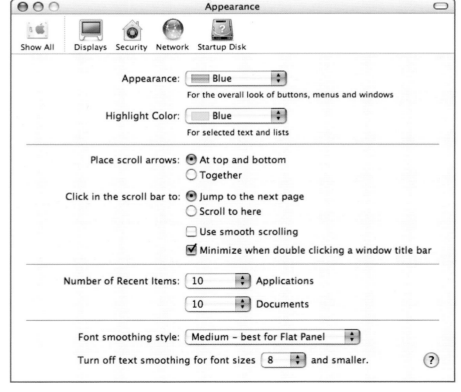

Figure 2-4: Use the controls on the Appearance sheet in System Preferences to subtly change the appearance of text and windows.

8. Clear the **Minimize When Double Clicking A Window Title Bar** check box if you don't want to be able to minimize a window by double-clicking its title bar.

9. In the Number of Recent Items area, use the **Applications** drop-down list box and the **Documents** drop-down list box to specify how many applications Mac OS X displays on the | Recent Items submenu.

10. Check that the setting in the **Font Smoothing Style** drop-down list box is suitable for your monitor. Apple recommends the Medium setting for LCD monitors and the Standard setting for CRT monitors. If you don't like the effect on your monitor, experiment with the other settings.

12. Use the **Turn Off Text Smoothing For Font Sizes** drop-down list box to specify the largest type size for which Mac OS X shouldn't use smoothing. (Smoothing on minuscule type tends to make it look smeary.)

13. Click **System Preferences** | **Quit System Preferences** to close System Preferences.

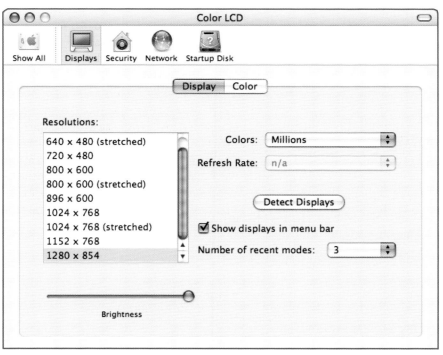

Change the Resolution and Color Depth

Depending on your Mac and monitor, you can display Mac OS X with varying resolutions and color quality. You can select the resolution and color depth on the Display tab of the Displays sheet in System Preferences.

1. Open and click **System Preferences**. The System Preferences window will be displayed.

2. Click **Displays**. The Displays sheet will appear. Its title bar shows the type of display—for example, Color LCD.

3. If the Color tab is displayed, click the **Display** tab button (see Figure 2-5).

Figure 2-5: Increasing the resolution lets you see more on the screen, but what you see is smaller.

NOTE

After changing your display, adding a display, or removing a display, you may need to click the **Detect Displays** button on the Display tab of the Displays sheet.

NOTE

Before performing an action with the Finder, you must activate the Finder so that its menus are displayed in the menu bar. If no other application is active, the Finder will already be active, and you won't need to activate it. If another application is active (either with one or more windows displayed or all its windows minimized), that application's menus will be displayed in the menu bar. When another application is active, you can activate the Finder by clicking open space or any object on the desktop. (This is because the desktop is technically part of the Finder.) You can also activate the Finder by clicking the Finder icon on the Dock. If no Finder window is open, Mac OS X will open a Finder window showing your default folder (typically, your Home folder) when you click the Finder icon on the Dock.

4. Select the resolution in the Resolutions drop-down list box.

5. Select the number of colors—256 Colors, Thousands, or Millions—in the Colors drop-down list box.

6. For a CRT, choose a refresh rate in the Refresh Rate drop-down list box. Refresh rates of 75 hertz (Hz) or higher reduce visible flicker on CRTs. The Refresh Rate drop-down list box is not available for LCDs, which don't suffer from flicker.

7. If you need to switch display resolution or color depth frequently, select the **Show Displays In Menu Bar** check box to add the displays menu to the menu bar. In the Number Of Recent Modes drop-down list box, specify how many modes (resolutions and color depths) the menu should include.

8. Drag the **Brightness** slider to change the brightness of the screen.

9. Click **System Preferences** | **Quit System Preferences** to close System Preferences.

Add Icons to Your Desktop

Because your desktop is always displayed, it can be a convenient place to keep icons for applications, folders, and documents you use frequently. You can customize the icons on your desktop to suit your needs.

CONTROL ICONS FOR DISKS AND DRIVES

By default, Mac OS X displays an icon on the desktop for:

- Your Mac's hard disk (which is always present)
- Any CD or DVD drive in which you have inserted a disc
- Any servers or network drives to which your Mac has established a connection

You can change these default settings:

1. Activate the **Finder**.

2. Open **Finder** and choose **Preferences**. The Preferences window for the Finder will be displayed.

General

General Labels Sidebar Advanced

Show these items on the Desktop:
- ☑ Hard disks
- ☑ CDs, DVDs and iPods
- ☑ Connected servers

New Finder windows open:

[🏠 Home ▲▼]

- ☐ Always open folders in a new window
- ☐ Open new windows in column view

- ☑ Spring-loaded folders and windows

  Delay: |———————◇————————|
  Short   Medium   Long

  Press Space Bar to open immediately

Figure 2-6: On the General tab of the Finder Preferences window, choose which categories of items appear on the desktop.

3. If the General tab (see Figure 2-6) isn't displayed, click the **General** tab button.
4. Select or clear the **Hard Disks** check box, the **CDs, DVDs and iPods** check box, and the **Connected Servers** check box, as appropriate.
5. Click the **Close** button (the red button) to close the Preferences window.

ADD OR REMOVE OTHER ICONS

As you'll see in Chapter 3, you can store folders and files directly on the desktop if you choose. You can also place on the desktop aliases (shortcuts) to applications, documents, and folders:

1. Activate the **Finder** and click a file or folder that you want on the desktop.
2. Open **File** and click **Make Alias**. Mac OS X creates an alias and assigns it the name of the file or folder and the word "alias." For example, an alias to the folder named My Songs receives the name "My Songs alias."
3. Mac OS X places an edit box around the default name. If you want, type a new name and press **RETURN**.
4. Drag the alias to your desktop.

Rearrange Desktop Icons

When you have the icons you want on the desktop, they may be a mess. You can drag the icons to where you want them or let Mac OS X arrange them for you.

LET MAC OS X ALIGN OR ARRANGE ICONS

When you drag the icons where you want them, it may be hard to align them, so let Mac OS X do that:

1. Activate the **Finder**.
2. Open **View** and click **Show View Options**. The Desktop window will be displayed (see Figure 2-7).

Desktop

Icon size: 64 x 64

|——————◇————|
Small   Large

Text size: [12 pt ▲▼]

Label position:
⦿ Bottom   ○ Right

- ☐ Snap to grid
- ☐ Show item info
- ☑ Show icon preview
- ☑ Keep arranged by

[Name ▲▼]

Figure 2-7: Use the options in the Desktop window to arrange and align icons on the desktop.

3. Select the **Snap To Grid** check box to make Mac OS X align the icons according to an underlying, invisible grid.

4. Select the **Keep Arranged By** check box to make Mac OS X arrange the icons automatically. In the drop-down list box, choose how to arrange them: Name, Date Modified, Date Created, Size, Kind, or Label.

Leave the Desktop window open for the moment in case you want to change the icon size, spacing, or labels.

CHOOSE ICON SIZE, TEXT SIZE, AND LABELS

1. Drag the **Icon Size** slider in the Desktop window to change icon size.

2. Select the text size (in points) in the Text Size drop-down list box.

3. To change the label position, select the **Bottom** option button or the **Right** option button.

4. Click the **Close** button (the red button) to close the Desktop window.

CHANGE LABEL COLOR

To make your icons easier to sort, you can assign them different label colors. You can then sort the icons by label (as described a moment ago) to put icons with the same color next to each other.

To change label color:

1. **CONTROL**+click or right-click the icon. The context menu appears.

2. Select the color in the Color Label area. (To remove the color, click the **X** button.)

Rename Desktop Icons

To rename a desktop icon:

1. Click the label. Mac OS X displays an edit box around it.

2. Type the new name and press **RETURN**.

Change the Dock

The Dock has several aspects you can customize, including its size, the number and selection of icons it contains, and its behavior.

You can perform major customization either from the Dock sheet of System Preferences (see Figure 2-8) or by using shortcuts. To display the Dock sheet, open ◆, highlight **Dock**, and click **Dock Preferences**, or open System Preferences and click **Dock**.

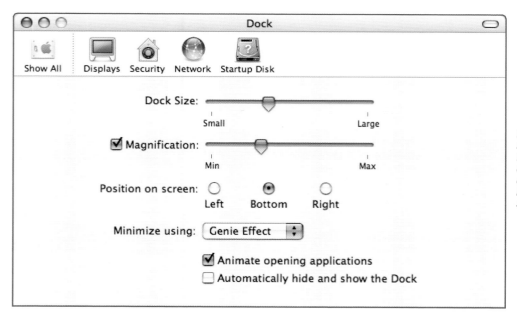

Figure 2-8: The Dock sheet of System Preferences is the central location for configuring the Dock, but you can also use shortcuts.

QUICKSTEPS

POSITIONING AND HIDING THE DOCK

CHANGE THE POSITION OF THE DOCK

You can change where the Dock is positioned, or hide the Dock when you don't need to see it.

- Press and hold **SHIFT** while dragging (**SHIFT**+drag) the **Dock divider line** to the desired side.

    –Or–

- Select the **Left** option button, the **Bottom** option button, or the **Right** option button opposite Position On Screen on the sheet.

    –Or–

- **CONTROL**+click or right-click the **Dock divider line**, highlight **Position On Screen**, and select the **Left** option button, the **Bottom** option button, or the **Right** option button on the Dock context menu.

    –Or–

- Open , highlight **Dock**, and click **Position On Left**, **Position On Bottom**, or **Position On Right**.

HIDE AND DISPLAY THE DOCK

By default, Mac OS X keeps the Dock displayed so that you can access it at any time. But you can configure the Dock to hide automatically so you have more space on screen.

- Select the **Automatically Hide And Show The Dock** check box on the Dock Preferences sheet.

    –Or–

- Open , highlight **Dock**, and choose **Turn Hiding On**.

    –Or–

- Press ⌘+**OPTION**+**D**.

The Dock then hides itself automatically. To display the Dock, move the mouse pointer to the side of the screen on which you've positioned the Dock.

To turn hiding off, clear the **Automatically Hide And Show The Dock** check box, choose **Turn Hiding Off**, or press ⌘+**OPTION**+**D** again.

CHANGE THE SIZE OF THE DOCK AND ITS ICONS

To change the size of the Dock:

- Drag the **Dock divider line** upward (to enlarge the Dock) or downward (to reduce it).

    –Or–

- Drag the **Dock Size** slider on the Dock sheet.

The Dock resizes proportionally. Its maximum length is controlled by the length of the side of the screen on which it's positioned. As you add more icons to the Dock, Mac OS X automatically shrinks the Dock as necessary to fit it on the screen with all its icons displayed.

TURN MAGNIFICATION ON OR OFF

The Dock's magnification feature lets you see the Dock icons easily even if you've reduced the Dock to a tiny size to accommodate many icons. When you pass the mouse pointer over a Dock icon, Mac OS X magnifies it, shown here:

To apply magnification, select the **Magnification** check box in the Dock Preferences dialog box, and drag the slider to specify the degree of magnification.

CHOOSE AN EFFECT FOR MINIMIZING AND RESTORING WINDOWS

Mac OS X offers a choice of two animations for minimizing and restoring windows. Choose **Genie Effect** (the default) or **Scale Effect** in the Minimize Using drop-down list box on the Dock sheet in System Preferences. The effects are hard to describe, but you'll see the difference easily when you try them.

You can toggle magnification on and off by opening , highlighting **Dock**, and clicking **Turn Magnification On** or **Turn Magnification Off**.

Press **SHIFT** as you minimize or restore a window to slow down the animation. For example, **SHIFT**+double-click the **title bar** to minimize a window, or **SHIFT**+click the icon for a minimized window to restore it.

As explained in Chapter 1, the portion of the Dock to the left of the divider line is for applications, and the portion to the right is for folders, documents, and minimized windows. When adding an icon to the Dock, you must drag it to the appropriate portion of the Dock.

ADD AN APPLICATION TO THE DOCK

To add an application to the dock, drag its icon to the left portion of the Dock. For example:

1. Activate the **Finder**.

2. Open **Go** and click **Applications**. A Finder window opens showing your Applications folder.

3. Drag an icon from the Applications folder to the left portion of the Dock.

ADD A DOCUMENT OR FOLDER TO THE DOCK

To add a document or folder to the Dock, drag its icon to the right portion of the Dock.

REARRANGE THE ICONS ON THE DOCK

To rearrange the icons on the Dock into your preferred order, drag an icon to its new position. Mac OS X makes space for the icon.

REMOVE AN ICON FROM THE DOCK

To remove an icon from the Dock, quit the application if it's running, and then drag the icon off the Dock. When you release the mouse button, the icon vanishes in a puff of logic.

ADDING ITEMS TO THE MENU BAR

The right end of the menu bar can display various icons for widely used features, such as the clock, modem status, or AirPort (wireless network) status. You can control the display of many of these icons from different System Preferences sheets.

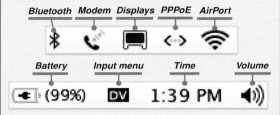

Bluetooth   Modem   Displays   PPPoE   AirPort

Battery   Input menu   Time   Volume

VOLUME ICON

Select or clear the **Show Volume In Menu Bar** check box on any tab of the Sound sheet.

BLUETOOTH ICON

Select or clear the **Show Bluetooth Status In The Menu Bar** check box on the Settings tab of the Bluetooth sheet. Alternatively, select or clear the **Show Bluetooth Status In Menu Bar** check box on the Bluetooth tab of the Keyboard & Mouse sheet. (The Bluetooth sheet and the Bluetooth tab are available only if your Mac has Bluetooth, a wireless networking technology, installed.)

DISPLAYS ICON

Select or clear the **Show Displays In Menu Bar** check box on the Display tab of the Displays sheet.

BATTERY STATUS ICON

Select or clear the **Show Battery Status In The Menu Bar** check box on any tab in the Energy Saver sheet. This check box is available only for PowerBooks and iBooks.

Continued...

Change How Mac OS X Operates

You can customize how Mac OS X operates to suit your preferences.

Set and Use the Date and Time

The time display at the right end of the menu bar may seem simple enough, but you can customize it out of all recognition—or dispense with it.

1. Click the **time readout** in the menu bar. The time menu is displayed, including the full date.

2. To switch the clock quickly between digital and analog, click the time readout in the menu bar and select **View As Analog** or **View As Digital**, as appropriate. The analog clock icon in the menu bar is hard to read, but you can also display the clock in a small window.

3. Click **Open Date & Time**. The Date & Time sheet in System Preferences will be displayed.

4. Click the **Clock** tab button.

5. Choose options for the clock:

   - The **Show The Date And Time** check box controls whether the clock appears at all.

   - Select the **Menu Bar** option button to display the clock on the menu bar. Select the **Window** option button to display the clock in a separate window. For a windowed clock, drag the **Transparency** slider to adjust the window's transparency.

   - Select the **Digital** option button or the **Analog** option button to control the format.

   - Choose other options, which include showing AM/PM, showing the day of the week, flashing time separators, and announcing the time out loud.

6. To change the time or date, click the **Date & Time** tab button to display the Date & Time tab (see Figure 2-10).

   - To set the date and time automatically using a time reference on the Internet, select the **Set Date & Time Automatically** check box, and choose the server in the drop-down list box.

   - To set the date and time manually, clear the **Set Date & Time Automatically** check box. Use the controls to set the date and time.

ADDING ITEMS TO THE MENU BAR
(Continued)

INPUT MENU ICON

Select or clear the **Show Input Menu In Menu Bar** check box on the Input Menu tab of the International sheet.

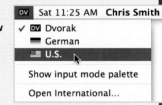

AIRPORT ICON

Select or clear the **Show AirPort Status In Menu Bar** check box on the AirPort tab of the Network sheet, with **AirPort** selected in the Show drop-down list. (The AirPort tab is available only if your Mac has an AirPort card.)

TIME DISPLAY

Select or clear the **Show The Date And Time** check box on the Clock tab of the Date & Time sheet. Select the **Menu Bar** option button.

PPPOE ICON

Select or clear the **Show PPPoE Status In Menu Bar** check box on the PPPoE tab of the Network sheet, with the appropriate network interface (for example, Built-in Ethernet) selected in the Show drop-down list box. (*PPPoE* stands for Point-to-Point Protocol Over Ethernet, a networking standard for fast Internet connections.)

MODEM ICON

Select or clear the **Show Modem Status In Menu Bar** check box on the Modem tab of the Network sheet, with the appropriate modem entry selected in the Show drop-down list box.

---

7. To specify the time zone, click the **Time Zone** tab button. Choose your location on the map or use the Closest City drop-down list box to specify your closest city (and thus your time zone).

8. Click **System Preferences** | **Quit System Preferences** to close System Preferences.

Improve Accessibility with Universal Access

Mac OS X's Universal Access feature provides alternatives to the normal way the mouse and keyboard are used as well as some settings that make the screen more readable (or make it audible).

1. Open and click **System Preferences**.

2. Click **Universal Access**. The Universal Access sheet will be displayed.

3. Select the options you want to use on the Seeing tab, Hearing tab, Keyboard tab, and Mouse tab (see Table 2-1). Figure 2-9 shows the Keyboard tab.

4. Click **System Preferences** | **Quit System Preferences** to close System Preferences.

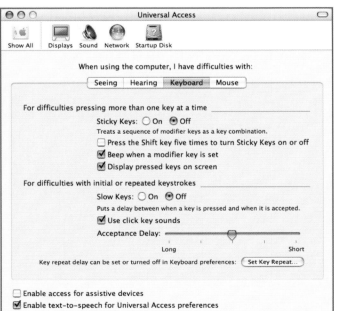

Figure 2-9: The Universal Access features let you access Mac OS X and the applications that run on it in different ways.

TABLE 1: UNIVERSAL ACCESS FEATURES

TAB	OPTION	DESCRIPTION	TURN ON OR OFF
Seeing	Zoom	Enables you to zoom the screen to a large size to see small items more easily.	Click **Turn On Zoom** or **Turn Off Zoom** on the Seeing tab, or press ⌘+OPTION+8.
Seeing	Zoom In	Zooms the display in.	Press ⌘+OPTION+=.
Seeing	Zoom Out	Zooms the display out.	Press ⌘+OPTION+– (hyphen).
Seeing	White On Black	Reverses the video to make the screen more visible.	Click **Switch To White On Black** or **Switch To Black On White** on the Seeing tab, or press ⌘+OPTION+CONTROL+8.
Seeing	Grayscale	Changes the display from color to grayscale to improve visibility of colors.	Click **Set Display To Grayscale** on the Seeing tab. Click **Set Display To Color** to restore color.
Seeing	Enhance Contrast	Increases the contrast to make the screen more visible.	Drag the **Enhance Contrast** slider on the Seeing tab or press ⌘+OPTION+CONTROL+. (period). Press ⌘+OPTION+CONTROL+, (comma) to reduce contrast again.
Hearing	Flash The Screen	Makes the screen flash once when Mac OS X plays an alert sound.	Select the **Flash The Screen When An Alert Sound Occur**s check box on the Hearing tab.
Keyboard	Sticky Keys	Simulates pressing a pair of keys, such as ⌘+A, by pressing one key at a time. The modifier keys ⌘, **OPTION**, **CONTROL**, and **SHIFT** "stick" down until the final key of the command sequence is pressed. This is interpreted as the key sequence pressed together. Select the **Beep When A Modifier Key Is Set** check box to make Mac OS X beep when you press a modifier key. Select the **Display Pressed Keys On Screen** check box to receive a visual readout of modifier key presses.	Select the **On** option button or the **Off** option button in the Sticky Keys area of the Keyboard tab. Alternatively, press **SHIFT** five times in succession when the Press The Shift Key Five Times To Turn Sticky Keys On Or Off check box is selected.
Keyboard	Slow Keys	Makes Mac OS X wait for the specified delay before it registers a keystroke. Drag the **Acceptance Delay** slider to set the delay. Select the **Use Click Key Sounds** check box to make Mac OS X play a click when it registers the keystroke.	Select the **On** option button or the **Off** option button in the Slow Keys area of the Keyboard tab.
Mouse	Mouse Keys	Enables you to use the numeric keypad instead of the mouse to move the pointer on the screen. Drag the **Initial Delay** slider to configure the delay before starting to move the mouse, and the **Maximum Speed** slider to set the maximum speed at which the mouse pointer moves.	Select the **On** option button or the **Off** option button in the Mouse Keys area of the Mouse tab. Alternatively, press **OPTION** five times in succession when the Press The Option Key Five Times To Turn Mouse Keys On Or Off check box is selected.
All tabs	Assistive Devices	Enables you to use extra assistive devices to control your Mac.	Select or clear the **Enable Access for Assistive Devices** check box at the bottom of the Universal Access sheet.
All tabs	Text-To-Speech For Universal Access Preferences	Announces the names of the Universal Access options you're choosing.	Select or clear the **Enable Text-To-Speech For Universal Access Preferences** check box at the bottom of the Universal Access sheet.

NOTE

If you have a PowerBook or an iBook, the Keyboard tab of the Keyboard & Mouse sheet also lets you choose between using the function keys as normal function keys or for custom actions (such as changing the screen brightness or the audio volume). Select the **Use The F1–F12 Keys For Custom Actions** check box to use the custom actions; you'll then need to press **FN** and the function key to use its default action (which will depend on the application that's active). Clear the check box to use the default actions. You'll then need to press **FN** and the function key to perform a custom action. This functionality was added in Mac OS X version 10.3.3, so if you have an earlier version of Mac OS X, you'll need to update to 10.3.3 or later to use it. See "Download and Apply Software Updates" in Chapter 5 for instructions on updating Mac OS X.

Customize the Keyboard

Mac OS X requires a keyboard for textual communications and typing. You can change the length of the delay before a key that is held down is repeated and the rate at which the key is repeated. On a PowerBook or an iBook, you can also choose whether to use the function keys primarily for default actions or for custom actions.

1. Open and click **System Preferences**. The System Preferences window will be displayed.

2. Click **Keyboard & Mouse**. The Keyboard & Mouse sheet will be displayed.

3. If the Keyboard tab isn't displayed, click the **Keyboard** tab button to display it (see Figure 2-10).

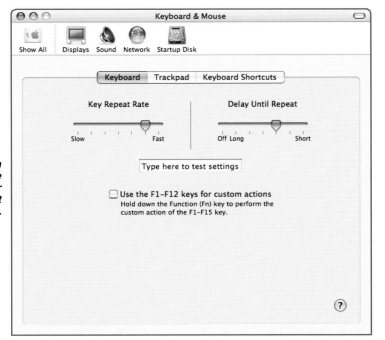

Figure 2-10: You can change the repeat rate and the repeat delay for your keyboard to suit your typing style.

Mac OS X also lets you apply a different logical layout, such as the Dvorak layout, to the keyboard. The keys themselves don't change, but they deliver different letters than normal. To apply a different layout, open , click **System Preferences**, click **International**, and click the **Input Menu** tab. Select the check box for each layout you want to use, and then click **System Preferences** | **Quit System Preferences** to close System Preferences. If you select two or more layouts, you can switch among them by using the input menu on the menu bar. Alternatively, press ⌘+SPACEBAR to switch between the last two layouts you've used, or press ⌘+OPTION+SPACEBAR to step through all the layouts in the input menu.

4. Click in the **Type Here To Test Settings** text box and type a few keystrokes to test the settings.

5. Drag the **Key Repeat Rate** slider to change the rate at which a key repeats when you hold it down. Test the setting.

6. Drag the **Delay Until Repeat** slider to change the delay until a key starts repeating. Test the setting.

7. When you have set up the keyboard the way you want, click **System Preferences** | **Quit System Preferences** to close System Preferences. Alternatively, if you want to customize other aspects of your system, click **Show All** to display all the categories.

Customize the Mouse and Trackpad

The mouse lets you interact with the screen and point at, select, and drag objects. It also lets you start and stop applications and close Mac OS X. While it is possible to control most aspects of Mac OS X without a mouse, it is much more difficult and usually slower to do so. This makes it vital to configure your mouse so that it works as comfortably as possible.

If you have a PowerBook or an iBook, you can configure its built-in trackpad for speed and comfort. This configuration is independent of the mouse configuration.

CUSTOMIZE THE MOUSE

1. Open and click **System Preferences** to open the System Preferences window.

2. Click **Keyboard & Mouse**. The Keyboard & Mouse sheet will be displayed.

3. Click the **Mouse** tab button. The Mouse tab contains the same controls as the upper part of the Trackpad tab, shown in Figure 2-11, later in this chapter.

4. Drag the **Tracking Speed** slider to control the speed at which the mouse pointer moves as you move the mouse.

5. Double-click a word in the Double-Click Here To Test text box to test the double-click speed. If Mac OS X registers a double-click, it selects and highlights the word you clicked. Drag the **Double-Click Speed** slider as necessary to change the speed, and double-click again in the text box to test it.

6. Click **System Preferences** | **Quit System Preferences** to close System Preferences.

CUSTOMIZE THE TRACKPAD

To configure the trackpad on your PowerBook or iBook:

1. Open and click **System Preferences**. The System Preferences window will be displayed.

2. Click **Keyboard & Mouse**. The Keyboard & Mouse sheet will be displayed.

3. Click the **Trackpad** tab button (see Figure 2-11).

4. Drag the **Tracking Speed** slider to control the speed at which the mouse pointer moves as you move your finger on the trackpad.

5. Double-click a word in the Double-Click Here To Test text box to test the double-click speed. If Mac OS X registers a double-click, it selects and highlights the word you clicked. Drag the **Double-Click Speed** slider as necessary to change the speed, and double-click again in the text box to test it.

Figure 2-11: If your Mac has a trackpad, configure it on the Trackpad tab of the Keyboard & Mouse sheet in System Preferences.

6. Choose whether to use the trackpad for clicking, dragging, and drag lock by selecting the **Clicking** check box, the **Dragging** check box, and the **Drag Lock** check box.

   ● You must select the **Clicking** check box to enable the Dragging check box, and you must select the **Dragging** check box to enable the Drag Lock check box.

   ● If you turn on dragging, tap twice with your finger on the trackpad and then move your finger to drag the object.

   ● If you turn on drag lock, tap twice with your finger on the trackpad to lock dragging on. Move your finger to drag the object, and then tap again to release the lock.

7. Select the **Ignore Accidental Trackpad Input** check box if you want Mac OS X to ignore trackpad movements it thinks are accidental. For example, you may brush the trackpad with the base of your thumbs while typing. This option is usually helpful.

8. Select the **Ignore Trackpad When Mouse Is Present** check box if you want Mac OS X to deactivate the trackpad when you plug a mouse into your PowerBook or iBook.

9. Click **System Preferences | Quit System Preferences** to close System Preferences.

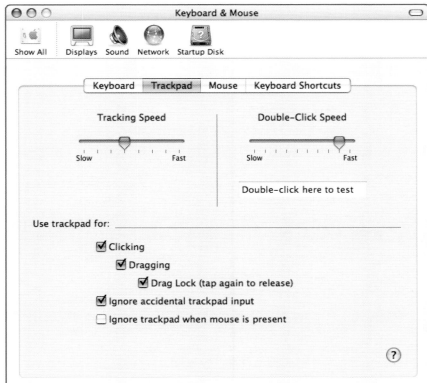

Change Sounds

Mac OS X plays an alert sound when you try to do something that doesn't work or when something happens that needs your attention. Mac OS X plays other sounds to give feedback for interface actions, such as moving files to the Trash or pressing the volume keys. You can change the alert sound or prevent Mac OS X from playing feedback sounds by using the Sound sheet in System Preferences.

1. Open and click **System Preferences**. The System Preferences window will be displayed.

2. Click **Sound**. The Sound sheet will be displayed.

3. If the Sound Effects tab (see Figure 2-12) isn't displayed, click the **Sound Effects** tab button to display it.

4. Click the sound in the **Choose An Alert Sound** list. Mac OS X will play the sound to help you choose a suitable one.

5. Drag the **Alert Volume** slider to set the volume for the alert sound relative to the other audio output (for example, music) on your Mac.

6. If you don't want Mac OS X to play feedback sounds for actions, clear the **Play User Interface Sound Effects** check box.

7. If you don't want Mac OS X to play feedback sounds when you press the volume keys, clear the **Play Feedback When Volume Keys Are Pressed** check box.

8. If you want to change the overall sound volume, drag the **Output Volume** slider to the left or right.

9. Click **System Preferences** | **Quit System Preferences** to close System Preferences.

Figure 2-12: On the Sound Effects tab of the Sound sheet in System Preferences, you can configure or suppress the alert sound that Mac OS X plays when it needs your attention.

Change Language and Regional Settings

Mac OS X lets you determine which language it uses for menus and dialog boxes as well as how numbers, dates, currency, and time are displayed and used.

CHANGE THE LANGUAGE

To change the language Mac OS X uses:

1. Open and click **System Preferences**. The System Preferences window will be displayed.

2. Click **International**. The International sheet will be displayed.

3. If the Language tab isn't displayed, click the **Language** tab button to display it.

4. To change the language, drag your desired language to the top of the Languages list box.

5. To change the selection of languages available, click **Edit**, select or clear check boxes as appropriate on the resulting sheet, and then click **OK**.

6. Click **System Preferences** | **Quit System Preferences** to close System Preferences.

7. Log out (open and click **Log Out**) to switch the Finder and your desktop to the language you chose.

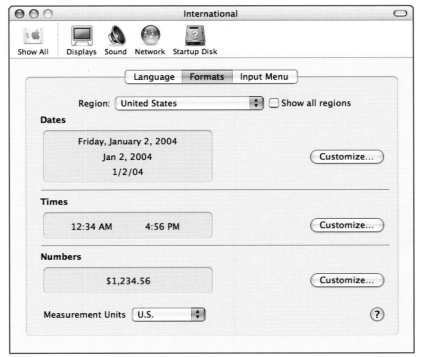

Figure 2-13: Choose your region and customize formats as necessary on the Formats tab of the International sheet in System Preferences.

NOTE

Mac OS X initially displays only the most widely used regions in the Region drop-down list box. To display all regions, select the **Show All Regions** check box.

CHANGE REGIONAL SETTINGS

To change the regional settings Mac OS X uses:

1. Open and click **System Preferences**. The System Preferences window will be displayed.

2. Click **International**. The International sheet will be displayed.

3. If the Formats tab isn't displayed, click the **Formats** tab button to display it (see Figure 2-13).

4. In the Region drop-down list box, select the region whose formats you want to use—for example, United States or Canada. The Dates readout, Times readout, and Numbers readout will display samples of those formats.

5. To change one of the formats, click the appropriate **Customize** button and work on the option sheet that Mac OS X displays. When you've finished choosing options, click **OK** to close the option sheet.

6. In the Measurement Units drop-down list box, select **U.S.** or **Metric** if you want to change the default setting for the region you chose.

7. Click **System Preferences** | **Quit System Preferences** to close System Preferences.

Chapter 3
Storing Information

The information on your Mac—documents, e-mail, photographs, music, and applications—is stored in *files*. So that your files are organized and can be found more easily, they are kept in *folders*, and folders can be placed in other folders for further segmentation. For example, a folder labeled "Movies" contains folders for Business, Family, and Personal. The Family folder contains folders for Events and Vacations. The Events folder contains a Mountain Mystery Hike folder, which in turn contains the folders and component files of a movie. Such a set of files and folders is shown in the Movies folder in Figure 3-1.

In this chapter, you'll see how to create, use, and manage files and folders like these. (In this chapter the term "objects" refers to any mix of files, folders, and disk drives.)

Display Files and Folders

The tool that Mac OS X provides to display and work with files and folders is called the *Finder*. The Finder is always running when Mac OS X is running; its icon (shown to the left here) appears by default at the left end of the Dock. The Finder has three views:

- **Icons view** displays a medium-size icon for each object:

- **List view** displays a list of objects with brief details:

Name	Date Modified	Size
ArK01	Jan 16, 2004, 10:21 AM	12 KB
AutoCorrect entries.doc	Oct 20, 2003, 6:18 PM	544 KB
CD Design 4.ai	Mar 17, 2004, 1:20 PM	4.5 MB
Crying Wolf.ppt	Jan 8, 2004, 11:29 AM	36 KB
Data-Only DVD.dvdproj	Feb 29, 2004, 1:44 PM	--
E*Trade Balance	Oct 28, 2003, 4:55 PM	8 KB
▶ eBooks	Mar 5, 2004, 5:13 PM	--

- **Columns view** (see Figure 3-2) shows a columnar display of the folder path (the route) to the selected object, together with a preview of the object and brief details.

Figure 3-1: The Finder in List view can show files in folders within other folders.

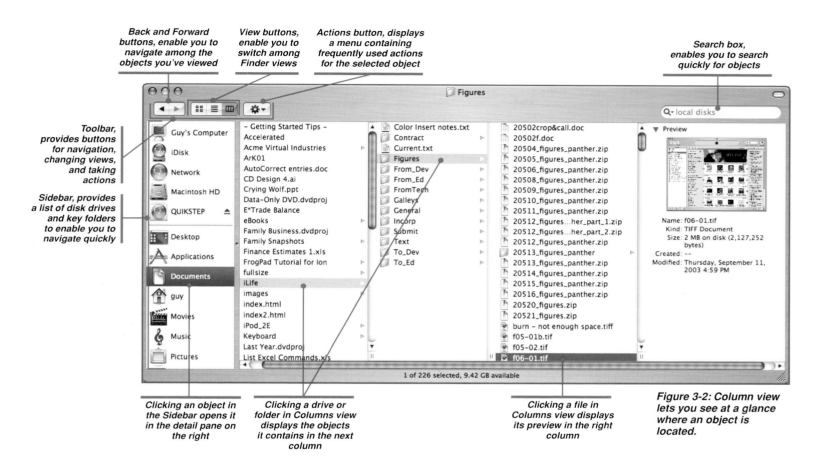

Back and Forward buttons, enable you to navigate among the objects you've viewed

View buttons, enable you to switch among Finder views

Actions button, displays a menu containing frequently used actions for the selected object

Search box, enables you to search quickly for objects

Toolbar, provides buttons for navigation, changing views, and taking actions

Sidebar, provides a list of disk drives and key folders to enable you to navigate quickly

Clicking an object in the Sidebar opens it in the detail pane on the right

Clicking a drive or folder in Columns view displays the objects it contains in the next column

Clicking a file in Columns view displays its preview in the right column

Figure 3-2: Column view lets you see at a glance where an object is located.

In each view, the Finder displays the Sidebar on its left side (see Figure 3-2). The Sidebar is a navigation tool that contains a list of disk drives and key folders on your computer. Click a drive or folder in the Sidebar to display its contents in the detail pane.

The Sidebar includes the following folders, which Mac OS X creates automatically for each user:

- Your **Home** folder, identified by your short user name, contains all your personal folders, including the Documents, Movies, Music, and Pictures folders.

- The **Desktop** folder contains items stored on your desktop.

- The **Applications** folder contains applications you can run.

- The **Documents** folder is the main folder for storing documents that aren't music, movies, or pictures. For example, if you create a document using Microsoft Word, Word uses the Documents folder by default.

- The **Movies** folder is the main folder for storing movie files. iMovie automatically uses this folder.

- The **Music** folder is the main folder for storing audio files. iTunes automatically uses this folder.

- The **Pictures** folder is the main folder for storing picture files. iPhoto automatically uses this folder.

Identify Disk Storage Devices

Files and folders are held on various physical storage devices called *disk drives*. Your Mac almost certainly has a primary hard disk and a primary CD drive or DVD drive. It may also have further hard disks or optical drives, and it may be connected to one or more network drives, either via a wired network or via a wireless network. Mac OS X also treats iPods as drives, so if you connect an iPod to your Mac, it will appear as a drive.

Mac OS X automatically mounts all disk drives that it detects (but see the Note to the left). By default, Mac OS X displays an icon for each mounted disk drive on your desktop, giving you instant access to them. You can also access the disk drives through the Finder or via common dialog boxes and sheets (such as the Open dialog box and the Save As sheet).

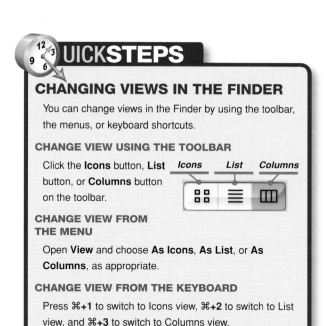
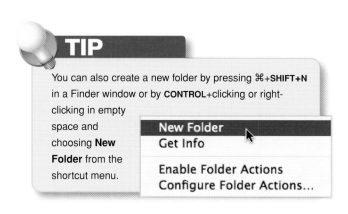
Select and Open Folders

When you open a Finder window, you see the disk drives and key folders on your computer in the Sidebar. You can:

- See the contents of a disk drive or key folder by clicking it in the Sidebar.
- Open a folder and display its contents in Icons or List view by double-clicking it.
- Display a folder's contents in the next column in Columns view by clicking it.

Create New Folders

While you could store all your files within the ready-made folders that Mac OS X provides for you—your Home, Documents, Movies, Music, and Pictures folders—you will probably want to make your files easier to find by creating some subsidiary folders.

For example, to create the Family folder discussed earlier:

1. Click the **Finder** button on the Dock to open a Finder window to your default folder for new windows.

2. In the Sidebar, click the **Movies** folder to display its contents.

3. Open **File** and click **New Folder**. Mac OS X will create a new folder, assign it the default name "untitled folder," and display an edit box around it so that you can change the name immediately.

untitled folder

4. Type the new name for the folder and either press **RETURN** or click elsewhere to apply the name.

5. Double-click the new folder to open it.

QUICKSTEPS

RENAMING AND DELETING FILES AND FOLDERS

RENAME A FILE OR FOLDER

In List view or Columns view:

1. Click the **file** or **folder** once to select it.
2. Click again. An edit box will be displayed around the name.
3. Type the new name or edit the existing name.
4. Press **RETURN** or click elsewhere to apply the new name.

In Icons view, click the icon's label once to display the edit box. Then follow steps 3 and 4 above.

MOVE A FILE OR FOLDER TO THE TRASH

To move a file or folder to the Trash, use any of these techniques:

- Drag the file or folder to the **Trash** icon on the Dock.

  –Or–

- Press ⌘+**DELETE**.

  –Or–

- Select the object. Open **File** and click **Move To Trash**.

  –Or–

- **CONTROL**+click or right-click the object. Click **Move To Trash** on the context menu.

RECOVER A FILE OR FOLDER FROM THE TRASH

To recover a file or folder that has been moved to the Trash:

Immediately after moving the file or folder to Trash, open **Edit** and choose **Undo Move Of** *filename*.

–Or–

Click the **Trash** icon on the Dock to display a Finder window showing the contents of the Trash. Drag the file or folder from the Trash to the desired location.

Customize the Finder

To make the Finder even quicker and easier to use, you can customize various aspects of its behavior, including Icons view, List view, Columns view, and the Sidebar.

Start by activating the **Finder** (for example, click the Finder icon on the Dock, or click the desktop) and choosing **Go | Home** to open a Finder window showing your Home folder.

CUSTOMIZE ICONS VIEW

1. If the Finder window isn't using Icons view, open **View** and click **As Icons** to switch to Icons view.

2. Open **View** and click **Show View Options**. The options window will open, showing the short name of your user account (in the example, "dana") in its title bar (because your Home folder is selected).

3. Make sure the **All Windows** option button is selected if you want this customization to affect all windows. To affect only this window, select the **This Window Only** option button.

4. Drag the **Icon Size** slider to make the icons your preferred size.

5. Use the **Text Size** drop-down list box to specify the text size.

6. Specify the label position by selecting the **Bottom** option button or the **Right** option button.

7. Select the **Snap To Grid** check box if you want Mac OS X to align the icons to the invisible underlying grid rather than letting you position them anywhere.

8. Select the **Show Item Info** check box if you want to display brief information about the contents of a folder with its icon.

9. Select the **Show Icon Preview** check box if you want graphics to be displayed as miniature versions of their contents rather than as generic icons. This option is useful for folders that contain pictures.

10. If you want Mac OS X to arrange the icons automatically, select the **Keep Arranged By** check box and specify the appropriate item in the drop-down list box.

11. In the Background area, specify the background for the folder by selecting the **White** option button, the **Color** option button, or the **Picture** option button.

- If you select Color, click the **Color** button, use the resulting Palette to pick the color, and click **OK**.

- If you select Picture, click the **Select** button, choose the picture in the Select A Picture dialog box, and click **OK**.

12. Leave the options window open so that you can perform further customization.

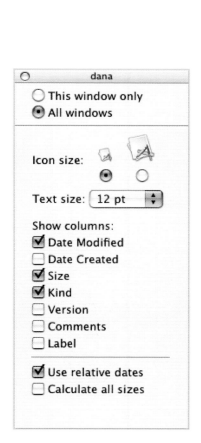

CUSTOMIZE LIST VIEW

1. With the options window still open, open **View** and click **As List** in the Finder window. The Finder window will switch to List view, and the options window will switch to displaying the options for List view.

2. Make sure the **All Windows** option button is selected if you want this customization to affect all windows. To affect only this window, select the **This Window Only** option button.

3. In the Icon Size area, click the option button for the size you prefer, large or small.

4. Use the **Text Size** drop-down list box to specify the text size.

5. In the **Show Columns** area, select the check boxes for the columns you want to have displayed in List view. The Name column is always displayed; you can't switch it off.

6. Select the **Use Relative Dates** check box if you want any date columns you display to use relative date descriptions, such as Today or Yesterday, instead of standard date formats (for example, 1 September 2004).

7. Select the **Calculate All Sizes** check box if you want Mac OS X to display the sizes of folders as well as files. Calculating the size of folders (especially those that contain many files) takes more processor cycles and may slow down the display of Finder windows.

8. Leave the options window open so that you can perform further customization.

CUSTOMIZE COLUMNS VIEW

1. With the options window still open, open **View** and click **As Columns** in the Finder window. The Finder window will switch to Columns view, and the options window will switch to displaying the options for Columns view.

2. Use the **Text Size** drop-down list box to specify the text size.

3. Select the **Show Icons** check box if you want to include icons in the listings. For a more compact display, clear this check box.

4. Select the **Show Preview Column** check box if you want to display the preview in the rightmost column. The preview is helpful for identifying files visually.

5. Click the **Close** button (the red button on the left).

Customize Finder Preferences

You can also customize various aspects of the Finder's look and behavior by using the Preferences window.

1. Open **Finder** and click **Preferences**. The Preferences window is displayed.

2. If the General sheet (see Figure 3-3) isn't displayed, click the **General** button to display it.

3. In the Show These Items On The Desktop area, choose which drives to show on the desktop by selecting or clearing the **Hard Disks** check box, the **CDs, DVDs And iPods** check box, and the **Connected Servers** check box.

4. In the New Finder Windows Open drop-down list box, choose the location you want each new Finder window to display: Computer, Macintosh HD, iDisk, Home, Documents, or another folder. The default is Home.

5. If you want each folder you open from a Finder window to be displayed in a new window instead of the same window, select the **Always Open Folders In A New Window** check box. If you prefer to use the Forward button and Back button to navigate among folders, clear this check box.

Figure 3-3: The General sheet of Finder's Preferences lets you specify which disk drives to show on the desktop, where and how new Finder windows open, and how to treat spring-loaded folders.

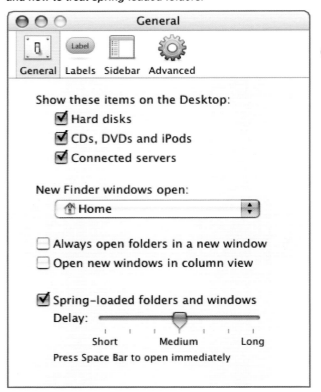

NOTE

Spring-loaded folders and windows are a Mac OS X feature that make moving and copying objects easier. Instead of having to open the destination before dragging an object, you can drag the object to the destination folder, wait a moment, and have Mac OS X open the folder automatically. Still dragging, you can open further folders inside that folder if necessary.

6. If you want new Finder windows always to use Columns view, select the **Open New Windows in Column View** check box.

7. Select the **Spring-Loaded Folders And Windows** check box if you want to use the spring-loaded folders feature. (See the Note.) Drag the **Delay** slider to specify how quickly the spring-loading works.

8. Click the **Labels** button to display the Labels sheet (see Figure 3-4), on which you can change the names used for the colored labels. (For example, you might change the name Red to "Urgent.")

Figure 3-4: On the Labels sheet of Finder Preferences, you can change the names used for the colored labels to better describe how you use them.

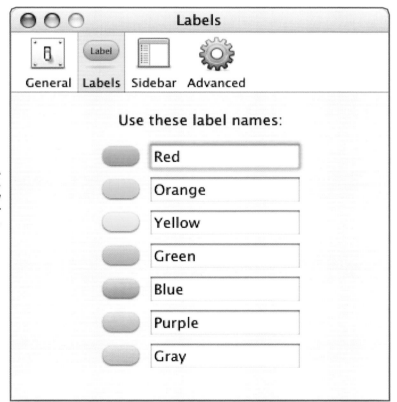

9. Click the **Sidebar** button to display the Sidebar sheet (see Figure 3-5).

10. Select the check boxes for the drives and folders you want the Sidebar to contain. Clear the check boxes for other items.

11. Click the **Advanced** button to display the Advanced sheet (see Figure 3-6).

12. Select the **Show All File Extensions** check box if you want Mac OS X to display all file extensions (instead of hiding most of them).

13. Clear the **Show Warning Before Emptying The Trash** check box if you don't want Mac OS X to display a confirmation message box when you empty the Trash. (See "Empty the Trash," later in this chapter.)

14. Click the **Close** button (the red button) to close the Preferences window.

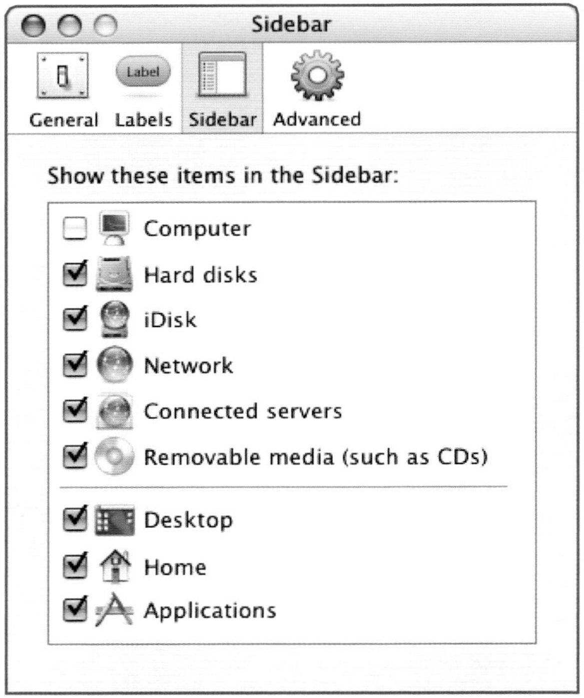

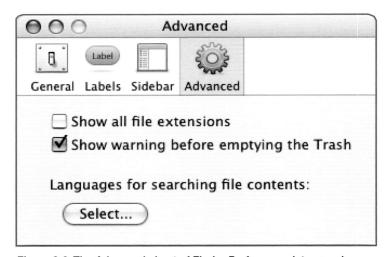

Figure 3-5: On the Sidebar sheet of Finder Preferences, choose which drives and folders to display in the Sidebar.

Figure 3-6: The Advanced sheet of Finder Preferences lets you choose whether to display file extensions and Trash warnings.

COPYING AND MOVING FILES AND FOLDERS

You can copy files and folders using the mouse, the menu, or the keyboard. You can move files and folders using the mouse.

COPY WITH THE MOUSE

To copy with the mouse, press and hold **OPTION** while dragging any file or folder from one folder to another on the same disk drive. To copy from a folder on one disk drive to a folder on another disk drive, drag without holding down OPTION.

MOVE WITH THE MOUSE

To move with the mouse, drag any file or folder from one folder to another on the same disk drive. To move from a folder on one disk drive to a folder on another disk drive, press and hold down ⌘ while dragging the object.

COPY USING THE MENU

To copy using the menu:

1. Select the object to copy.
2. Open **Edit** and click **Copy "*object*,"** where *object* is the object's name.
3. Navigate to the destination.
4. Open **Edit** and click **Paste Item**.

COPY USING THE KEYBOARD

To copy using the keyboard:

1. Select the object to copy.
2. Press ⌘+**C** to copy the object.
3. Navigate to the destination.
4. Press ⌘+**V** to paste the object.

Select Multiple Files or Folders

Often, you will want to perform one or more operations—such as copy, move, or delete—on several files and/or folders at the same time. You can select objects using any of several techniques:

- In Icon view, move the mouse pointer to just beyond the corner of the block of icons you want to select. Drag the mouse across the icons, creating a selection box around the icons and making Mac OS X select them. You can drag in whichever direction you find easiest.

    –Or–

- In List view or Columns view, drag up or down through the objects you want to select.

    –Or–

- Click the first object, hold down **SHIFT**, and click the last object. Mac OS X selects both of those objects and the objects between them. This method works best for selecting contiguous objects in List view or Columns view.

    –Or–

- Click the first object, hold down ⌘, and click each of the other objects. You can use this technique in any view. ⌘+click a selected object to deselect it.

Use the Trash

The Mac operating system has long used the metaphor of trash for deleting items. Instead of deleting an object immediately (and removing it from your Mac's hard disk so that you can never retrieve it again), you move the object to the Trash. An object remains in the Trash until you empty the Trash, at which point you can't retrieve it any more. This two-stage process is not only clear and familiar but helps you avoid deleting objects permanently by making hasty choices in the Finder.

The Trash is a special system folder that can contain both files and folders. You can open the Trash in a Finder window by clicking the **Trash** button on the Dock. Figure 3-7 shows the Trash open in List view. You can sort the Trash and search through it as you would any other folder.

EMPTY THE TRASH

Before emptying the Trash, you may want to double-check that you haven't moved any valuable files to it by mistake. Then:

1. Activate the **Finder**.

2. Open **Finder** and click **Empty Trash**. Mac OS X displays a confirmation message box.

3. Click **OK**. Mac OS X empties the Trash, permanently deleting all the objects it contains.

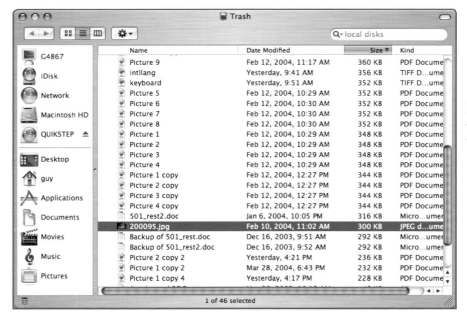

Figure 3-7: The Trash is a special folder that holds files and folders you've deleted until you empty it.

NOTE

You can turn off the confirmation message box by clearing the **Show Warning Before Emptying The Trash** check box on the Advanced sheet of Finder Preferences (Finder | Preferences).

CAUTION

You can also empty the Trash by **CONTROL**+clicking or right-clicking the **Trash** icon on the Dock and choosing **Empty Trash** from the shortcut menu. When you use this technique, however, Mac OS X doesn't display the confirmation message box.

NOTE

You can tell if an object is an alias in two ways. First, the lower-left corner of its icon bears a curling black arrow. Second, if you display the Info window for the object (for example, **CONTROL**+click or right-click it and choose **Get Info**), the Kind readout says *Alias*.

Mundane Tasks

USE THE SECURE EMPTY TRASH FEATURE

Emptying the Trash by using the technique described in the previous section gets rid of the files and folders well enough for conventional purposes, but the files leave fragments that computer recovery experts might be able to reassemble. If you need to ensure that your deleted material cannot be recovered like this, use the Secure Empty Trash feature instead of emptying the Trash.

1. Activate the **Finder** if it isn't already.
2. Open **Finder** and click **Secure Empty Trash**. Mac OS X displays a confirmation message box.
3. Click **OK**. Mac OS X empties the Trash, permanently deleting all the objects it contains and overwriting the disk sectors that contained them.

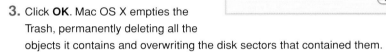

Are you sure you want to erase the items in the Trash permanently using Secure Empty Trash?

If you choose Secure Empty Trash, you cannot recover the files.

Cancel   OK

Secure Empty Trash takes longer than emptying the Trash in the conventional way.

Create Aliases

Aliases allow you to quickly access files from places other than where the files are stored. For example, you can start an application from the Dock even though the actual application file is stored in another folder. Similarly, you can store aliases for the documents you need most frequently in a convenient location, such as on your desktop (or on the Dock).

To create an alias:

1. Select the file or folder.
2. Open **File** and click **Make Alias**. Mac OS X will create an alias to the object and assign it the object's name and the word "alias." For example, an alias to the file named "Work Plans" receives the name "Work Plans alias."

TIP

You can also create an alias by holding down ⌘ and **OPTION** as you drag an object from its location to where you want to create the alias.

TIP

You can create multiple aliases to the same file or folder. If you move the original file or folder, Mac OS X automatically changes the aliases so that they refer to its new location.

NOTE

You can also search quickly by using the Search box on the Finder toolbar. Click the icon at the left end of the box and select the location to search—Local Disks, Home, Selection, or Everywhere. Then type your search term in the Search box. The Finder displays matching items as you type. Click the **X** button to clear the Search box of your last search.

3. Mac OS X places an edit box around the default name. If you want, type a new name and press **RETURN**.

4. Drag the alias to where you want to keep it.

Search for Files and Folders

It's often difficult to find files and folders on a computer, especially if it has a large hard disk (or several of them) and one or more network drives. The Finder provides a capable Find feature to help you locate the objects you need.

1. Activate the **Finder**.

2. Open **File** and click **Find**. The Find window is displayed, showing basic search settings (see Figure 3-8).

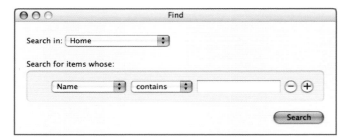

Figure 3-8: Mac OS X's Find feature quickly locates files matching the criteria you specify.

3. Use the **Search In** drop-down list box to tell Mac OS X where to search:

- **Home** searches your Home folder and all the folders it contains. If you store your documents in your Home folder, this is the quickest and easiest search option.

- **Everywhere** searches all the disk drives your Mac has access to: all local disks and all network drives. The resulting search is extremely thorough but may take a long time.

- **Local Disks** searches all your Mac's local disk drives: its hard disk drives, any optical drives that contain CDs or DVDs, any removable drives (for example, an iPod) that are connected, and any floppy drives that contain disks. This search will take a relatively long time (but not as long as an Everywhere search).

Specific Places displays extra controls for you to designate which disk drives or folders to search. Add a place by clicking **Add**, choosing the drive or folder in the Choose A Folder dialog box, and clicking **Choose**. Remove a place by selecting it in the list box and clicking **Remove**.

4. In the **Search For Items Whose** area, use the first line of controls to specify the first search criterion (see Table 3-1).

TABLE 1: SEARCH CRITERIA FOR FINDING OBJECTS WITH FIND

ITEM	COMPARISON	COMMENTS
Name	Contains Starts With Ends With Is	Specify the comparison and the appropriate text string. For example, you might specify Contains Jane to find files and folders whose names contain "Jane."
Content	Includes	Specify the text to find in the file's contents.
Date Modified	Is Today Is Within Is Before Is After Is Exactly	Use the drop-down list and (if needed) the text box to specify the time frame in which the object was last modified.
Date Created	Is Today Is Within Is Before Is After Is Exactly	Use the drop-down list and (if needed) the text box to specify the time frame in which the object was created.
Kind	Is Is Not	Specify the type: Alias, Application, Folder, Document, Audio, Image, Movie.
Label	Is Is Not	Specify the label color.
Size	Is Less Than Is Greater Than	Specify the size.
Extension	Is	Specify the extension (for example, .doc).
Visibility	Visible Items Invisible Items Visible And Invisible Items	Specify whether you're searching for visible or invisible objects.
Type	Is	Specify the object type.
Creator	Is	Specify the name of the user who created the object.

TIP

The better you target your searches, the faster they will be. If you know roughly where a file is stored, use a Specific Places search. Make your criteria as specific as possible so that you'll find only the documents you need.

TIP

You can also close a Finder window by opening **File** and clicking **Close Window** or by pressing ⌘+W.

5. To add another search criterion, click the **+** button. The Find window adds a second line of controls. Specify the next criterion using the same technique. This is an AND search: the search result must meet all the criteria you specify. Therefore, each criterion you add restricts the search further.

6. Click **Search**. Mac OS X displays a Search Results window (see Figure 3-9). The Parent column shows the folder that contains each object found. Click an object to display a partial tree diagram showing the object's location in the lower part of the window.

7. Double-click an object to open it. Double-click a folder in the tree diagram to open that folder.

8. Click the **Close** button (the red button) on the Search Results window to close it.

9. Click the **Close** button (the red button) on the Find window to close it.

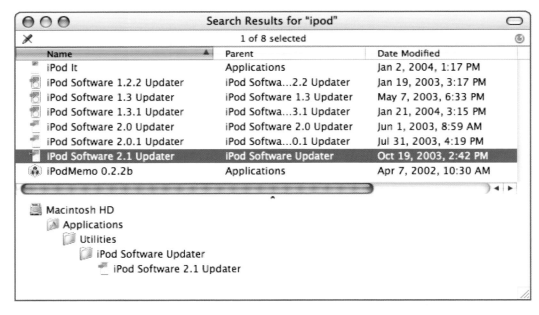

Figure 3-9: From the Search Results window, you can check the location of an object or double-click the object to open it.

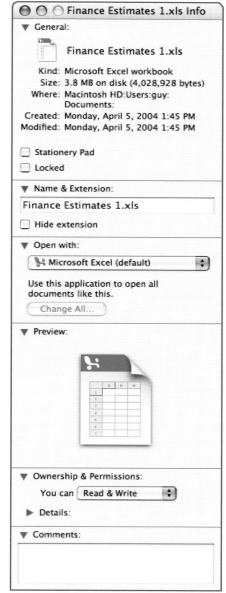

Figure 3-10: The Info window provides full information about an object.

Get Info About a File or Folder

List view displays some information about the selected object (such as its kind, its size, and the date it was last modified), and the Preview pane in Columns view displays substantially more information. But to get a full set of information about an object, you need to display its Info window:

1. Select the object in a Finder window or on the desktop.

2. Open **File** and click **Get Info**. The Info window will be displayed (see Figure 3-10).

3. Verify the information you want to know. You can expand and collapse the different sections of the window by clicking the gray triangles.

4. Click the **Close** button (the red button) to close the Info window.

Work with Ownership and Permissions

For security, Mac OS X assigns different levels of permissions to different objects. These permissions control what each user can do with an object: whether the user can see it but not change it (Read Only permission), see it and change it (Read & Write permission), not see it but add files to it (Write Only, which is used for public folders in which users can deposit files), or not access it at all (No Access permission). Each object also has an *owner*, a user or system process that has ultimate control over the object. For a file or folder that you create, you are the owner. For a system folder, the system is the owner.

Mac OS X's permissions are set up to give you free rein over your Home folder and its contents, keep you out of other users' folders (and keep them out of yours), and prevent you from damaging system folders. Administrator users have wider-reaching privileges than Standard users, who in turn have more privileges than Simplified users. (See Chapter 8 for a discussion of the different types of users.)

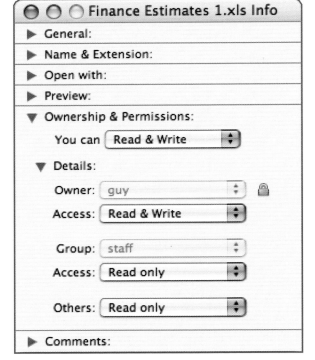

Figure 3-11: Use the Ownership & Permissions section of the Info dialog box to check and change permissions for an object.

CHECK AN OBJECT'S OWNERSHIP AND PERMISSIONS

To check an object's ownership and permissions, display the Info window for the object (click **File | Get Info**) and expand the Ownership & Permissions section (if necessary) by clicking the **Ownership & Permissions** gray triangle and the **Details** gray triangle. Figure 3-11 shows an example.

CHANGE AN OBJECT'S PERMISSIONS AND OWNERSHIP

Sometimes, you may need to change the permissions on an object—for example, to upgrade a user from Read Only access to Read & Write access so that the user can change a file. You'll need to be an administrator to do this.

1. If the **Lock** icon shows a closed lock, click it to open it.

2. In the Group drop-down list box, select the user or the group whose permission you want to change.

3. In the Access drop-down list box, select the necessary level of permission—for example, Read Only or Read & Write.

4. If Mac OS X displays the Authenticate dialog box, type your administrator password and click **OK**.

5. If you want to apply the permission change to the objects contained in the object you're changing (for example, the files in a folder), click the **Apply To Enclosed Items** button. Mac OS X will display a confirmation dialog box.

6. Click **OK**.

7. Click the **Lock** icon to change it from an open lock to a closed lock.

CREATING ZIP ARCHIVES OF FILES AND FOLDERS

Mac OS X enables you to create compressed archive files in the zip format:

1. In the Finder, select the files or folders you want to put in the archive.

2. Open **File** and click **Create Archive**. (The name of the command varies depending on the objects selected.) Mac OS X will create an archive file.

   • If the archive contains two or more objects, Mac OS X will name it Archive.zip.

   • If the archive contains only one object, Mac OS X gives the archive the same name as the object but adds the .zip extension.

3. If necessary, click the object's name once (in Icons view) or twice with a pause (in List view or Columns view), type the new name, and press **RETURN**.

To open a zip archive, double-click it.

CAUTION

Once you encrypt your file with FileVault, the ONLY way to retrieve your file is with the password. If you forget or lose your password, you have effectively lost your file.

More rarely, you may need to change an object's ownership:

1. If the **Lock** icon shows a closed lock, click it to open the lock.

2. In the Owner drop-down list box, select the new owner for the object. Mac OS X will display the Authenticate dialog box.

3. Type your administrator password and click **OK**.

4. Click the **Lock** icon to change it from an open lock to a closed lock.

5. Click the **Close** button (the red button) to close the Info window.

Encrypt Your Home Folder with FileVault

Mac OS X versions 10.3 (Panther) and later have a feature named FileVault, which can automatically encrypt all the objects stored in your Home folder using a security protocol that's extremely hard to crack.

DECIDE WHETHER TO USE FILEVAULT

FileVault is turned off by default because, while it's extremely secure, if you forget your password, you can lose access to your own files—permanently. Before turning on FileVault, evaluate whether you really need it. If your Mac contains secret or sensitive information, and if the risk of losing your Mac is even moderately high (for example, because you have a PowerBook or iBook), consider FileVault. If your Mac contains only mundane information, FileVault probably isn't worth the effort.

Apart from the potential for losing your files, FileVault's other disadvantage is that it slows down your Mac a little. If your Mac is slow anyway, you may find FileVault's added burden a problem. If your Mac normally runs quickly, you may not notice the difference.

When you log in, FileVault decrypts your folders and files so that you can use them. When you log out (or shut down your Mac), FileVault encrypts the folders and files again. So, FileVault ensures only that your folders and files are secure only when you're logged out. If you leave your Mac running without logging out, anyone can access your folders and files using your credentials.

Figure 3-12: On the Security sheet of System Preferences, encrypt your Home folder with FileVault.

SET A MASTER PASSWORD FOR YOUR MAC

Before you turn on FileVault, you must create a master password for your Mac. The master password enables an administrator to turn off FileVault for any user of the Mac. So, if a user who isn't an administrator forgets his or her FileVault password, the administrator can use the master password to rescue that user's files.

To set the master password:

1. Open ♦ and click **System Preferences**. The System Preferences window will be displayed.
2. Click **Security**. The Security sheet will be displayed (see Figure 3-12).
3. Click **Set Master Password**. Mac OS X will display the sheet shown in Figure 3-13.
4. Type the password in the Master Password text box and in the Verify text box, and enter a reminder in the Hint text box if you want to. (Make the hint oblique enough that it helps only you, not anyone looking to break into your Mac.)
5. Click **OK**.

Figure 3-13: Set a master password for your Mac so that you can recover your files if your forget your account password.

TURN ON FILEVAULT

After setting the master password, you can turn on FileVault:

1. Click **Turn On FileVault**. FileVault will prompt you for your password:

2. Type your password and click **OK**. FileVault will display a warning dialog box to ensure you understand the consequences of what you're doing:

3. Click **Turn On FileVault**. Mac OS X will log you out so that FileVault can encrypt your Home folder. You will see the FileVault screen (shown here) while FileVault works.

4. When FileVault has finished encrypting your Home folder, Mac OS X will display the login screen. Log in as usual.

> ## NOTE
>
> FileVault ties in with the other security settings that Mac OS X offers. Chapter 8 discusses how to control security on your Mac.

TURN OFF FILEVAULT

If you decide that FileVault doesn't suit you, turn it off:

1. Open and click **System Preferences**. The System Preferences window will be displayed.

2. Click **Security**. The Security sheet will be displayed.

3. Click **Turn Off FileVault**. FileVault will prompt you for your password.

4. Type your password and click **OK**. FileVault will display a confirmation message box.

5. Click **Turn Off FileVault**. Mac OS X will log you out so that FileVault can decrypt your Home folder. You'll see a FileVault screen during the decryption.

6. When FileVault has finished decrypting your Home folder, Mac OS X will display the login screen. Log in as usual.

Back Up Files and Folders

Backing up copies important files and folders on your disk and writes them on another device, such as a recordable CD, recordable DVD, or a Zip disk.

If you have a membership with Apple's .Mac service, you can download the free Backup utility and use it to back up your data either to a local disk or to your .Mac iDisk, as described in this section. If you don't have a .Mac membership, you may prefer another backup utility (such as Retrospect from Dantz). Alternatively, you can use the Finder to burn copies of files and folders to CD or DVD as a backup (see the next section).

GET AND INSTALL BACKUP

Download Backup from the .Mac web site (www.mac.com), double-click the resulting installer package (Backup.pkg) to run it, and follow through the installation routine. You'll need to supply an administrator's name and password in the Authenticate dialog box before you can install Backup. See Chapter 4 for how to access and use the Internet and how to download files across it.

RUN AND ACTIVATE BACKUP

1. Activate the **Finder**.

2. Open **Go** and click **Applications**. A Finder window showing your Applications folder will be displayed.

3. Double-click **Backup**. Backup will launch, contact the iDisk server (if an Internet connection is available), and activate itself.

4. Click **OK**. Backup will appear (see Figure 3-14), suggesting a default selection of key information (such as your Address Book contacts and your password Keychain) for backup to your iDisk.

Back Up	Items	Size	Last Backed Up
☑	Address Book contacts	660K	--
☑	Stickies notes	4K	--
☑	iCal calendars	32K	--
☑	Safari settings	652K	--
☑	Internet Explorer settings	248K	--
☑	Keychain (for passwords)	36K	--
☐	Preference files for applications	--	--
☐	AppleWorks files in Home folder	--	--
☐	Excel files in Home folder	--	--
☐	iPhoto library	--	--
☐	iTunes library	--	--
☑	iTunes purchased music	50.9M	--
☐	Mail messages and settings	--	--
☐	PowerPoint files in Home folder	--	--
☐	Word files in Home folder	--	--
☐	Files on Desktop	--	--
☑	Documents	744M	--
☑	GarageBand	536M	--

Backup — Back up to CD/DVD

Est. Required Discs: 3 CDs or 1 DVD   9 Items, 1.30 GB used

Backup Now

Figure 3-14: Backup is a straightforward application for backing up your files and folders to a hard drive, to CD or DVD, or to your iDisk.

USE BACKUP TO BACK UP DATA

To back up data with Backup:

1. Start Backup as described in the previous section. Figure 3-14 shows the Backup window with settings chosen for a backup to CD or DVD.

2. In the drop-down list box at the top of the window, select the backup destination: Back Up To iDisk, Back Up To CD/DVD, or Back Up To Drive.

3. Select the check boxes for the default items you want to back up.

4. Add further folders by dragging them from a Finder window (or from your desktop) or by clicking the + button, using the resulting sheet to specify a folder, and clicking **Choose**.

5. Remove an existing item if necessary by selecting it and choosing **Edit | Remove From List**.

6. Check the readout at the bottom of the window to see how much space the backup will require. Make sure your backup medium has enough space.

7. Click **Backup Now**. Backup will prompt you to name your backup.

8. Accept the default name or type your preferred name, then click **Begin Backup**.

9. Follow any prompts to designate the disk drive or supply CDs or DVDs—as shown here, for example:

10. Backup will notify you when the backup is complete:

11. Click **OK**.

NOTE

You must have a paid membership in .Mac (currently $99 per year) to use Backup to back up data to a CD/DVD.

QUICKSTEPS

MANAGING DISKS

Mac OS X makes managing disks as straightforward as possible.

ADD A DISK TO YOUR MAC

You can add most disks to your Mac by simply inserting them or plugging them in. For example:

1. Insert a CD or DVD in your CD drive or DVD drive. Mac OS X will mount it (installs it) automatically and display an icon on the desktop for it, and will start playing its content (if your preferences are set to do so).

2. Plug in a hot-pluggable drive such as a USB drive, a FireWire drive, a memory-card reader, or an iPod. (*Hot-pluggable* means that you can attach the drive while your Mac is running, instead of having to shut your Mac down first.) Mac OS X will mount the drive automatically and display an icon for it on the desktop.

REMOVE A DISK FROM YOUR MAC

You can remove most kinds of disks from your Mac by dragging them to the Trash. If you find this concept peculiar or the action awkward, select the disk, open **File** and click **Eject** *Disk Name* (where *Disk Name* is the name of the disk). Some keyboards have an eject button in the upper-right corner for ejecting a disk from a CD or DVD drive.

ERASE A REWRITABLE CD OR DVD

After writing data to a rewritable CD or DVD, you must erase the disc's contents before you can write data to it again.

1. Activate the **Finder**.

2. Open **Go** and click **Utilities**. A Finder window showing your Utilities folder will be displayed.

3. Double-click **Disk Utility**. Disk Utility will open.

Continued...

RESTORE DATA FROM BACKUP

Backup is a tedious but necessary chore that becomes exciting only when you need to restore data from backup after suffering data loss. To restore data from backup:

1. Activate the **Finder**.

2. Open **Go** and click **Applications**. A Finder window showing your Applications folder will be displayed.

3. Double-click **Backup**. Backup will launch.

4. In the drop-down list box at the top of the window, select the restore source: Restore From iDisk, Restore From CD/DVD, or Restore From Drive.

5. Follow the prompts to specify the disk drive or supply the master disc of the backup set—as shown here, for example:

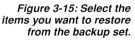

6. After reading the restore source, Backup displays the items available (see Figure 3-15).

7. Select the check boxes for the items you want to restore.

Figure 3-15: Select the items you want to restore from the backup set.

MANAGING DISKS

ERASE A REWRITABLE CD OR DVD *(Continued)*

4. Click the **Erase** tab button to display the Erase tab (see Figure 3-16).

5. Select the entry for the disc in the list box.

6. Click **Erase**. Disk Utility will display a confirmation sheet:

Erase Optical Media

Erasing an optical disc (CD-RW, DVD-RW, etc.) will destroy all information on the disc. Are you sure you wish to erase the optical disc "MATSHITADVD-R UJ -815"?

Cancel   Erase

7. Click **Erase**. Disk Utility erases the disc.

8. The Finder displays a dialog box asking what you want to do with the disc. Click **Eject** to eject it, or select **Open Finder** in the Action drop-down list box and click **OK** if you want to write data to the disc immediately.

9. Click **Disk Utility | Quit Disk Utility** to close Disk Utility.

8. Click **Restore Now**. Backup will begin the restore operation, checking with you before overwriting files or folders, as shown here:

Are you sure you want to replace the item "bass guitar.aif"?

This will replace the item on your hard disk with an identically named item from the backup.

☑ Apply to All   Show In Finder   Replace   Skip

9. Click **Replace** to replace a file or **Skip** to skip replacing it. Select the **Apply To All** check box to apply your choice to all the files or folders.

10. Open **Backup** and click **Quit Backup** to close Backup.

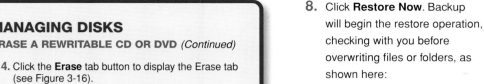

Figure 3-16: Use the Erase tab of Disk Utility to erase a rewritable disc so that you can use it again.

Write Files and Folders to a CD or DVD

Mac OS X allows you to copy ("burn," or record) files to a writable or rewritable CD or DVD. You must have a CD-R (writable) or CD-RW (rewritable) drive and suitable blank media to burn CDs. To burn DVDs, you need an Apple SuperDrive or a compatible DVD burner and writable or rewritable blank media.

TIP

When buying writable or recordable media, put quality above price. If your data is valuable, there's no point in using low-quality discs that won't preserve it perfectly, no matter how much of a bargain those discs may appear to be.

1. Insert a blank CD or DVD (as appropriate) into your CD burner or DVD burner. Mac OS X will display a dialog box asking what you want to do with the disc:

2. Select **Open Finder** in the Action drop-down list box.

3. Click **OK**. Mac OS X will mount the disc as a drive on the desktop with a name such as *untitled CD*.

4. Click the disc's name to select it, type the desired name, and press **RETURN**.

5. Double-click the disc's icon to open a Finder window showing its contents (nothing yet).

6. Drag files and folders to the CD from another Finder window or from your desktop. Rearrange the files and folders in the CD Finder window as desired.

7. When you're ready to burn the CD, open **File** and click **Burn Disc**. Mac OS X will display a confirmation dialog box, as shown here:

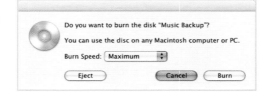

8. Click **Burn**. Mac OS X will burn the disc and then mount it on the desktop.

9. Drag the disk to the Trash to eject it, and then label it.

Chapter 4
Using the Internet

The Internet provides a major means for worldwide communications between both individuals and organizations, and for locating and sharing information. To use the Internet, you must have a connection to it, either a dial-up connection or a broadband connection. You can then send and receive e-mail, access the World Wide Web, and use instant messaging.

Connect to the Internet

You can connect to the Internet using a telephone line, a cable TV connection, or a satellite link. With a telephone, you can connect with either a dial-up connection or a DSL (digital subscriber line) connection (see comparison in Table 4-1). DSL, cable TV, and satellite connections are called broadband connections because of their higher (than dial-up) speed and common setup (see comparison in Table 4-2). You must have access to at least one of these forms of communication in order to connect to the Internet. You must also set up the Internet connection itself.

TABLE 4-1: *Comparison of Dial-Up and DSL Connections*

FEATURE	DIAL-UP	DSL
Cost	Average $20/month	Average $40/month
Speed	Up to 48 Kbps* download**, 33 Kbps upload	Most common: 768 Kbps download, 128 Kbs upload
Connection	Dial up each time	Always connected
Use of line	Ties up line, may want a second line	Line can be used for voice and fax while connected to the Internet

* **Kbps is Kilobits (thousands of bits, 1 or 0) per second.**
** **Download is receiving information from the Internet on your computer.**

TABLE 4-2: *Representative Speeds, Costs, and Reliability for Internet Connections*

SERVICE	DOWNLOAD SPEED	UPLOAD SPEED	MONTHLY COST	RELIABILITY
Dial-Up	48 Kbps	33.6 Kbps	$20	Fair
DSL	768 Kbps	128 Kbps	$40	Good
Cable Internet	1 Mbps	500 Kbps	$40	Good
Satellite Internet	1 Mbps	150 Kbps	$60	Fair

NOTE

To connect to the Internet, you must have an existing account with an Internet service provider (ISP), and you must know your ISP's phone number for your modem to dial. You also need to know the user name and password for your account. This information is provided by your ISP when you establish your account.

Set Up Communications

Communications is the physical link between your Mac and the Internet. To set up connections, you must first choose between a dial-up and a broadband connection.

SET UP A DIAL-UP CONNECTION

To set up a *dial-up connection* that uses the modem to dial and connect to another computer at the other end of the phone line:

1. Open and click **System Preferences**. The System Preferences window will be displayed.
2. Click **Network**. The Network sheet will be displayed.
3. Select **Internal Modem** in the Show drop-down list box. The Internal Modem controls will be displayed.

4. If the PPP tab (see Figure 4-1) isn't displayed, click the **PPP** tab button. (PPP is the abbreviation for Point-to-Point Protocol, the network protocol used for connecting to the Internet via dial-up.)

Figure 4-1: A dial-up connection requires an account name, password, and phone number.

5. Enter the service provider name, account name, password, and telephone number in the boxes provided. If your ISP gave you an alternate dial-up number, enter that in the Alternate Number box.

6. Click **PPP Options** to display the dialog box shown in Figure 4-2.

Figure 4-2: Choose connection and disconnection options for your internet connection.

7. Choose suitable options for your needs in the Session Options area. You can decide:

- Whether Mac OS X connects automatically when needed (for example, when you open an application that requires an Internet connection)
- Whether to disconnect after a specified interval of inactivity or when you log out
- Whether (and if so, how many times) to redial the connection if it's busy

8. Click **OK** to close the dialog box.

9. Click **Apply Now** to apply your settings.

10. Click the **Modem** tab button to display the Modem tab (see Figure 4-3).

11. Check that the settings are suitable for the connection. The settings required vary by ISP, but the following settings are fairly typical:

- Select the **Enable Error Correction And Compression In Modem** check box.
- Select the **Wait For Dial Tone Before Dialing** check box.
- In the Dialing area, select the **Tone** option button unless you have pulse dialing (in which case, select the **Pulse** option button). If in doubt, pick up your phone and press any of the higher numeric keys (7, 8, or 9). If you hear a single beep, select the **Tone** option button. If you hear rapid clicks, select the **Pulse** option button.
- In the Sound area, select the **On** option button so that you can hear your modem dialing. Hearing the modem is helpful when setting up your connection. When the connection is working reliably, you may prefer to turn the sound off by selecting the **Off** option button.
- In the Connection area, choose whether to have Mac OS X notify you of incoming phone calls when you're online.
- Select the **Show Modem Status In Menu Bar** check box to make modem details appear in the menu bar. (This enables you to quickly check the status of your connection.)

12. Click **Apply Now** to apply your settings.

13. Press ⌘+Q or choose **System Preferences | Quit System Preferences** to close System Preferences.

Figure 4-3: Configure settings for your modem on the Modem tab.

TIP

To connect quickly, click the **modem** icon in the menu bar and choose **Connect**. The modem icon displays information about the progress of the connection.

CONNECT TO THE INTERNET

You're now ready to connect to the Internet:

1. Click the **Modem** icon in the menu bar and choose **Open Internet Connect** from the menu. The Internet Connect application opens, displaying the Internal Modem sheet (see Figure 4-4).

2. Click **Connect**. Mac OS X dials your ISP, establishes the connection, and registers your Mac on the Internet. Internet Connect displays information about the progress of the connection. You will hear the modem dialing and going through the *handshaking* (beeps and pinging sounds) with the ISP's modem.

3. To disconnect, click the **Modem** icon in the menu bar and choose **Disconnect**. Alternatively, click **Disconnect** in Internet Connect.

4. Open **Internet Connect** and click **Quit Internet Connect** to close Internet Connect.

Modem: Idle

Connect

✓ Internal Modem

✓ Show time connected
✓ Show status while connecting

Open Internet Connect...

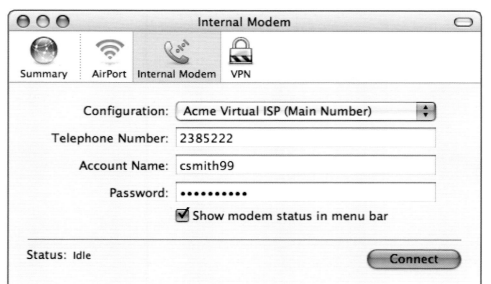

Figure 4-4: Use the Internet Connect application to connect to the Internet.

NOTE

Sometimes a DSL or TV cable connecting device is called a "modem," but it is not an analog-to-digital converter, which is the major point of a **mo**dulator-**dem**odulator. For this reason, this book doesn't describe DSL and cable connecting devices as modems.

NOTE

Because Safari is Mac OS X's default browser, this book assumes that you will use Safari to access the Web.

CAUTION

Unless you use a custom redirection service such as Anonymizer (www.anonymizer.com), each web site you visit can learn your Mac's Internet Protocol (IP) address, and your ISP keeps records of the IP address assigned to your Mac in your online sessions. Beyond this relatively straightforward, join-the-dots method of identification (which the FBI can subpoena from ISPs under the Communications Assistance for Law Enforcement Act, or CALEA), the National Security Agency (NSA) actively monitors massive amounts of worldwide Internet traffic.

SET UP A BROADBAND CONNECTION

A broadband connection—which uses a DSL phone line, a TV cable, or a satellite connection—is normally made with a device that connects to your local area network (LAN) and allows several computers on the network to use the connection. (See Chapter 9 for instructions on setting up a network.) With a network set up, your computer connected to the network, and a broadband service connected to the network, your computer is connected to the broadband service. There is nothing else you need to do to set up a broadband connection.

Test Your Internet Connection

By now, you should have configured your Internet connection. The easiest way to test that it's working is to try to connect to the Internet by clicking the **Safari** icon on the Dock. If an Internet web page is displayed, then you are connected and you need do no more. If you did not connect to the Internet and you know that your dial-up or broadband and network connections are all working properly, you will need to change some parameters of your Internet connection.

Use the World Wide Web

The *World Wide Web* (or just the *Web*) is the sum of all the web sites in the world—examples of which are CNN, EBay, and the Apple web site. The World Wide Web is what you can access with a *web browser*, such as Safari, which comes with Mac OS X and is Mac OS X's default web browser.

Search the Internet

You can search the Internet in two ways: by using the search facility built into Safari (which is powered by Google, a major search site) and by using an independent search facility on the Web.

Click the **Erase Search Text** icon (the X icon) in the Search text box to clear the box's contents. To reuse one of your recent searches, click the arrow button at the left end of the box and choose the search from the pop-up menu.

SEARCH FROM SAFARI

To search using Safari's built-in Google search facility:

1. Click the **Safari** icon on the Dock to start Safari.

2. Click in the **Search** text box in the upper-right corner of the Safari window.

3. Type what you want to search for.

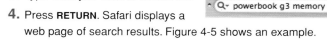

4. Press **RETURN**. Safari displays a web page of search results. Figure 4-5 shows an example.

5. Click a result to display its page.

Figure 4-5: The results of a search using Safari's built-in Google search facility

BROWSING THE INTERNET

Browsing the Internet uses a browser, such as Safari, to go from one web site to another to see the sites' contents. You can browse to a site by directly entering a site address, or *URL* (uniform resource locator), by navigating to a site from another site, or by using the browser controls. First, you must start the browser.

STARTING A BROWSER

To start Safari, click the **Safari** icon on the Dock or activate the **Finder**, click **Go | Applications**, and double-click **Safari**.

ENTER A WEB SITE DIRECTLY

To go directly to a web site:

1. Start Safari.

2. Click the icon at the left end of the Address text box to select the entire address.

3. Type the address of the web site you want to open and press **RETURN**.

USING SITE NAVIGATION

Site navigation means to use a combination of links and menus on one web page to locate and open another web page, either in the same site or in another site.

- **Links** are words, phrases, sentences, or graphics that you click to display the linked pages. When you position the mouse pointer over a link, the pointer changes to display a hand icon with the forefinger pointing upward. Links are often underlined.

- **Menus** contain one or a few words, in either a horizontal or vertical list, that you click to display the linked pages.

Continued...

SEARCH FROM AN INTERNET SEARCH SITE

There are many independent Internet search sites. A popular one is Yahoo!

1. Click the **Safari** icon on the Dock to open Safari.

2. Click the icon at the left end of the Address text box (the blue icon in the example shown here) to select the address.

3. Type www.yahoo.com and press **RETURN** to go to the Yahoo! site.

4. In the **Search The Web** text box on the Yahoo! site, type the text you want to search for.

5. Press **RETURN** or click the **Yahoo! Search** button on the site. Safari displays a web page of search results.

6. Click the link of your choice to go to that page.

Keep Bookmarks of Your Favorite Sites

Sometimes you visit a site that you would like to return to quickly or often. Safari provides a feature called "bookmarks" that you can use to save markers to specific pages on sites so that you can access them quickly. You can access bookmarks via the Bookmarks bar, which Safari displays below the Address bar by default, the Bookmarks menu, or the Bookmarks window. You can add a limited number of bookmarks (a dozen or two) to the Bookmarks bar, which Safari displays below the Address bar by default. You can add more bookmarks to the Bookmarks menu, and an unlimited number to the Bookmarks window. Use the Bookmarks bar for your primary bookmarks, the Bookmarks menu for your secondary bookmarks, and the Bookmarks window for the remainder of them.

CREATE A BOOKMARK ON THE BOOKMARKS BAR

To create a bookmark on the Bookmarks bar:

1. Navigate to the web page you want to bookmark.

2. Drag the icon at the left end of the Address text box to the Bookmarks bar.

3. Safari will display a naming sheet showing the page's title. Type the name you want (keep it short so that it doesn't waste space on the Bookmarks bar), and click **OK**.

BROWSING THE INTERNET *Continued...*

USE BROWSER NAVIGATION

Browser navigation means using the controls within your browser to go to another web page:

- Click the **Back** button to go to the previous page in the stack of pages you have viewed.

- Click the **Forward** button to move forward again.

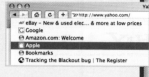

- To navigate quickly, click the **Back** button or the **Forward** button and hold down the mouse button for a second to display a menu of the recent pages available. Drag down to select the page you want.

- Press **DELETE** to go back to the previous page. Press **SHIFT+DELETE** to go forward to the next page.

USE WINDOWS AND TABS

Safari lets you open multiple windows, so that you can view two or more web pages in different windows at the same time. With default settings, you can open a link in a new window by holding down ⌘ as you click a link.

Safari also enables you to use multiple tabs in the same window. You must first enable tabbed browsing by choosing **Safari | Preferences**, clicking the **Tabs** button, selecting the **Enable Tabbed Browsing** check box, and clicking the **Close** button (the red button).

Once you've done this, you can open a link on a new tab in the current window by holding down ⌘ as you click the link. (When you switch on tabbed browsing, this shortcut opens the link on a new tab instead of in a new window.) Safari selects the new tab.

When you open the first new tab, Safari displays the tab bar below the Address bar and the Bookmarks bar. You can navigate to another tab by clicking it.

CREATE A BOOKMARK

To create a bookmark:

1. Navigate to the web page you want to bookmark.

2. Choose **Bookmarks | Add Bookmark**. Safari will display a naming sheet showing the page's title.

3. Edit the name or type a new name. Make the name as compact yet descriptive as possible so that you can grasp instantly what the web page contains.

4. Use the drop-down list box to specify where to save the bookmark:

    - Choose **Bookmarks Menu** to create the bookmark as an entry on the Bookmarks menu. Doing this makes the bookmark quickly accessible, but your Bookmarks menu will soon grow long.

    - Choose a folder or subfolder to create the bookmark in that folder. You can then access the bookmark through the Bookmarks window.

5. Click **Add**.

REARRANGE BOOKMARKS ON THE BOOKMARKS BAR

To move a bookmark on the Bookmarks bar, drag it to the new position.

To remove a bookmark from the Bookmarks bar, drag it into the Safari window.

OPEN A BOOKMARKED PAGE

To open a bookmarked page:

- Click the appropriate button on the Bookmarks bar.

  –Or–

- Open **Bookmarks** and click the bookmark's item.

  –Or–

- Display the Bookmarks window, select the category, and double-click the bookmark.

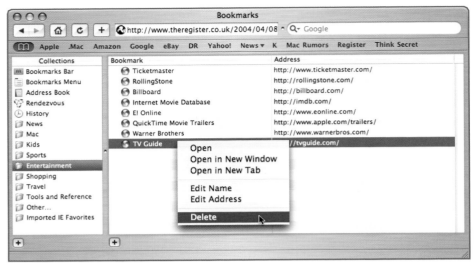

Figure 4-6: Use the Bookmarks window to navigate through and manage your full set of bookmarks.

USE THE BOOKMARKS WINDOW

To see all your bookmarks, open **Bookmarks** and click **Show All Bookmarks**. Safari displays the Bookmarks window (see Figure 4-6).

Click a collection in the Collections pane to display its contents. Then:

- Double-click a bookmark to open it.

    –Or–

- **CONTROL**+click or right-click a bookmark and choose **Delete** to delete it.

To leave the Bookmarks window, open **Bookmarks** and click **Hide All Bookmarks.**

TIP

If you have a slow connection, there's a tab trick you can benefit from: Hold down ⌘+SHIFT as you click a link to open the linked page on a new tab but keep the current tab displayed. When you're ready, click the new tab to switch to it.

To close a tab, click the X button on it. OPTION+click a tab's X button to close all the other tabs.

Change Your Home Page

Each time you start Safari, it automatically opens a specific web page called your "home page." (You can also display your home page by clicking the **Home** icon on the toolbar. If this icon doesn't appear on the toolbar, open **View** and click **Home** to add it.) To change your home page:

1. Click the **Safari** icon on the Dock to open Safari.

2. Go to the page you want to use as your home page.

3. Choose **Safari | Preferences**. The Preferences window will open.

4. Click the **General** button. The General sheet will be displayed.

5. Click **Set To Current Page** to make the current page your home page.

6. Click the **Close** button (the red button) to close the Preferences window.

CONTROLLING INTERNET SECURITY

Safari allows you to control several aspects of Internet security to help keep your browsing sessions safe. To configure settings for these features, display the Security sheet of the Preferences window:

1. Click the **Safari** button on the Dock. Safari will launch.
2. Choose **Safari | Preferences**. The Preferences window will be displayed.
3. Click the **Security** button. The Security sheet will be displayed (see Figure 4-7).

HANDLE COOKIES

Cookies are small files containing text data that web sites store on your computer so that they can identify your Mac when you return to the web site. Cookies have a positive side: they can save you from having to enter your name and ID frequently. Many e-commerce web sites (sites where you can execute a payment transaction over the Web) require cookies for their shopping carts and payment mechanisms to work at all.

Cookies can also be dangerous, enabling web sites to identify you when you do not want them to be able to do so, and potentially letting outsiders access sensitive information on your Mac. Safari lets you choose whether to accept or reject requests to store cookies on your Mac.

To determine whether Safari accepts cookies, select the **Always** option button, the **Never** option button, or the **Only From Sites You Navigate To** option button in the Accept Cookies area of the Security sheet.

The default setting is Only From Sites You Navigate To, which makes Safari accept cookies from sites you actively navigate to (for example, by clicking a link) but reject cookies from other sites, such as advertisers on

Continued...

Access Your Browsing History

Safari keeps a history of the web pages you visit so that you can easily return to a site you've visited in the past. Safari keeps about a week's worth of history (the period will be shorter if you visit very many web pages each day). You can clear your history.

USE HISTORY

To use History, open **History** and choose the page from the History menu or from one of the submenus named by day and date.

CLEAR HISTORY

You may want to clear your history so that nobody who can access your Mac can see which pages you've visited. To clear your history, open **History** and click **Clear History**.

Figure 4-7: Use the options on the Security sheet of Safari's Preferences window to control how Safari handles cookies, web content, and pop-up windows.

Use SnapBack

In addition to History, Safari provides SnapBack, a feature that lets you quickly return to the SnapBack page for each window. The SnapBack page is:

- The first page you opened in a window (until you change it)
- The last page you opened in this window by typing its address in the Address text box
- The last page you opened in this window from History or using a bookmark
- The last page you marked as a SnapBack page by choosing **History** | **Mark Page For SnapBack**

When a SnapBack page is available in a window, Safari displays an orange icon with a white arrow at the right end of the Address text box. Click this icon to return to the SnapBack page:

Copy Information from the Internet

You'll sometimes find information on the Internet that you want to copy—a picture, some text, or a web page.

COPY A PICTURE FROM A WEB PAGE

To copy a picture from the current web page to your hard disk:

1. **CONTROL+**click or right-click the picture and click **Save Image As**. Safari will display a Save As sheet.

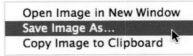

2. In the Save As text box, change the picture's default name if you want. (For example, you might assign a more descriptive name.)

3. In the Where drop-down list box, choose the folder in which you want to save the picture.

4. Click **Save**.

COPY TEXT FROM THE INTERNET

To copy some text from the current web page to a text editor or word processor:

1. Drag across the text to select it.
2. CONTROL+click or right-click the selection, and choose **Copy**.
3. Open or switch to a text editing application (for example, Text Editor) or the word processor (for example, Microsoft Word).
4. CONTROL+click or right-click where you want the text to appear, and choose **Paste**.

COPY A WEB PAGE FROM THE INTERNET

To copy the current web page and store it on your hard disk:

1. Choose **File** | **Save As**. Safari will display a Save sheet.
2. In the Save As text box, change the page's default name if you want. (For example, you might assign a more descriptive name to help you identify the page.)
3. In the Where drop-down list box, choose the folder in which you want to save the picture.
4. Click **Save**.

Play Internet Audio and Video

You can play audio and video from the Internet with Safari by clicking an audio or video link on a web page. Safari launches the appropriate plug-in or helper application for the content.

Chapter 7 discusses working with audio and video in depth.

Use Internet E-Mail

Mac OS X includes a powerful e-mail application named Mail that allows you to send and receive e-mail.

NOTE

If your Dock doesn't include a Mail icon, click the **desktop**, choose **Go | Applications** to open a Finder window showing your Applications folder, and then double-click the **Mail** icon. Alternatively, drag the **Mail** icon to the Dock to add it, and then click the icon you just added.

Establish an E-Mail Account

To send and receive e-mail, you must establish an e-mail account with an Internet service provider (ISP) and configure that account in Mail. To set up your e-mail account, you need to know the following information, which your ISP will provide:

- Your e-mail address (for example, <u>csmith6446@example.com</u>)
- Your account name with the e-mail provider (for example, <u>csmith</u>)
- Your password
- The incoming mail server's name (for example, <u>pop3.example.com</u>) and its type (POP3, IMAP, or HTTP)
- The outgoing mail server's name (for example, <u>smtp.example.com</u>)

With an Internet connection established and with this information, you can set up an account in Mail:

1. Click the **Mail** icon on the Dock. The first time you start Mail it will display several messages, and then it will display the Welcome To Mail dialog box (see Figure 4-8)—unless you have already set up an e-mail account, as you may have when installing Mac OS X.

2. Enter the account details in the text boxes and click **OK**. Mail will quickly check the information to see if it can access the account. If all is well, Mail will display this Import Mailboxes dialog box:

Welcome to Mail

You have no email accounts configured to use Mail. Please enter the following information to send and receive email.

Full Name:	Chris Smith
Email Address:	chris__smith@mac.com
Incoming Mail Server:	mail.mac.com
Account Type:	IMAP
User Name:	chris__smith@mac.com
Password:	••••••••••••
Outgoing Mail Server (SMTP):	smtp.mac.com

(?)   (Quit)   (OK)

Figure 4-8: Enter the details of your e-mail account in the Welcome To Mail dialog box.

3. If you need to import mailboxes from another e-mail application, click **Yes** and follow through the resulting series of Import windows. Otherwise, click **No**. Mail will open, displaying the Inbox (see Figure 4-9).

Create and Send E-Mail

To create and send an e-mail message:

1. Open or activate **Mail** and click **New** on the toolbar. The New Message window will open (see Figure 4-10).

New

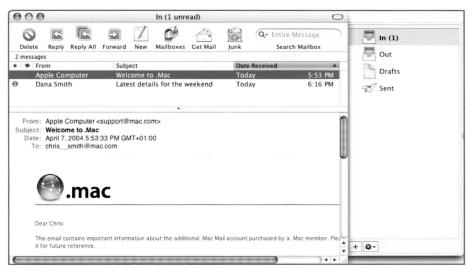

Figure 4-9: Mail is a straightforward but powerful e-mail application.

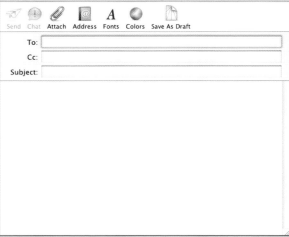

Figure 4-10: Sending e-mail messages is a fast and easy way to communicate

2. Start to type a name in the To text box. If Mail recognizes the name as one you've previously sent a message to, or as an entry in your address book (see the "Using Address Book" QuickSteps, later in this chapter), it suggests the match or matches.

- To select the single match offered (after typing, for example, "chr" as shown on the left here), press **RETURN**. Mail creates a button for the address (as shown on the right here).

- To select one of multiple matches, either continue typing to narrow down the list or click the correct match in the list. Mail creates a button for the address.

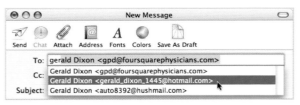

- If Mail has no suggestions, finish typing the address.

3. To send the message to more than one addressee, type a comma after the first address, and then type the second address. If Mail has created an address button for the first addressee, you needn't type the comma.

4. If you want to differentiate the addressees to whom the message is principally being sent from those for whom it is being copied for information, press **TAB** (or click in the Cc text box) and enter the other addressees' addresses there.

5. Press **TAB** (or click in the Subject text box) and type the subject of the message.

6. Press **TAB** again (or click in the large text box) and type your message.

7. When you have completed your message, click **Send** in the upper-left corner. Mail will contact your outgoing mail server and send the message, complete with sound effects.

8. If you're ready to close Mail, choose **Mail | Quit Mail**.

CAUTION

E-mail often appears to be an informal means of communication, an impression enhanced by the speed with which you can dash off a message and send it in moments to one or more people. But it's worth remembering that e-mail, like other written forms of communication, can easily be kept and stored by the recipient, and can come back to haunt the sender many years later. Worse, unlike other written forms of communications, an e-mail can also be forwarded instantly to people you never intended should read it. So before you send a "quick" e-mail message, read it through again to check that you won't regret sending it.

Receive E-Mail

Depending on how Mail is configured, it may automatically receive any e-mail destined for you when your Mac is connected to your ISP. If not, or if you need to dial to connect to your ISP, click **Get Mail** on the toolbar. In either case, the mail you receive will go into your Inbox. To open and read your mail:

To: chris__smith@mac.com
▶ 🖉 1 Attachment, 433 KB (Save All...)

1. Open **Mail**. Mail displays the Inbox.

2. Click a message in the Inbox to read it in the Preview pane at the bottom of the window, or double-click a message to open the message in its own window (see Figure 4-11).

Figure 4-11: To see as much as possible of a message you've received, open it in its own window rather than reading it in the Inbox's Preview pane.

3. Choose what action (if any) to take with the message:

- Respond to it as described in the next section.
- Print it by clicking **Print** in a message window or by choosing **File | Print** in the Inbox.
- Drag it to a mail folder.
- Delete it by clicking **Delete** in either a message window or the Inbox.

4. If you're ready to close Mail, choose **Mail | Quit Mail**.

Respond to E-Mail

You can respond to messages you receive in three ways. First, click the message in your Inbox (or open it in its own window), and then:

- Click **Reply** to return a message to only the person who sent the original message.

  –Or–

Reply

- Click **Reply All** to return a message to all the people who were addressees (both To and Cc) in the original message.

  –Or–

Reply All

- Click **Forward** to send on a message to people not shown as addressees on the original message.

Forward

When you take any of these actions, Mail opens a window very similar to the New Message window and allows you to add or change addressees and the subject, and add a message. Click **Send** to send the message.

If you see an address in an e-mail message that you want to add to your address book, **CONTROL+**click or right-click the address and click **Add To Address Book**. Mail causes Address Book to create a new entry for that address. Switch to **Address Book**, select the new entry, and click **Edit** to enter further information you have for that person.

Not all e-mail applications can properly receive formatted e-mail messages, resulting in messages that are not very readable. However, most e-mail applications released in the last five years can handle formatted e-mail properly.

Apply Formatting to an E-Mail Message

The simplest e-mail messages are sent in plain text without any formatting. These messages take the least bandwidth and are the quickest and easiest to receive. If you wish, you can send messages with formatting using HTML, the Internet's Hypertext Markup Language with which many web sites have been created. You can do this for an individual message or for all messages.

CHOOSE WHETHER TO APPLY FORMATTING TO ALL MESSAGES

1. Choose **Mail | Preferences**. The Preferences window will open.
2. Click **Composing** to display the Composing sheet.
3. In the Format drop-down list box, choose **Rich Text** if you want to apply formatting. Choose **Plain Text** to send plain text messages.
4. Click the **Close** button (the red button) to close the window.

CHOOSE WHETHER TO APPLY FORMATTING TO AN INDIVIDUAL MESSAGE

You can override your default setting (specified in the previous section) for applying formatting:

1. From the main Mail window, click the **New** button on the toolbar to open a new message window.
2. Open **Format** and click **Make Plain Text** or **Make Rich Text** as appropriate.
3. Address, compose, and send the message as usual.

Attach Files to E-Mail Messages

You can attach and send files, such as documents or images, with e-mail messages:

1. In Mail, click the **New** button on the toolbar. A New Message window will be displayed.
2. Click **Attach** on the toolbar. In the resulting dialog box, navigate to and select the file you want to send.

Attach

3. If you're sending the file to someone using a Windows computer, select the **Send Windows Friendly Attachments** check box.

QUICKSTEPS

USING ADDRESS BOOK

Mac OS X's Address Book, shown in Figure 4-12, enables you to collect addresses and other information about your contacts.

OPEN ADDRESS BOOK

To open Address Book, click the **Address Book** icon on the Dock.

ADD A NEW ADDRESS

To add a new address to Address Book:

1. Open **File** and click **New Card**. Address Book will add a card with the provisional name, *No Name*, will open the card for editing in the right column, and will select the First field.

2. Enter as much of the information as you have or want. Use TAB or the mouse to move from field to field. For e-mail, you need a name and an e-mail address. You can have multiple e-mail addresses for each contact. To add another e-mail address, click the **green +** button next to the existing addresses, and choose the type of address in the pop-up menu to the left of the e-mail address box.

3. When you've finished entering address information, click **Edit**.

ADD A GROUP OF ADDRESSES

To add a group of addresses that you want to be able to send a single message to:

1. Open **File** and click **New Group**. Address Book will add an entry to the Group column and will display an edit box around the default name, *Group Name*.

2. Type the name for the group and press **RETURN**. Address Book will apply the name and will leave the new group selected.

Continued…

4. Click **Choose File**. Mail will close the dialog box and add details of the file to the message.

5. Address, type, and send the message as you normally would.

Receive Files Attached to E-Mail Messages

When someone sends you a message with a file attached, Mail displays information about the attachment in the Preview pane and in the message window:

Click **Save All**, use the resulting dialog box to choose the folder in which to save the file, and click **Save**.

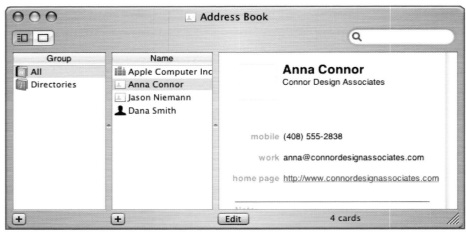

Figure 4-12: Address Book provides a place to store information about the people you correspond with.

3. Click the **All** group entry or another group's entries that contains contacts you want to add to the new group. Drag an entry from the Name column and drop it on the new group to add that contact to the group.

After you have created a group like this, you can address a new message to the group by starting to type the group's name in the To box in the New Message window. When you complete the name, or accept Mail's suggestion for completing it automatically, Mail inserts the names of the group members in the To box.

NOTE

The easiest video camera to use with iChat is Apple's iSight, which comes with stands for mounting on PowerBooks and iBooks, desktop Macs, or your (physical) desktop. But you can also use a digital video camcorder that attaches to your Mac via FireWire.

Use iChat

iChat is an application for *instant messaging*, or *IM*—instantly sending and receiving messages with others who are online at the same time as you. (Instant messaging is often referred to as "chat"—hence, iChat's name.) iChat can also handle teleconferencing, the live, remote interaction of several people complete with audio and video transmission.

To use iChat, you need to have an account with Apple's .Mac online service or an AOL Instant Messenger (AIM) screen name and password. To transmit audio, your Mac must have a microphone; and for you to hear audio, your Mac must have speakers. To send video, you must have a video camera connected to your Mac via FireWire.

Set Up iChat

To set up iChat:

1. If you plan to use a video camera with iChat, attach it to your Mac. If the camera has a power control, turn it on.

2. Click the **iChat** icon in the Dock. iChat will display a Welcome To iChat AV dialog box.

3. Click **Continue**. iChat will display the Set Up A New iChat Account dialog box (see Figure 4-13).

Figure 4-13: Enter your .Mac or AIM details to set up a new iChat account.

QUICKSTEPS

CONFIGURING ICHAT

iChat contains several dozen configurable options that enable you to customize its behavior to suit your needs and preferences. To start configuration, open **iChat** and click **Preferences**. The Preferences window will open. Click the button for the sheet you want to work with.

GENERAL SHEET OPTIONS

Options on the General sheet include controlling whether iChat automatically logs you in when it opens, choosing whether to show your status in the menu bar, specifying what iChat should do when you return to your Mac and your status is Away, and deciding where to save files you receive.

ACCOUNTS SHEET OPTIONS

On the Accounts sheet, you can change the AIM screen name you're using for iChat.

MESSAGES SHEET OPTIONS

On the Messages sheet, you can choose colors and fonts for your text balloons and senders' text balloons, choose whether to confirm the sending of files, and decide whether to automatically save chat transcripts (which can be useful for work and love).

ALERTS SHEET OPTIONS

On the Alerts sheet, you can choose what kinds of alerts iChat uses when a particular event occurs. For example, when a buddy becomes available, you might choose to have iChat bounce its icon in the Dock and announce out loud that your buddy is now online.

Continued...

4. Enter your details and click **Continue**. iChat will display the Set Up Rendezvous Messaging dialog box. Rendezvous is an Apple technology for exchanging messages and data with other users of your local network (as opposed to exchanging messages and data across the Internet).

5. If you want to use iChat with other local users, click the **Use Rendezvous Messaging** option button. If not, make sure the **Do Not Use Rendezvous Messaging** option button is selected.

6. Click **Continue**. iChat will display the Set Up iChat AV dialog box, on which you can check that your web camera is working. If iChat doesn't detect a camera attached to your Mac, it warns you of this. Likewise, if your Mac doesn't support video conferencing, iChat lets you know.

7. Click **Continue**. iChat will display the Conclusion dialog box.

8. Click **Done**. iChat will open.

Use iChat

Now that iChat is set up, you're ready to use it. First, you must enter contacts, or *buddies*, with whom you want to communicate:

ADD BUDDIES TO ICHAT

1. If iChat isn't running, click the **iChat** icon on the Dock to launch it. iChat will display the Buddy List window.

2. Click the **+** button. iChat will display a dialog box for selecting an address from your address book.

CONFIGURING ICHAT *(Continued)*

PRIVACY SHEET OPTIONS

On the Privacy sheet, you can control which people
can see you are online and send you messages: Allow
Anyone, Allow People In My Buddy List, Allow Specific
People (you specify who), Block Everyone, or Block
Specific People (again, you specify who). You can also
choose to block others from seeing that you are idle.

VIDEO SHEET OPTIONS

The Video sheet lets you check the video camera
you're using, choose which microphone to use, control
the bandwidth iChat uses (for example, to prevent it
from hogging your Internet connection), automatically
open iChat when you turn on the camera, and play the
repeated ring sound when you're invited to a conference.

After choosing suitable options in the Preferences
window, click the **Close** button (the red button) to close
the window.

3. If the buddy is in your address book, select the name and click **Select Buddy**. If not,
   click **New Person** to display a dialog box for entering the person's details (see Figure
   4-14). You must enter at least the account type (.Mac or AIM) and the account name;
   usually it's helpful to add the first and last names and the e-mail address as well. Click
   Add to add the new person.

4. Your buddies will appear in the Buddy List, together with an icon indicating their status
   if they're online: a green dot for online and active, a yellow dot for online but inactive, a
   red dot for online but away, and no dot if they're offline (see Figure 4-14).

*Figure 4-14: iChat uses colored dots to give
a rough indication of each buddy's status.*

NOTE

If your buddy's Mac doesn't have a microphone, the Invite To Audio Chat item will be unavailable, and the Invite To One-Way Audio Chat item will be available instead. This item lets your buddy hear you and respond using text.

NOTE

If your buddy's Mac doesn't have a video camera, the Invite To Video Chat item will be unavailable, and the Invite To One-Way Video Chat item will be available instead. This item lets your buddy see you and respond verbally.

TIP

If you want to check your video camera before starting a call, click the **green-and-white camera** button at the top of the Buddy List window. iChat will display a window showing you what the camera is seeing.

START AN AUDIO CHAT

To start an audio chat:

1. CONTROL+click or right-click a buddy who's online and click **Invite To Audio Chat**.

2. iChat will display an Audio Chat window while it waits for your buddy to reply:

3. If your buddy accepts the invitation, iChat will establish audio contact. Speak to your buddy as you would in a telephone conversation.

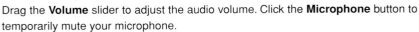

   Drag the **Volume** slider to adjust the audio volume. Click the **Microphone** button to temporarily mute your microphone.

4. To end the chat, click the **Close** button (the red button).

START A VIDEO CHAT

To start a video chat:

1. CONTROL+click or right-click a buddy who's online and click **Invite To Video Chat**. iChat will display a Video Chat window while it waits for your buddy to reply.

2. If your buddy accepts the invitation, iChat will establish audio and video contact. Chat as you would on a normal video phone. Click the **Microphone** button to temporarily mute your microphone. Click the **Full-Screen Mode** button (the button with two arrows) to zoom the Video Chat window to full screen. Double-click anywhere to exit full-screen mode.

3. To end the chat, click the **Close** button (the red button).

START A TEXT CHAT

To start a text chat:

1. **CONTROL**+click or right-click a buddy who's online and click **Send An Instant Message**. iChat will display an Instant Message window.

2. If your buddy responds, iChat shows the responses on the other side of the window from yours.

3. Type messages and press **RETURN** to send them. To send an *emoticon*, or "smiley," click the symbol at the right end of the text box and choose from the panel. The text below the panel shows the name of the emoticon and the key sequence for entering it from the keyboard.

4. When you've finished chatting, click the **Close** button (the red button).

SEND A FILE

To send a file to a buddy:

1. During a chat, open **Buddies** and click **Send File**. Use the resulting dialog box to select the file, and then click **Open**. Type any necessary message and press **RETURN** to send the message and the file.

2. To send a file without starting a chat, **CONTROL**+click or right-click your buddy's entry in the Buddy List window, and then click **Send File**. Use the resulting dialog box to select the file, and then click **Open.**

In either case, your buddy can choose whether to accept the file (by clicking **Save File**) or decline it (by clicking **Decline**).

RESPOND TO CHAT INVITATIONS

1. When a buddy sends you an invitation, iChat displays a pop-up window to let you know. Here's an example of an audio invitation:

2. Click the **pop-up window** to display more detail:

3. Click **Accept** to accept the invitation. iChat sets up the connection.

4. When you've finished chatting, click the **Close** button (the red button).

CONTROL YOUR STATUS

To control how iChat shows your status, click the **status** button in the toolbar and choose the appropriate entry from the pop-up menu. Click one of the Custom entries to display a text box in which you can type your preferred descriptor, for example, *Caffeinated*, *Bored*, or *Pretending to work*.

If you leave your Mac unused for a while, iChat changes your status to Idle (meaning that the Mac is idle—not necessarily that it thinks you're idle); after a long while, iChat changes your status to Away. If your Mac goes to sleep, iChat changes your status to Offline.

After you return from being away, iChat offers to change your status back to Available. Click **Available** if you want to accept this offer. Otherwise, click **No**.

Select the **Don't Show Again** check box if you don't want to see this prompt again.

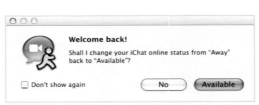

Chapter 5

Managing Mac OS X

Running applications is one of Mac OS X's major functions. Managing Mac OS X entails setting up the starting and stopping of applications in a number of different ways. Managing also includes maintaining and enhancing Mac OS X.

Start and Stop Applications

Previous chapters have discussed starting applications from the Dock, from aliases on the desktop, and from the Applications folder. All of these methods of starting applications require a direct action from you. Mac OS X also provides several ways to start applications automatically and to monitor and manage them while they are running.

Start and Stop Mac OS X Automatically

Mac OS X allows you to start it and stop it automatically at times you specify:

1. Open and click **System Preferences**. The System Preferences window will be displayed.

NOTE

Figure 5-1 is shown for PowerBook or iBook laptop (battery-powered) computers. Desktop computers do not have the two drop-down list boxes for Optimized Energy Settings and Settings For the type of power (battery or power adapter).

2. Click **Energy Saver**. The Energy Saver sheet will be displayed.

3. Click the **Schedule** tab button (see Figure 5-1).

4. To start your Mac automatically, select the **Start Up The Computer** check box and use the controls to its right to specify which days (Weekdays, Weekends, Every Day, or a specific day of the week) and the time.

5. To make your Mac shut down or sleep, select the lower check box, click **Shut Down** or **Sleep** in the drop-down list, and use the controls to its right to specify which days and the time.

6. Click **System Preferences** | **Quit System Preferences** to close System Preferences.

If you choose to shut your Mac down or put it to sleep, Mac OS X gives you ten minutes' notice at the specified time in case you're still working. Click **Shut Down** (or **Sleep**) to shut down (or sleep) immediately; click **Cancel** to cancel the shutdown or nap; or just leave Mac OS X to complete the countdown and shut down or sleep.

Energy Saver

Show All   Displays   Sound   Network   Startup Disk

Optimize Energy Settings: Highest Performance

Settings for: Power Adapter

Sleep   Schedule   Options

☑ Start up the computer   Weekdays   at   7 : 30 AM

☑ Shut Down   Weekdays   at   6 : 00 PM

These settings are optimized for highest performance whether the computer is plugged in or not. Current battery charge is 91 percent.

☑ Show battery status in the menu bar

🔓 Click the lock to prevent further changes.   (Hide Details)

This computer has been scheduled to shut down automatically.
If you do nothing, the system will shut down automatically in 567 seconds.

(Cancel)   (Shut Down)

Figure 5-1: You can configure Mac OS X to start up and shut down (or sleep) automatically at specific times.

Start Applications Automatically When You Log In

Sometimes you will want to start an application automatically every time you start your Mac. For example, you might start an antivirus application automatically and have it run in the background. Or you might want, each time you log in, to open all the applications you use in a typical session. You can also open specific documents when you log in, which can save a fair amount of clicking at the start of a work session.

1. Open and click **System Preferences**. The System Preferences window will be displayed.

2. Click **Accounts**. The Accounts sheet will be displayed.

3. Select your account in the list box on the left.

4. Click the **Startup Items** tab (see Figure 5-2).

5. To add an item to the list, click the **+** button beneath the These Items Will Open Automatically When You Log In list box, select the item in the resulting dialog box, and click **Add**.

6. Drag the items into the order in which you want them to be opened. (The first item in the list will be opened first.)

7. To remove an item from the list, click it and then click the **–** button beneath the list box.

8. To make Mac OS X hide an item after opening it (instead of displaying the item in a window), select the **Hide** check box in the item's row.".

9. Click **System Preferences | Quit System Preferences** to close System Preferences.

Figure 5-2: Use the Startup Items tab of the Accounts sheet to specify which applications and documents are to open automatically when you log in.

SWITCHING APPLICATIONS

Like most modern operating systems, Mac OS X lets you have multiple applications open at the same time. Mac OS X makes it easy to switch from one open application to another.

SWITCH USING EXPOSÉ

The easiest way to switch to another application is to click its window—if you can see it. To enable you to see all open windows, Mac OS X 10.3 (Panther) introduced Exposé, a new means of switching applications.

Press **F9** to reduce all your open windows and display them at a smaller size on screen. Move the mouse over a window to see its title (see Figure 5-3). Click a window to restore the screen display to normal size with the window you clicked at the front.

Press **F10** to reduce all the open windows in the active application and arrange them so that you can see them (see Figure 5-4). Mac OS X grays out the other applications in the background. Click the window you want to bring to the front. Exposé then restores the rest of the screen display to normal size and displays the window you clicked at the front.

Press **F11** to move all open windows to the edges of the desktop so that you can access items on the desktop. Press **F11** again to restore the windows to their previous positions.

You can press **SHIFT** with any of these keystrokes to slow down the animation for visual entertainment.

CONFIGURE EXPOSÉ

If the Exposé keystrokes conflict with keyboard shortcuts in the applications you use, configure Exposé to use

Continued…

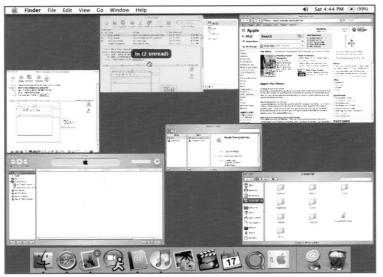

Figure 5-3: Pressing F9 makes Exposé shrink all open windows so that you can see them all at once and pick the one you want.

Figure 5-4: Pressing F10 makes Exposé shrink the open windows in the active application so that you can pick the one you want.

SWITCHING APPLICATIONS *(Continued)*

different keystrokes, active screen corners, or mouse shortcuts. Mouse shortcuts are available only for mice that have two or more buttons.

1. Open and click **System Preferences**. The System Preferences window will be displayed.

2. Click **Exposé**. The Exposé sheet will be displayed (see Figure 5-5).

3. Choose the methods of executing Exposé's All Windows, Application Windows, and Desktop commands. For example, open one of the menus in the Active Screen Corners box and choose the appropriate command from it.

4. Click **System Preferences | Quit System Preferences** to close System Preferences.

SWITCH USING THE HEADS-UP DISPLAY

You can also switch applications by pressing ⌘+**TAB** or ⌘+**SHIFT**+**TAB**. When you press one of these shortcuts, Mac OS X displays the Head-Up Display (shown here)— a bar showing an icon for each running application.

Holding down ⌘,
press

TAB to
move the highlight to the next icon, or press **SHIFT+TAB** to move the highlight to the previous icon. Release the keys to display that application.

Alternatively, hold down ⌘ to keep the Heads-Up Display on screen, and click the application you want to display.

Press ⌘+**TAB** once to switch to the last application you were using. You can then press ⌘+**TAB** again to switch back to the application you switched from, toggling between two applications.

Continued...

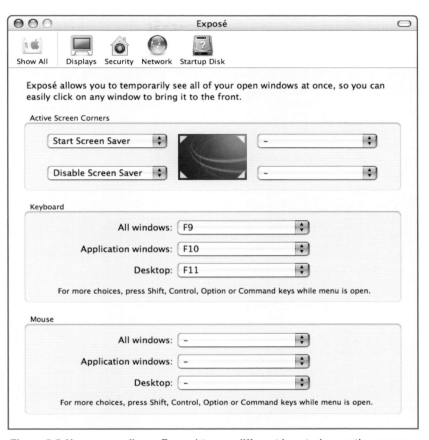

Figure 5-5: You can configure Exposé to use different keystrokes, active screen corners, or mouse shortcuts.

TIP

You can execute whatever feature you put in Active Screen Corners by simply moving the mouse to that corner until the mouse pointer disappears. You don't have to click.

CAUTION

When you close an application forcibly, you lose any unsaved data in the application. For this reason, never close an application forcibly unless you must.

TIP

You can force-quit the foreground application by pressing **⌘+OPTION+SHIFT+ESC** or by opening ****, holding down **SHIFT**, and clicking **Force Quit**.

Hide and Show Applications

Instead of minimizing an application window to an icon on the right side of the Dock, you can hide the application so that it's not visible, even though it's still running. To hide an application, open its application menu (for example, open the **Address Book** menu when Address Book is the active application) and click the **Hide** command. The command is named Hide *application*, where *application* is the application's name—for example, Hide Address Book.

To hide all applications *except* the active application, open the application menu and click **Hide Others**.

To show all hidden applications, open the application menu of the active application and click **Show All**. Alternatively, use the Heads-Up Display (press ⌘+**TAB**) to display one application.

Quit an Application When It Goes Wrong

When an application won't respond to the mouse or keyboard, you will have to quit it forcibly by using the Force Quit Command or the Force Quit Applications window.

Usually, it's easy to tell when an application isn't responding: Mac OS X displays a spinning, colored disc in place of the mouse pointer, and you can't perform any actions with the mouse. (Mac users know this disc semi-affectionately as the *Spinning Beachball of Death*, or SBOD.) Neither will you be able to take any actions from the keyboard in the application that's stopped responding.

QUIT AN APPLICATION USING THE FORCE QUIT COMMAND

Your first tool for quitting an application forcibly is the Force Quit command. **OPTION**+click the application's icon in the Dock and click **Force Quit** on the menu.

Mac OS X will force the application to quit. If this command doesn't work, try using the Force Quit Applications window.

QUICKSTEPS

QUITTING APPLICATIONS

When you've finished using an application, quit it so that it stops taking up memory and processor cycles.

USE QUIT FROM A MENU

The standard way of quitting an application is to open the application menu (the menu that bears the application's name) and click the **Quit** command (which also bears the application's name). For example, to quit Mail, open the **Mail** menu and click **Quit Mail**.

QUIT USING THE KEYBOARD

Press ⌘+Q.

QUIT FROM THE DOCK

CONTROL+click or right-click the icon for a running application in the Dock and click **Quit** on the resulting menu. You can also display this menu by clicking and holding down the mouse button for a couple of seconds.

If none of these options work, see "Quit an Application When It Goes Wrong."

TIP

If you can't use the mouse to open the menu, press ⌘+**OPTION**+**ESC** to display the Force Quit Applications window.

NOTE

Because Mac OS X requires the Finder to run all the time, the Force Quit button changes to a Relaunch button when you select the Finder in the Force Quit Applications window. Click **Relaunch** to relaunch the Finder.

QUIT AN APPLICATION USING THE FORCE QUIT APPLICATIONS WINDOW

1. Open and click **Force Quit**. Mac OS X will display the Force Quit Applications window (see Figure 5-6).

2. Select the application that's not responding.

3. Click **Force Quit**. Mac OS X will force the application to quit.

4. Click the **Close** button (the red button) to close the Force Quit Applications window.

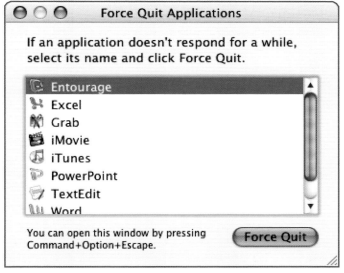

Figure 5-6: Use the Force Quit Applications window to quit an application that won't respond.

Start an Application from the Terminal

Underneath its stunning interface, Mac OS X runs on UNIX, a powerful and stable operating system first developed in the 1970s and updated continuously since then. Darwin, the version of UNIX under Mac OS X, includes many applications that use a *command-line interface*—an interface with which you interact by typing commands rather than by using a mouse to manipulate graphical objects.

Should you need to, you can run UNIX commands from Mac OS X by using the Terminal application. You'll seldom need to do this unless you know UNIX and you need to perform an operation that Mac OS X and its applications can't manage. But here's a quick example for you to try:

1. Click the **Finder** icon on the Dock.

2. Open **Go** and click **Utilities**. The Finder window will display the contents of the Utilities folder (which is located inside the Applications folder).

3. Double-click **Terminal**. A Terminal window will be displayed (see Figure 5-7).

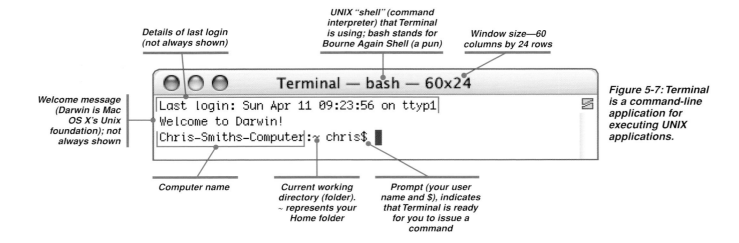

Details of last login (not always shown)

UNIX "shell" (command interpreter) that Terminal is using; bash stands for Bourne Again Shell (a pun)

Window size—60 columns by 24 rows

Welcome message (Darwin is Mac OS X's Unix foundation); not always shown

```
Last login: Sun Apr 11 09:23:56 on ttyp1
Welcome to Darwin!
Chris-Smiths-Computer:~ chris$ 
```

Terminal — bash — 60x24

Computer name

Current working directory (folder). ~ represents your Home folder

Prompt (your user name and $), indicates that Terminal is ready for you to issue a command

Figure 5-7: Terminal is a command-line application for executing UNIX applications.

4. Type <u>ls</u> and press **RETURN**. *ls* stands for "list" and is a command that lists the files and folders in the current directory. Terminal will display a list of the directory's contents, followed by the prompt to indicate that it is ready (see Figure 5-8).

5. Type <u>cd Documents</u> and press **RETURN** to change directory to your Documents folder, which is contained in your Home folder. UNIX is case sensitive, so use that capitalization—any other capitalization, such as **cd documents**, won't work.

6. Type <u>ls</u> and press **RETURN** to list the contents of your Documents folder. Here you can see an example of a sparsely populated Documents folder. Your Documents folder will have different contents.

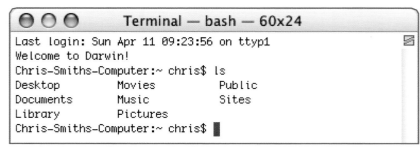

Figure 5-8: Using the ls command to list the contents of a folder.

RUNNING ACCESSORY APPLICATIONS

Mac OS X comes with several small applications (located in your Applications folder—open a **Finder** window and click **Applications** in the Sidebar) that you can use to perform common tasks. Most of these applications are discussed elsewhere in this book, but Calculator, Stickies, and TextEdit will be looked at here.

CALCULATOR

The Calculator has two views: Basic view (click **View | Basic**) shows a standard desktop calculator, while Advanced view (click **View | Advanced**; see Figure 5-9) shows a powerful scientific calculator. To use the calculator, click the numbers on screen or type them on the keyboard.

Calculator can also speak the buttons you've pressed and/or speak the total, which can be helpful for confirming what you're doing; open the **Speech** menu and click **Speak Button Pressed** or **Speak Total**, as appropriate. Calculator can also display a window showing the calculations you've performed, which helps you track your work and identify errors; open the **View** menu and click **Paper Tape** to display this window.

STICKIES

Stickies is a sticky-note application that you can use to take quick notes and post reminders. Create a note by opening **File** and clicking **New Note**, then type text into it or drag in other content, such as a picture or a movie clip, from a Finder window (or your desktop) or another application. Drag the note to wherever you want to

Continued...

---

7. Choose a file (not a folder) to copy as an example. Type <u>cp</u> (which stands for *copy*), a space, the file's name, another space, and the name you want to assign to the copy. If the file's name or the copy's name contains spaces, put the name in double quotation marks ("")—for example, <u>cp "General notes.rtf" "Copy of General notes.rtf"</u>. Otherwise, type just its name—for example, <u>cp testfile1 testfile2</u>.

```
Chris-Smiths-Computer:~/Documents chris$ ls
Business              Letters
General notes.rtf     My Novel
Chris-Smiths-Computer:~/Documents chris$ cp "General notes.r
tf" "Copy of General notes.rtf"
Chris-Smiths-Computer:~/Documents chris$ ▮
```

8. Type <u>ls</u> and press **RETURN** to list the contents of the Documents folder again. The copy you created will be included in the list.

```
Chris-Smiths-Computer:~/Documents chris$ ls
Business
Copy of General notes.rtf
General notes.rtf
Letters
My Novel
Chris-Smiths-Computer:~/Documents chris$ ▮
```

9. Delete the copy by typing <u>rm</u> (which stands for *remove*) and the file name, using double quotation marks again if the name contains spaces—for example, <u>rm "Copy of General notes.rtf"</u> or <u>rm testfile2</u>. The copy is deleted without confirmation.

10. Press ⌘+Q, or open **Terminal** and click **Quit Terminal** to close Terminal.

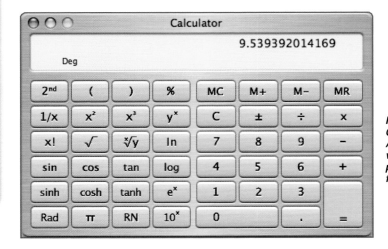

Figure 5-9: The Calculator's Advanced view provides powerful scientific functions.

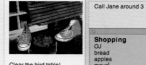
Run System 9 Applications on Classic

Mac OS X is a completely different operating system from earlier versions of Mac OS, such as System 8 and System 9, and requires applications to be written especially for it. However, Mac OS X includes a feature called Classic that enables you to run applications written for System 9.

Classic is an *emulator*—software that fools the application into thinking it's running on the earlier version of Mac OS. In layperson's terms, Mac OS X creates Classic by running a copy of System 9 on top of Mac OS X, so your Mac needs plenty of RAM (at least 256 MB, and preferably 512 MB or more) to run demanding applications at a good speed in Classic.

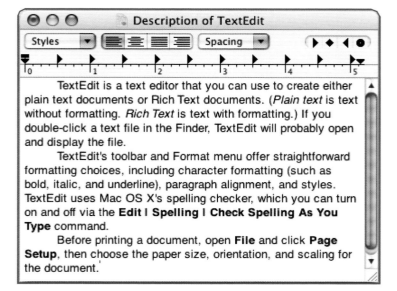

Figure 5-10: TextEdit supports character and paragraph formatting, and uses Mac OS X's built-in spelling checker.

Mac OS X automatically launches Classic when you open an application that needs it. You'll see what appears to be System 9 starting up in a new window (see Figure 5-11), and then the application you opened will appear. Work in it as usual, and then close it.

After you launch Classic, it stays running even when you close the application or applications that required it. Mac OS X will close Classic when you log out or shut down. However, you can also close Classic manually, restart it, or force quit it if it stops responding:

Figure 5-11: Classic mode enables you to run System 9 applications on Mac OS X.

1. Open ★ and click **System Preferences**. The System Preferences window will be displayed.
2. Click **Classic**. The Classic sheet will be displayed.
3. Click the **Start/Stop** tab if it's not displayed (see Figure 5-12).
4. Click **Stop**, **Restart**, or **Force Quit** as appropriate.
5. Click **System Preferences | Quit System Preferences** to close System Preferences.

Maintain Mac OS X

Maintaining Mac OS X consists of periodic updates for fixes and new features, restoring Mac OS X when hardware or other software damages it, getting information about it, and installing new hardware and software.

Figure 5-12: You can shut down Classic manually from the Start/Stop tab of the Classic sheet in System Preferences.

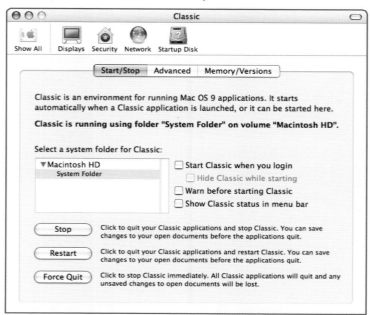

Keep Mac OS X Up-to-Date

Mac OS X's Software Update feature helps you to keep Mac OS X and key applications up-to-date. You can run Software Update manually, configure it to run automatically, or do both.

CHECK MANUALLY FOR UPDATES

To check immediately for updates, open ★ and click **Software Update**. You'll see the Update window shown here while Software Update checks.

NOTE

Depending on the updates you're installing, you may need to agree to a license agreement.

Figure 5-13: In the New Software Is Available For Your Computer dialog box, choose which updates you want to download and install.

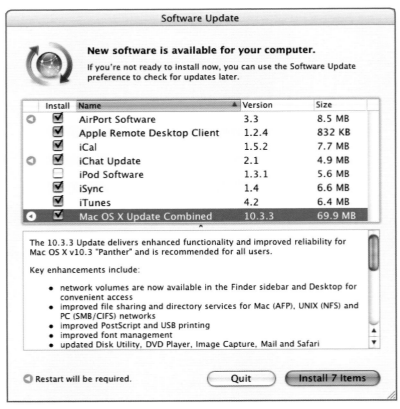

If updates are available, Software Update displays the New Software Is Available For Your Computer dialog box (see Figure 5-13). Clear the check boxes for any updates that you don't want to install. For example, if you don't have an iPod, you can probably live without updates to the iPod Software; if your Mac doesn't have an AirPort, you won't need updates for that either. Sometimes, you may also not want to download a particular update right now—for example, because its file size is so large that the download will take several hours over your dial-up connection.

Click the **Install Items** button (its name changes to show the number of updates: Install 1 Item, Install 2 Items, and so on) to install the updates. Mac OS X will display the Authenticate dialog box.

Type your password and click **OK**. Software Update then downloads the updates and installs them. After installing the updates, you may need to restart your Mac. If so, Software Update will prompt you, as shown here. Save any unsaved work in other applications, and then click **Restart** to restart your Mac. (You can also click **Shut Down** to shut down your Mac, and then restart it when you want to.)

If there are no updates available, Software Update displays a message box telling you so. Click **OK**, and Software Update will close itself.

IGNORE UPDATES

After you choose not to install an update, Software Update will present it to you again the next time it checks to see which updates are available. If you never want a particular update, you must tell Software Update to ignore it:

1. Select the update from the list in the New Software Is Available For Your Computer dialog box.

2. Open **Update** and click **Ignore Update**. A confirmation dialog box will be displayed:

3. Click **OK**.

> Are you sure you want to remove the update "AirPort Software" from the list?
>
> You will no longer be notified of new versions of this update. To see this update again, choose Reset Ignored Updates from the application menu.
>
> Cancel   OK

RESET IGNORED UPDATES

After ignoring updates, you can reset ignored updates so that Software Update will notice them again. Open the **Software Update** menu and click **Reset Ignored Updates**. Software Update will check immediately for updates, will find those you've ignored, and will offer them in the New Software Is Available For Your Computer dialog box.

Figure 5-14: You can configure Software Update's behavior on the Update Software tab of the Software Update sheet of System Preferences.

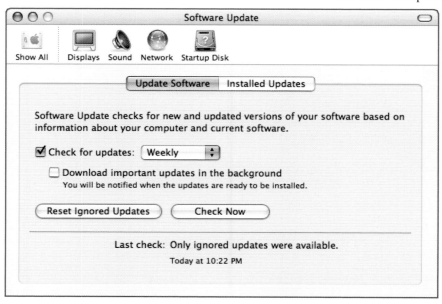

Configure Software Update

To configure how often Software Update checks for updates:

1. Open and click **System Preferences**. The System Preferences window will be displayed.

2. Click **Software Update**. The Software Update sheet will be displayed.

3. If the **Update Software** tab isn't displayed, click it (see Figure 5-14).

4. To make Software Update check automatically for updates, select the **Check For Updates** check box and choose **Daily**, **Weekly**, or **Monthly** in the drop-down list box.

5. To make Software Update automatically download important updates and then notify you about them, select the **Download Important Updates In The Background** check box. This check box is available only if you select the **Check For Updates** check box.

6. Open **System Preferences** and click **Quit System Preferences** to close System Preferences.

Get System Information

To get quick information about your Mac, open and click **About This Mac**. The About This Mac window will be displayed (see Figure 5-15), showing the version of Mac OS X (for example, 10.3.3) and your Mac's processor and memory.

If you need no more information, click the **Close** button (the red button) to close the About This Mac window. You can close the window and make Software

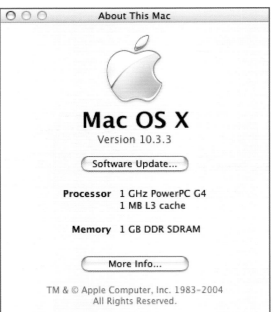

Update automatically check for updates by clicking **Software Update**. But what you'll probably want to do is click **More Info** to launch the System Profiler application, which presents detailed information on various aspects of your Mac's hardware and software.

Figure 5-15: The About This Mac window shows details of your Mac's Mac OS X version, processor, and memory.

Select the category of information in the Contents pane on the left. Figure 5-16 shows an example of the Network category for a PowerBook. After checking the information you need, open the **System Profiler** menu and click **Quit System Profiler** to close System Profiler.

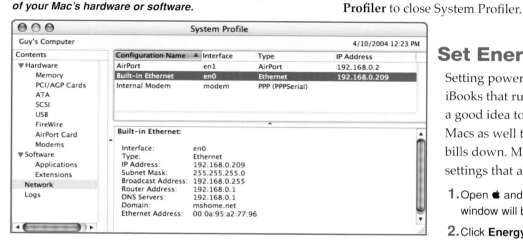

Figure 5-16: Use System Profiler to check the details of your Mac's hardware or software.

Set Energy Saver Options

Setting power options is most important on PowerBook and iBooks that run at least some of the time on batteries, but it's a good idea to configure suitable power options for desktop Macs as well to conserve power and keep your electricity bills down. Mac OS X's Energy Saver options provide several settings that allow you to manage your Mac's use of power.

1. Open ⌘ and click **System Preferences**. The System Preferences window will be displayed.

2. Click **Energy Saver**. The Energy Saver sheet will be displayed. Figure 5-17 shows the Energy Saver sheet for a PowerBook or iBook. The Energy Saver sheet for a desktop Mac offers fewer controls: it doesn't have the Optimize Energy Settings drop-down list box or the Settings For drop-down list box, and the Sleep tab doesn't have the Show Details/Hide Details button.

3. If the Energy Saver sheet is shown at its small size (smaller than in Figure 5-17), click **Show Details**. The sheet will be displayed at its full size.

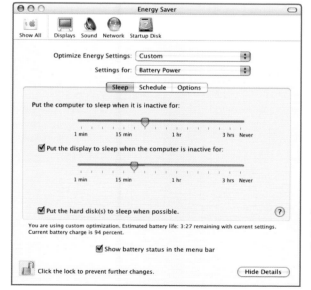

Figure 5-17: Configure power options on the Energy Saver sheet in System Preferences (shown for a PowerBook or iBook).

NOTE

The DVD Playback option prevents the screen from going to sleep, puts the hard disk to sleep when possible (because it's seldom used during DVD playback), and puts the Mac to sleep after three hours. The Presentations option prevents the Mac and its display from going to sleep but puts the hard disk to sleep when possible. This option is for using your Mac to display a presentation continually—for example, at a trade show.

NOTE

If your 'Book is plugged in, Mac OS X selects the Power Adapter item in the Settings For drop-down list box; if it's on battery power, Mac OS X selects the Battery Power item. On a desktop Mac, Mac OS X doesn't display the Settings For drop-down list box.

NOTE

For a PowerBook or iBook, you can select the **Show Battery Status In The Menu Bar** check box to display a battery readout in the menu bar.

4. In the Optimize Energy Settings drop-down list box, select the setting that best describes the power configuration you want: **Automatic** (Mac OS X handles decisions for you), **Highest Performance**, **Longest Battery Life**, **DVD Playback**, **Presentations**, or **Custom**.

5. If your Mac is a PowerBook or an iBook, choose **Power Adapter** or **Battery Power** in the Settings For drop-down list to specify which settings you want to configure. (Typically, you'll want different settings for when your 'Book is plugged in than when it's running on battery power.)

6. If the Sleep tab isn't displayed, click the **Sleep** tab.

7. Drag the **Put The Computer To Sleep When It Is Inactive For** slider to specify how long Mac OS X should wait before putting your Mac to sleep when it detects no input on the keyboard or mouse.

8. Select the **Put The Display To Sleep When The Computer Is Inactive For** check box if you want to put the display to sleep sooner than the computer. Drag the slider to specify the length of time. Putting the display to sleep soon is especially good for PowerBooks and iBooks running on battery power (the display uses a lot of power) and for LCDs (the lamp eventually burns out).

9. Select the **Put The Hard Disk(s) To Sleep When Possible** check box if you want Mac OS X to put the hard disk to sleep whenever it can. This saves power (and reduces noise) but decreases performance.

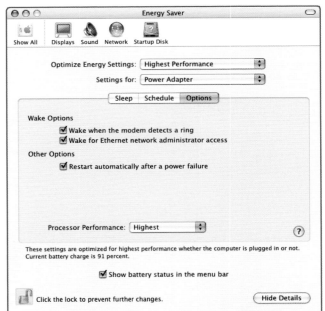

Figure 5-18: You can configure your Mac to wake when the phone rings or the network prompts it, to make it restart automatically after a power failure, and to change the processor performance.

10. To choose other power options, click the **Options** tab button. Figure 5-18 shows the Options tab for a PowerBook or iBook. The Energy Saver sheet for a desktop Mac doesn't have the Optimize Energy Settings drop-down list box or the Settings For drop-down list box. The Options tab doesn't include the Processor Performance drop-down list box, but it may include an Allow Power Button To Sleep The Computer check box (depending on your Mac).

   - Choose whether to have your Mac wake from sleep when the modem detects a ring (so as to receive faxes) or wake via a prompt across an Ethernet network from an administrator.

   - Select the **Restart Automatically After A Power Failure** check box if you want your Mac to restart automatically after a power outage. This option is primarily useful for desktop Macs providing services (for example, sharing a printer or an iTunes music library) to other Macs. The battery in a PowerBook or iBook normally allows it to ride out short power outages without a problem.

   - In the Processor Performance drop-down list box, you can choose **Reduced** performance instead of Highest performance to increase battery life on a PowerBook or iBook or to make action games designed for older, slower Macs run at a less frenetic pace.

11. For a PowerBook or iBook, return to step 6, choose the other setting in the Settings For drop-down list box (Power Adapter or Battery Power), and choose suitable settings.

12. Click **System Preferences | Quit System Preferences** to close System Preferences.

USE AN UNINTERRUPTIBLE POWER SUPPLY

The battery in a PowerBook or iBook enables it to ride out power outages of up to several hours, depending on how fully the battery is charged and how much power the 'Book is consuming. With a desktop Mac, you can use an uninterruptible power supply, or UPS, to prevent your Mac from crashing when the power goes out. Your Mac's power cord plugs into the UPS, which in turn plugs into a wall outlet. The UPS contains batteries that will supply power to your Mac for a short time (from 5 to 30 minutes), enough to get you through brief power interruptions or allow you to shut down your Mac "gracefully" (under control) on longer outages.

TIP

If you find the underside of your PowerBook gets uncomfortably hot, try using the **Reduced** processor performance setting to decrease the amount of heat being output. Alternatively, get a notebook fan.

TIP

Before buying a UPS, calculate how much power your Mac needs. The easiest way to calculate the power is to use a template such as the one at American Power Conversion Corp. (www.apcc.com/template/size/apc/; this web site requires your browser to accept cookies in order to work). Select a model that connects to your Mac and that supports software for shutting down your Mac automatically if you're not present to shut it down manually when a power outage occurs.

QUICKSTEPS

GETTING MAXIMUM BATTERY LIFE

If your Mac is a PowerBook or an iBook, you're likely sometimes to want to make the battery last as long as possible. Apple has provided you with various ways to do so.

USE THE BATTERY STATUS MENU

First, put the battery status menu on your menu bar so that you can see the battery's status. Open the **Energy Saver** sheet of System Preferences, and select the **Show Battery Status In The Menu Bar** check box.

- The charging icon shows that the battery is charging. The time display shows the estimated time left to complete the charge.

- When your PowerBook or iBook is running on battery power, the display shows a battery icon with a black bar indicating approximately how much battery power is left. For more detail, click the icon, click **Show** on the menu, and choose **Time** to display the time left or **Percentage** to show the percentage left.

REDUCE THE BRIGHTNESS OF THE DISPLAY

The display accounts for a large proportion of the power your PowerBook or iBook consumes. To reduce the brightness of the display:

1. Press **F1** on the keyboard to reduce the brightness one step at a time. (Press **F2** to increase the brightness.)

   —Or—

2. Open and click **System Preferences**, click **Displays**, click the **Display** tab button, and drag the **Brightness** slider to the left.

Continued…

Some UPSs connect to your Mac via a USB (Universal Serial Bus) connection so that they can notify your Mac of power problems and even shut it down automatically if you're not there to do so yourself. Depending on the UPS, you may control it, either through the UPS tab in the Energy Saver sheet of System Preferences or via its own software.

Add and Remove Software

Today, almost all application and utility software comes in one of two ways: on a CD or DVD, or downloaded from the Internet.

If you get software on a CD or DVD, insert the CD or DVD in your optical drive. Mac OS X will mount the disc and display a window showing its contents, as in the example shown in Figure 5-19.

Figure 5-19: Mac OS X mounts a CD or DVD so that you can install the software it contains.

Most software that you download from the Internet is packed into a file called a *disk image*, which is then compressed to make it as small as possible. If you download a compressed disk image from the Internet by using Safari, Safari will save the compressed file to your desktop, uncompress the disk image automatically and save it to the desktop too, mount the disk image on your desktop, and open a window showing its contents. Figure 5-20 shows an example of a disk image on the desktop.

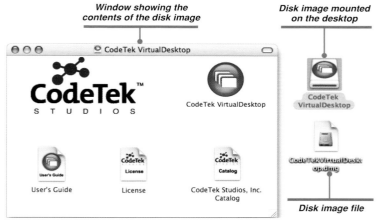

Figure 5-20: When you download a disk image file containing software from the Internet, Safari automatically displays a window showing its contents.

From a window such as this, you install the software in one of two ways: by dragging it to your Applications folder or by running the Installer. Which technique you need depends on the software:

- If the software has a file named Install (like the file in Figure 5-19), you must use the installer.
- If the software simply has a file with the application's name, you typically install it by dragging.
- If in doubt, read any instructions that came with the software, either as a leaflet accompanying a software CD or a file that appears in the software's window.

GETTING MAXIMUM BATTERY
LIFE (Continued)

SWITCH OFF HARDWARE FEATURES
YOU'RE NOT USING

Switch off any hardware features you're not using,
such as the AirPort wireless network (click the
AirPort icon on the menu bar, and click **Turn AirPort
Off**) or Bluetooth networking (click the **Bluetooth** icon
on the menu bar, and click **Turn Bluetooth Off**).

USE HEADPHONES

When listening to audio on your 'Book, use
headphones rather than your Mac's built-in speakers.
Headphones require much less power to drive.

USE AGGRESSIVE POWER MANAGEMENT

Configure Energy Saver (see "Set Energy Saver
Options," earlier in this chapter) to put your display,
hard disk, and your 'Book to sleep as quickly as
makes sense. For example, you might make the
display sleep after one minute, the hard disk after five
minutes, and your 'Book after ten minutes.

INSTALL SOFTWARE BY DRAGGING

If the window that contains the new software doesn't have the toolbar
displayed (as in Figure 5-20), open **View** and click **Show Toolbar**. Mac OS X
will display the toolbar and the Sidebar.

1. Drag the icon for the software to your Applications folder in the Sidebar.
2. Click the **Applications** folder in the Sidebar to display its contents.
3. Double-click the icon for the software to run the software.
4. In the Sidebar, click the **Eject** icon next to the disk image to eject the disk image.

INSTALL SOFTWARE USING AN INSTALLER

Double-click the icon for the installer file to launch the installation routine, and
then follow the displayed instructions. Figure 5-21 shows an example of the
beginning of an installation routine.

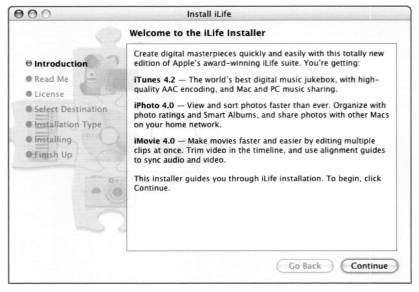

Figure 5-21: Run the installer to install an application.

After installing the software, eject the CD or DVD or unmount the disk image by dragging it to the Trash. If you downloaded the disk image from the Internet, you can now either move the disk image file to the Trash (drag it there) or move it to another folder for safe storage in case you need it again (for example, to install on another Mac). If there's a compressed file as well (which will typically have a .sit, .tar, .gz, or .tgz extension), drag this to the Trash too.

REMOVE SOFTWARE

1. Click the **Finder** icon on the Dock. A Finder window will open.
2. Click **Applications** in the Sidebar. The contents of the Applications folder will be displayed.
3. Drag the application or the folder containing it to the Trash.

Add Hardware

Most hardware today is *Plug and Play*. This means you can plug it in and immediately use it. When you first turn on your Mac after installing the hardware, Mac OS X may notify you that it has discovered the hardware; however, Mac OS X may simply install the *drivers* (the software that enables Mac OS X to communicate with the hardware) without comment. For example, if you insert a PC Card FireWire adapter in the PC slot of a PowerBook that doesn't have FireWire, Mac OS X makes no comment; but if you open System Profiler, you can see that the FireWire capability has been added.

Beyond being Plug and Play, most peripheral hardware that connects via FireWire or USB is *hot pluggable*: you can plug it in or remove it while Mac OS X is running instead of having to shut down Mac OS X before installing the

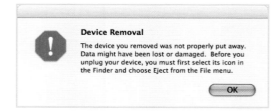

hardware. You don't need to warn Mac OS X before you plug in a hot-pluggable device, such as an iPod or memory-card reader, but you must eject the device (usually by dragging it to the Trash) before disconnecting it. If you don't, you may lose data, and Mac OS X will display a warning, like the example shown here. Click **OK** (there's nothing else you can do).

Some hardware requires you to install drivers provided by the manufacturer. Typically, you'll either receive these drivers on a CD in the hardware box or have to download them from a web site:

- The **manufacturer** of the device is generally the best source of drivers for a current product.

- **Apple's Downloads site** (http://www.apple.com/downloads/macosx/drivers/) provides a collection of drivers for widely used devices.

- **Third-party driver sites** can be good sources of drivers for older hardware, although many older hardware devices that worked with earlier versions of Mac OS (such as System 8 and System 9) do not work with Mac OS X because nobody has written drivers for them. The best way to find driver sites is to search using a search engine such as Google (www.google.com) or Yahoo! (www.yahoo.com).

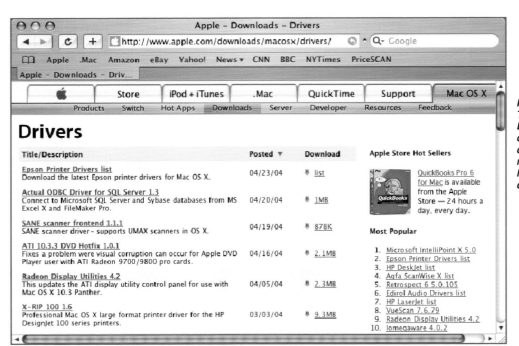

Figure 5-22:
The Apple Downloads site offers a number of drivers for many different hardware components.

Chapter 6
Working with Documents and Pictures

In this chapter you will discover the many aspects of creating documents and pictures and how to install and use printers with documents and pictures. You will also learn how to set up and use Mac OS X's built-in fax capability with documents and pictures.

Create Documents and Pictures

Creating documents and pictures is primarily done with applications outside of Mac OS X. For example, many Mac users run word processing applications, such as Microsoft Word or the OpenOffice.org word processor, to create text-based documents; and they use drawing applications and image-editing applications, such as Adobe Illustrator and Adobe Photoshop, to create and manipulate pictures.

All new Macs, however, include iPhoto, a powerful but straightforward application for importing, editing, and exporting photos. iPhoto is included in

ACQUIRING A DOCUMENT

The documents on your Mac got there because they were created with an application on your Mac, they were brought to your Mac on a disk, they were transferred across a local area network (LAN), or they were downloaded from the Internet.

CREATE A DOCUMENT WITH AN APPLICATION

1. Start the application. For example, start Microsoft Word by activating the **Finder**, opening **Go**, clicking **Applications**, and then double-clicking the **Microsoft Word** icon in the Microsoft Office folder.

2. Create the document using the application's features. In Word, for example, type the document, formatting it with Word's formatting tools.

3. Save the document (again, in Word) by opening **File** and choosing **Save**, choosing the name and folder for the document, and clicking **Save** (see Figure 6-1).

Figure 6-1: Most applications in which you can create documents let you choose where to save the files you create.

4. Close the application used to create the file (for example, click the **Quit** command on the menu that bears the application's name).

IMPORT A DOCUMENT FROM A DISK

Use the Finder to bring in a document from a disk or another removable storage device:

1. Insert the disk in the appropriate drive on your Mac. For example, insert a CD or DVD in an optical drive,

Continued...

---

iLife '04, Apple's set of multimedia applications that comes bundled with new Macs. Apple distributed earlier versions of iLife (before iLife '04) for free, so if you have any Mac but the most recent, you may well have earlier versions of the iLife applications installed on your Mac. If you don't have iLife '04, or if you have an earlier version, you can get iLife '04 for $49.99 from the Apple Store (http://store.apple.com) or a computer store.

Mac OS X provides strong features for bringing documents and pictures in from other computers, from the Internet, and from scanners and cameras.

Create a Picture

Pictures are really just documents that contain an image, and they can be created or brought into your Mac in the same way as any other document (see the "Acquiring a Document" QuickSteps).

For example, if you have a drawing application such as Adobe Illustrator installed on your Mac, you can create a picture by taking these general steps:

1. Open the application by clicking its icon on the Dock, or open a Finder window to the Applications folder and double-click the application's icon in that folder.

2. Use the New command to create a new file. For example, depending on the application, you might open **File** and click **New**.

3. Create the picture using the tools in the application.

4. Save the document by opening **File** and choosing **Save** or **Save As** (depending on the application), specifying the location and file name in the Save As dialog box, and clicking the **Save** button.

5. Open the application's application menu and click **Quit** to close the application.

Install Cameras and Scanners

How you install a digital camera or scanner depends on whether the device is Plug and Play (plug it in and it starts to function), what type of connection it has, and whether Mac OS X already has a driver for it.

INSTALL A USB CAMERA OR MEDIA READER

Many digital cameras can connect to your Mac via USB (Universal Serial Bus). If your camera doesn't connect via USB, chances are good that the camera has a storage card (such as a CompactFlash card or a Memory Stick card) that can be removed from the camera and inserted in a card reader that is connected to your Mac via USB.

When you connect a digital camera or a storage card containing photos via USB, Mac OS X recognizes the camera or storage card as a removable disk drive and mounts it on the desktop so that you can access its contents. Mac OS X also automatically starts iPhoto, the photo-editing application included in the iLife multimedia suite, and switches iPhoto into Import mode so that you can easily import the pictures into your Photo Library in iPhoto. (See "Transfer Pictures from a Camera," later in this chapter.)

INSTALL A SCANNER

Most recent scanners designed for the consumer market connect to your Mac via USB. Some more expensive scanners connect via FireWire, the high-speed data-transfer technology that Apple favors over USB. Older scanners, and some scanners intended for professional use (and professional purchasing power), connect via SCSI (Small Computer Systems Interface), an older technology for connecting hard drives and fast peripherals to a computer. Mac OS X 10.3 includes drivers for many popular models of scanners and for scanners that use the TWAIN scanning technology.

If the scanner came with a driver for Mac OS X and/or with custom scanning software and there are manufacturer's instructions for installing the scanner with Mac OS X, follow those instructions. Otherwise, use these instructions:

1. Install the driver or software.

2. Connect the scanner to your Mac.

3. Run the scanning software (if any).

DOWNLOAD A DOCUMENT FROM THE INTERNET

Use Safari to bring in a document from a site on the Internet:

1. Click the **Safari** icon on the Dock. Safari will launch.

2. Type an address in the Address bar, search, or browse to a site and page from which you can download the document file.

3. Click the document file's link on the web page to begin downloading the file. Safari will save the file to your desktop.

4. Drag the file to a Finder window and use the Spring-Loaded Folders feature to navigate to the folder in which you want to store the file.

5. Open **Safari** and click **Quit Safari** to close Safari.

TIP

If your scanner came with custom scanning software, use that software in preference to Image Capture, as it will probably be designed to make better use of your scanner's capabilities than Image Capture. Also, you may not be able to use Image Capture.

If you don't have a driver for the scanner:

1. Connect the scanner to your Mac via the interface it uses—USB, FireWire, or SCSI.

2. Turn on the scanner and put a document on its scanning surface.

3. Press the button on your scanner that starts the scanning operation.

4. If Mac OS X opens the Image Capture application, you're all set. If not, check the scanner manufacturer's web site to see if a driver for Mac OS X is available.

Scan Pictures Using Image Capture

Scanners enable you to take printed images and convert them to digital images on your Mac. The scanner must first be installed, as described in the previous section. To scan a picture using Image Capture, Mac OS X's default scanning application:

1. Turn on the scanner.

2. Place the document carefully on the scanning surface.

3. Press the button on your scanner that starts the scanning operation. Either your scanner's software or Image Capture will open. The scanner will scan the document, and the overview (a preliminary scan) will appear in your software or in Image Capture. Figure 6-2 shows Image Capture with its Drawer open.

4. To choose settings for the scan in Image Capture, click **Drawer**. Image Capture displays the Drawer, in which you can specify:

   - The source for the scan: Flatbed or Transparency

   - The document type: Text, B/W Photo, or Color Photo

   - The resolution in dots per inch (dpi), which controls the file size

   - The source size (in inches, centimeters, or pixels)

   - Any scaling needed: enter the percentage in the Scaling box, and Image Capture will indicate the resulting size in the New Size boxes

   - Whether to use image correction: None, Automatic, or Manual (If you select the Manual option button, Image Capture displays the Brightness, Tint, and Hue sliders, which you drag to specify settings).

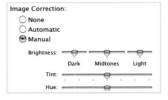

NOTE

TWAIN is widely supposed to be an acronym for Technology Without An Interesting Name, but computer scholars claim it's actually taken from "never the twain shall meet" in Kipling's "Ballad of East and West." TWAIN was a brave attempt to bring the incompatible worlds of scanners and computers together.

5. To make the overview fit in the window, click the **Size Overview To Fit** button.

6. Use the **Zoom In** and **Zoom Out** buttons if you need to zoom the picture, or use the **Rotate Left** and **Rotate Right** button to rotate it.

7. Drag across the preview to specify which part of it you want to capture.

8. Click **Scan**. Image Capture causes the scanner to scan the picture and then saves the file in the folder you specified, assigning it an automatic name consisting of "scan" and the date and time—for example, scan20040930_201831.tif for a scan performed at 8:18:31 PM on September 30, 2004.

9. Open **Image Capture** and click **Quit Image Capture** to close Image Capture.

10. Open a Finder window to the scanned picture, click the name, type a more descriptive name, and press **RETURN**.

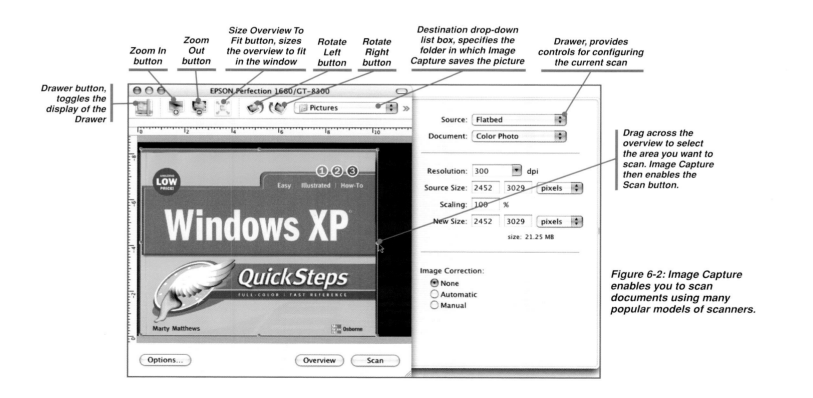

Figure 6-2: Image Capture enables you to scan documents using many popular models of scanners.

Transfer Pictures from a Camera

As mentioned in "Install a USB Camera or Media Reader" (earlier in this chapter), when you connect your camera or its memory card via USB, Mac OS X automatically mounts the device on the desktop and opens iPhoto in Import mode, as shown at the bottom of Figure 6-3.

IMPORT ALL PICTURES AUTOMATICALLY

The easiest way to proceed is to import all pictures automatically, and then review them in iPhoto and delete the duds. To import the pictures:

TIP

If iPhoto doesn't open automatically, click the **iPhoto** icon on the Dock to open it, and then click the **Import** mode button below the main window.

Source pane, shows your
Photo Library (at the top)
and your albums

Viewing area, displays
one or more pictures

Figure 6-3: Mac OS X automatically opens iPhoto and switches it to Import mode when it detects you've plugged in a digital camera or a storage card that contains digital pictures.

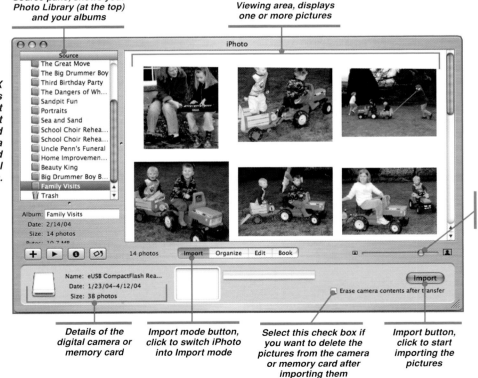

Size slider, changes
the size of pictures
displayed in the
Viewing area

Details of the
digital camera or
memory card

Import mode button,
click to switch iPhoto
into Import mode

Select this check box if
you want to delete the
pictures from the camera
or memory card after
importing them

Import button,
click to start
importing the
pictures

1. In the lower-right corner of the iPhoto window, select the **Erase Camera Contents After Transfer** check box if you want iPhoto to delete the pictures from the camera after importing them. Usually, it's safer to delete them manually.

2. Click the **Import** button in the lower-right corner of the iPhoto window.

3. If you selected the Erase Camera Contents After Transfer check box, iPhoto displays the Confirm Move dialog box. Click **Delete Originals** if you're sure you want to delete them from the camera. Click **Keep Originals** if you've changed your mind.

4. iPhoto will import the pictures, showing you a preview of the current photo and a readout of its progress.

5. If any of the pictures are duplicates of pictures you've imported before (for example, because you left them on your camera after importing them), iPhoto displays the Duplicate Photo dialog box (see Figure 6-4). Select the **Applies To All Duplicates** check box if you want your decision to apply to all duplicate pictures rather than just the one currently displayed, and then click **Yes** or **No**.

6. After importing all your pictures, iPhoto switches automatically to Organize mode so that you can review the pictures. See "Sort Through Your Last Roll Quickly," later in this section, for details.

Figure 6-4: Choose whether or not to import pictures that are duplicates of pictures already in your Photo Library.

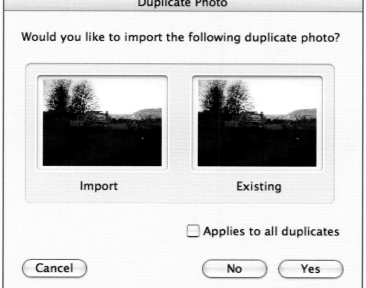

NOTE

If you see generic icons rather than thumbnails in Icons view in the Finder, open **View** and click **Show View Options** to display the options window. Select the **All Windows** option button, select the **Show Icon Preview** check box, and then click the **Close** button (the red button).

TIP

You can also drag the pictures to a specific album. iPhoto will add the pictures to your Photo Library and will create references to them in that album so that they appear in the album.

IMPORT SOME PICTURES MANUALLY

If you don't want to import all your pictures at once, you can import them manually:

1. Click the **Organize** button below the main picture window in iPhoto to put iPhoto back into Organize mode.

2. Double-click the icon for the camera or media reader on the desktop to open a Finder window showing its contents.

3. Open the folders on the camera or media reader until you can see the picture files.

4. If the Finder window is using List view or Columns view, open **View** and click **As Icons** to change to Icons view so that you can see thumbnails of the pictures.

5. Position the Finder window so that you can see some of the iPhoto window.

6. In the Finder window, select the pictures that you want to import:

   ● To select multiple contiguous pictures, click the first picture, then **SHIFT**+click the last picture.

   ● To select multiple noncontiguous pictures, click the first picture, then ⌘+click each of the other pictures.

   ● ⌘+click a selected picture to deselect it.

7. Drag the pictures to the iPhoto window and drop them there. iPhoto will switch to Import mode automatically, import the pictures, and then switch to Organize mode.

EJECT THE CAMERA OR MEMORY CARD

After importing the pictures either automatically or manually, eject the camera or memory card by dragging its icon on the desktop to the Trash icon on the Dock. You can then unplug the camera or memory card from your Mac without causing an error.

Sort Through Your Last Roll Quickly

iPhoto stores details of the last batch of pictures you imported in the Last Roll album, which appears by default just beneath the Photo Library entry in the Source pane. After importing pictures, you can use Last Roll and iPhoto's Slideshow feature to sort through them quickly, as follows:

If you find the Last Roll feature useful, you can increase the number of rolls it contains. Open **iPhoto** and click **Preferences**, click the **General** button, then increase the number in the **Show Last *NN* Roll Album** box (where *NN* is the number). If you don't use Last Roll, clear its check box to remove it from the Source list. Click the **Close** button (the red button) to close the Preferences window.

1. Click **Last Roll** in the Source (left) pane. The last pictures you imported will be displayed.

2. Click **Slideshow** in the toolbar at the bottom of the window. The Slideshow dialog box will be displayed (see Figure 6-5).

3. Unless you want to see the slideshow over and over, make sure the **Repeat Slideshow** check box is cleared.

4. Click **Play**. iPhoto starts a full-screen slideshow of the pictures, using default settings.

5. To take an action, move the mouse. iPhoto will display the Control bar (see Figure 6-6), which you can use to navigate among pictures, rotate the current picture, assign a rating to the current picture (from no stars to five stars) by dragging along the line of five dots, or delete it.

6. At the end of the slideshow, iPhoto displays its main window again. If you chose to repeat the slideshow, you may press **ESC** to stop it.

Figure 6-5: The Slideshow dialog box lets you quickly start a slideshow with default settings or create a customized show with your preferred music.

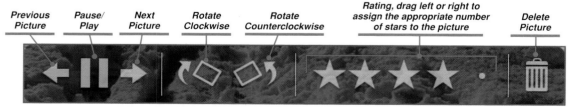

Figure 6-6: Use the Control bar to rotate, delete, or rate pictures.

Edit and Manage Your Pictures with iPhoto

After culling out the dud pictures from your roll, you can edit the remaining pictures in iPhoto and sort them into albums.

EDIT A PICTURE

To edit a picture, **CONTROL**+click or right-click it and click **Edit In Separate Window**. iPhoto will open the picture in a separate window for editing (see Figure 6-7). You can then:

- Click the **Zoom** buttons to zoom in and out.
- Click the **Fit** button to zoom the picture to fit into the window.
- Click the **Rotate** button to rotate the picture. **OPTION**+click the **Rotate** button to rotate the picture the opposite way.

NOTE

iPhoto lets you edit a picture either in the main window or in a separate window. Editing in a separate window tends to be more flexible, as you can open two or more pictures for editing at the same time; but you may prefer editing in the same window to keep your screen uncluttered. To choose which editing method iPhoto uses when you double-click a picture, click **iPhoto | Preferences**, click the **General** tab button, and choose the **Changes To Edit View** option button or the **Opens Photo In Edit Window** option button in the Double-Click Photo area. Click the **Close** button (the red button) to close the Preferences window.

Figure 6-7: iPhoto provides easy but effective tools for editing your pictures.

- Use the **Constrain** drop-down list box to constrain cropping to a particular size ratio. (See the "Cropping Pictures to Fit Your Desktop" QuickSteps.)

- To crop a picture, select a constraint in the Constrain drop-down list box if necessary, then drag with the mouse on the picture to select the area. Drag a border of the selected area to move that border, or drag in the middle of the selected area to move the whole area. Click **Crop** when you're ready.

- To enhance the picture, letting iPhoto tweak the colors, click **Enhance** one or more times.

- To remove red-eye from flash pictures, drag a rectangle that includes the eyes but leaves some of the face selected, and then click **Red-Eye**.

- To change the brightness or contrast, drag the **Brightness/Contrast** sliders.

- To temporarily remove the changes you've made, press **CONTROL**. Toggling the changes off like this helps you judge how successful they are.

- To undo a change, open **Edit** and choose the **Undo** command. (The Undo menu item specifies what will be undone—for example, "Undo Enhance Photo.") You can undo multiple actions until you switch to another picture.

- To revert to the original picture, open **Photos** and click **Revert To Original**. iPhoto will display a confirmation dialog box. Click **OK**.

After editing the picture, click the **Close** button (the red button) to close its window. iPhoto will return you to the main window.

WORK WITH ALBUMS

iPhoto stores all your pictures in its Photo Library, so you can access any picture by selecting Photo Library in the Source pane. But what you'll typically want to do is arrange your pictures into albums for topics or occasions.

1. To create a new album, open **File** and click **New Album**, type the name in the resulting dialog box, and click **OK**. iPhoto will add the album to the Source pane.

Please enter a name for the new Album:

Family Disasters

Cancel   OK

NOTE

iPhoto stores all your pictures in the Photo Library rather than in the albums. Each album consists only of references to the pictures you've told iPhoto to display in it. This means that when you edit a picture that appears in an album, you're actually editing the version of the picture that appears in the Photo Library—so your edits will carry through to every album that contains the picture. This centralization makes for economical editing, but you may sometimes want to edit the same picture in different ways for different albums or for use on your desktop or elsewhere. In this case, select the picture, open **Photos** and click **Duplicate** to duplicate it, and then work with the duplicate.

QUICKSTEPS

CROPPING PICTURES TO FIT YOUR DESKTOP

As explained in "Change the Desktop from iPhoto" in Chapter 2, you can quickly put pictures on your desktop from iPhoto. But before you do so, you may need to crop the pictures so that they're the right dimensions.

1. Click the **iPhoto** icon on the Dock. iPhoto will open.

2. In the Source list, click the album that contains the picture.

3. In the Detail pane, **CONTROL**+click or right-click the picture you want to crop and click **Edit In Separate Window**. iPhoto will open the picture in an editing window.

4. In the Constrain drop-down list, select the item that says (Display)—for example, "1280 × 854 (Display)." iPhoto displays a shaded area how the crop will turn out (see Figure 6-8).

5. To move the crop area, click in it and drag it.

6. Click the **Crop** button to crop the picture.

7. Click the **Close** button (the red button) to close the editing window.

2. To add a picture to the album, drag it from the Photo Library (or another album) to the destination album. iPhoto will add to the album a reference to the picture, which remains stored in the Photo Library but now appears in the album as well.

3. To display an album's pictures, click the album in the Source pane.

4. To delete an album, select it in the Source pane and press **DELETE**. iPhoto will display a confirmation dialog box. Click **Remove**.

Constrain drop-down list box, select the (Display) item to crop a picture to fit your desktop

Crop area

Figure 6-8: Choose the (Display) item in the Constrain drop-down list box to crop a picture to fit your desktop exactly.

Print Documents and Pictures

Before you can transfer your digital documents and pictures to paper, you must install and configure a printer.

Install a Printer

To install either a local printer or a network printer in Mac OS X, you use the Printer Setup Utility. This section explains the process of installing a local printer separately from the process of installing a network printer, as there are several differences between the two processes.

Before installing a local printer, work through the following checklist.

CHECKLIST BEFORE INSTALLING A PRINTER

A local printer is one that is attached to your Mac with a cable or a wireless connection. Make sure your printer meets the following conditions *before* you begin to install it in Mac OS X:

- It is plugged into the correct port on your Mac. Most inkjet printers and personal laser printers connect to your Mac directly via a USB cable. Most laser printers designed for multiple users connect via an Ethernet connection: both the printer and your Mac connect to the network's hub or switch via standard Ethernet cables or a wireless AirPort, and they communicate through the hub or switch.
- It is plugged into an electrical outlet.
- Fresh ink, toner, or ribbon is correctly installed.
- It is loaded with paper.

INSTALL A LOCAL PRINTER

Installing a local printer is usually pretty straightforward:

1. With the printer turned off, connect it to your Mac. Then make sure the other points in the above checklist are satisfied.
2. Turn on the printer.

TIP

You can also connect an Ethernet laser printer directly to your Mac by using a *crossover* cable, a special cable that reverses the wires in the cable from their standard arrangement.

NOTE

Some printers connect to your Mac via a wireless connection. This arrangement is typically used for PowerBooks and iBooks, for which it offers the most benefits, but it can be used with desktop Macs as well. In this case, "plugging the printer into your Mac" means that you should establish the appropriate wireless connection.

3. Activate the **Finder**.

4. Open **Go** and click **Utilities**. The contents of the Utilities folder will be displayed.

5. Double-click **Printer Setup Utility**. Printer Setup Utility will open and will display the Printer List window. If you haven't set up a printer on this Mac before, Printer Setup Utility displays a message inviting you to add a printer.

6. Click **Add**. (If Printer Setup Utility doesn't display this message, click the **Add** button in the toolbar.) Printer Setup Utility displays a dialog box for selecting the printer.

7. In the top drop-down list box, select **USB** for a USB-connected printer or **AppleTalk** for an Ethernet-connected printer.

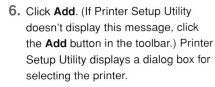

8. Printer Setup Utility searches for connected printers and displays the names of any it finds.

9. Click the printer name. Printer Setup Utility automatically selects the appropriate printer model in the Printer Model drop-down list box.

10. Click **Add**. Printer Setup Utility adds the printer to the Printer List window. If this is the first printer you've added, Printer Setup Utility automatically makes the printer the default printer.

11. Open the **Printer Setup Utility** menu and click **Quit Printer Setup Utility** to close Printer Setup Utility.

You're ready to test your printer. Go to "Test the Printer," later in this chapter.

Network printers are not directly connected to your Mac but are available to you by being shared through the network to which your Mac is connected. There are three types of network printers:

- Printers connected to someone else's computer and shared by that computer
- Printers connected to a dedicated print server (a special-purpose computer whose function is to share and manage printers on a network)
- Printers directly connected to a network (these printers have a built-in print server)

NOTE

If you don't know the details of the network printer you're connecting to, consult your network administrator.

To connect to a network printer:

1. Connect your Mac to the network if it's not already connected.

2. Activate the **Finder**, open **Go** and click **Utilities**, and then double-click **Printer Setup Utility**.

3. Click **Add** either in the message box that suggests you add a printer or on the toolbar in Printer Setup Utility.

4. Specify the details of the printer:

- To connect to a line printer (typically on a corporate or college network), select **IP Printing** in the top drop-down list box (see Figure 6-9). Enter the IP (Internet Protocol) address of the printer in the **Printer Address** text box, enter the queue name in the **Queue Name** text box (or leave it blank to use the default queue), and use the **Printer Model** drop-down list box and the list under it to specify the printer mode. Click **Add**.

- To connect to a network printer shared using Apple's AppleTalk protocol, select **AppleTalk** in the top drop-down list box. In the second list box, select the AppleTalk zone—for example, **Local AppleTalk Zone**. Select the printer by name in the list box. Printer Setup Utility should select the printer model automatically in the **Printer Model** drop-down list box; if not, select it manually. Then click **Add**.

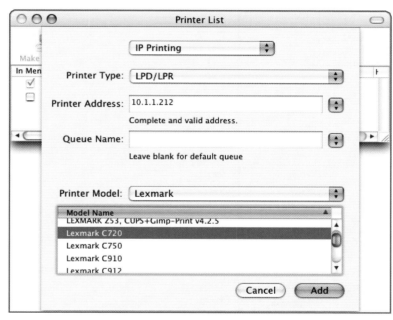

Figure 6-9: Use the IP Printing choice to connect to a line printer.

- To connect to a printer shared by a Windows computer, select **Windows Print-ing** in the top list box. In the second list box, select the name of the Windows workgroup if Printer Setup Utility hasn't selected it automatically. The list box displays the computers available on the network. Double-click the computer that's sharing the printer. (Enter a user name and password if requested and click **OK**.) Printer Setup Utility will display the list of printers (see Figure 6-10). Select the printer in the middle list box, specify the manufacturer in the **Printer Model** drop-down list box, and then specify the model in the lower list box. (If your printer isn't listed, consult the manufacturer.) Click **Add**.

5. Printer Setup Utility adds the printer to the Printer List window. If this is the first printer you've added, Printer Setup Utility automatically makes the printer the default printer.

6. Open the **Printer Setup Utility** menu and click **Quit Printer Setup Utility** to close Printer Setup Utility.

Test the printer as described next.

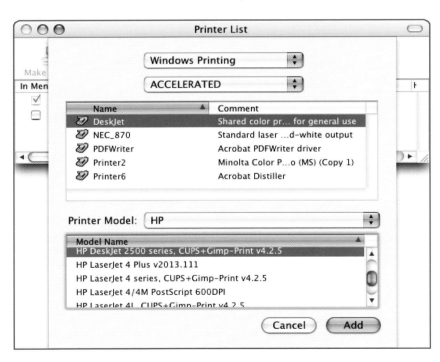

Figure 6-10: Open the entry for the Windows computer that's sharing the printer (here, ACCELERATED) so that you can select the printer and specify which model it is.

After adding your printer, test it by printing a document. For example:

1. Click the **iPhoto** icon on the Dock. iPhoto will open.

2. Select a picture you want to print.

3. Click **Print** on the toolbar at the bottom of the window. The Print dialog box will open (see Figure 6-11).

4. Ensure the correct printer is selected in the Printer drop-down list.

5. In the Style drop-down list, select **Standard Prints**.

6. In the options area below the Style drop-down list, select the **One Photo Per Page** check box.

7. Click **Print**. iPhoto sends the page to the printer, which prints it.

Figure 6-11: Print a document (such as a picture from iPhoto) to check that your printer is working correctly.

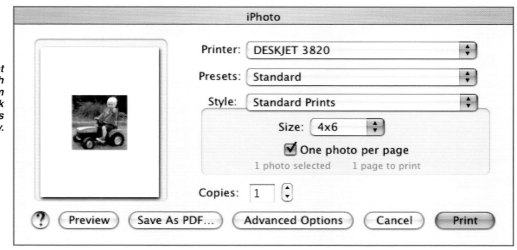

PRINTING

Most printing is done from within an application. Here's an example using Microsoft Word, whose Print dialog box is shown in Figure 6-12.

PRINT DOCUMENTS

To print:

1. Open **File** and choose **Print** to display the Print dialog box.
2. Click **Print** to print using the default settings.

CHOOSE A PRINTER

To choose which printer you want to use:

1. Open **File** and choose **Print** to display the Print dialog box.
2. Open the **Printer** drop-down list box and choose the printer you want.

SPECIFY WHICH PAGES TO PRINT

In the Pages area of the Print dialog box you can:

1. Select the **All** option button to print all pages in the document. (This is the default setting.)
2. Select the **Current Page** option button to print only the current page.
3. Select the **From** option button, specify the starting page in the **From** text box, and specify the ending page in the **To** text box.
4. Print a series of individual pages, and/or one or more ranges of pages, by specifying the individual pages separated by commas, and specifying each range with a hyphen. For example, entering 4,6,8-10,12 will print pages 4, 6, 8, 9, 10, and 12.

IDENTIFY A DEFAULT PRINTER

If you add two or more printers, you need to tell Mac OS X which is the default. To do so:

1. Activate the **Finder**, open **Go** and click **Utilities**, and then double-click **Printer Setup Utility**.
2. Select the printer in the list box.

Make Default

3. Click **Make Default**.
4. Open the **Printer Setup Utility** menu and click **Quit Printer Setup Utility** to close Printer Setup Utility.

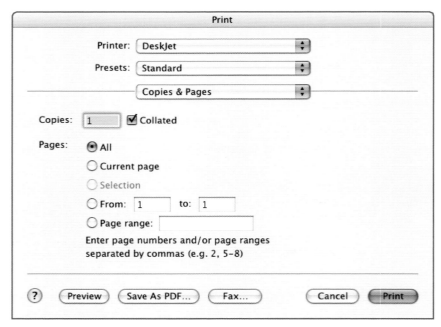

Figure 6-12: The Print dialog box in Microsoft Word is similar to those in many other applications.

Print to a PDF File

Instead of printing a document on a piece of paper, you can print it to a file in Adobe's Portable Document Format (PDF) format. There are two primary reasons for printing to a PDF:

- To create a file that you can take to a remote printer. For example, you might create a PDF file so that you could have it printed on a specialist item, such as a T-shirt, at a service bureau.

- To create a file that you can send to someone who is using a different computer platform (for example, Windows or Linux) and be confident that they will be able not only to open the document but also see it exactly as you laid it out.

Because Adobe has promoted the PDF format vigorously and has produced and distributed free versions of its Acrobat Reader software for all significant computer operating systems, almost anybody with an Internet connection should be able to open a PDF and view it as its creator intended.

To create a PDF file:

1. Open the file from which you want to create the PDF file in the appropriate application. For example, open **iPhoto** and select a picture.

2. Open **File** and choose **Print** to display the Print dialog box.

3. Choose printing options.

4. Click **Save As PDF**. The application displays the Save To File dialog box (see Figure 6-13).

5. Enter the file name and choose the folder in which to save it.

6. Click **Save**.

7. Open the application's application menu and click the **Quit** command to close the application. For example, open **iPhoto** and click **Quit iPhoto** to close iPhoto.

Figure 6-13: The Save To File dialog box lets you create a PDF file of a document in the folder you choose.

Print Web Pages

Printing web pages works the same way as printing from any other application:

1. Click the **Safari** icon on the Dock. Safari will open.
2. Browse to the page you want to print.
3. Open **File**, click **Print**, and select the printer and other options in the Print dialog box.
4. Click **Print** to print the page.
5. Open **Safari** and click **Quit Safari** to close Safari.

Control Printing

When a document is printed, the *print job* (the information required to print the document) is sent to the printer, where it is stored temporarily in a holding area called the *print queue*. When the printer is ready, it starts to print the document. If further documents are sent to the printer while the printer is busy printing, they wait their turn in the print queue. You can control the print process by manipulating jobs in the print queue. For example, you might need to place a lower-priority print job on hold in order to get an urgent print job printed.

To control printing:

1. Open **Go** and click **Utilities**. The contents of the Utilities folder will be displayed.
2. Double-click **Printer Setup Utility**. Printer Setup Utility will be displayed, showing the status of the printer:

- **Printing** indicates that the printer is currently printing.
- **Stopped** indicates that the printer has been stopped (for example, by an administrator).
- A blank indicates that the printer is functional but waiting for print jobs to be sent to it.
3. In the list box, select the printer you want to control.

NOTE

You cannot change the order in which print jobs are being printed by putting on hold the document that is currently being printed. You must either complete printing the current document or cancel it. You can, however, use hold to get around intermediate documents that are not currently printing. For example, suppose you want to print the third document in the queue immediately, but the first document is currently printing. You must either let the first document finish printing or cancel it. You can then pause the second document before it starts printing, and the third document will begin printing when the first document is out of the way.

QUICKSTEPS

MANAGING FONTS

A *font* is a set of characters with the same design, size, weight, and style. A font is a member of a *typeface* family, all with the same design. The font 12-point Arial bold italic is a member of the Arial typeface family with a 12-point size, bold weight, and italic style. Mac OS X comes with a good variety of fonts, which you can manipulate by using the Font Book application (see Figure 6-14):

1. Activate the **Finder**.
2. Click **Applications** in the Sidebar.
3. Double-click **Font Book**.

ADD FONTS

1. Activate the **Finder**.
2. Open the folder that contains the font file.
3. Double-click the font file. Font Book will display a window showing the font.
4. Click **Install Font**. Font Book installs the font to your User font folder and displays its main window.
5. If you want the font to be available to all users of your Mac rather than just to you, drag the font to the Computer item under the All Fonts collection.

Continued...

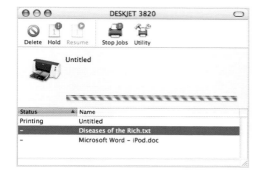

4. To quickly stop all print jobs on the printer, open the **Printers** menu and click **Stop Jobs**. (You might want to do this if you notice a problem with the printer.) You can then restart the jobs by opening the **Printers** menu and clicking **Start Jobs**.

5. For greater control, open **Printers** and click **Show Jobs**. A window for the printer will be displayed:

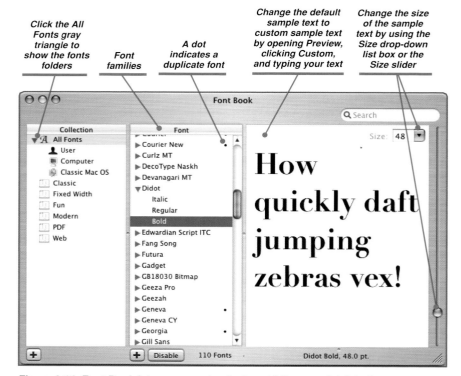

Figure 6-14: Font Book lets you examine fonts, add them, and delete them.

MANAGING FONTS *(Continued)*

DISABLE FONTS

If you want to reduce temporarily the number of fonts you have available without deleting the fonts, you can *disable* the fonts:

1. Open **Font Book** and click the font in the Font list.
2. Click the **Disable** button at the bottom of the Font list. Font Book will display a confirmation dialog box.
3. Click **Disable**. Font Book will disable the font and will display Off next to it in the Font list.

To enable a font you've disabled, click the font in the Font list and click the **Enable** button at the bottom of the Font list.

DELETE FONTS

To delete a font:

1. Open **Font Book** and click the font in the Font list.
2. Press **DELETE**. Font Book will display a confirmation dialog box.
3. Click **Remove**. Font Book will delete the font file.

USE FONTS

Fonts are used or specified from within an application. In Microsoft Word, for example, you can select one or more characters and then open the Font menu (as shown here) or the Font dialog box (open **Format** and click **Font**) to apply the font you want. Other applications use similar features to let you choose fonts. One nice feature in recent versions of Word is that the list shows what the fonts look like instead of simply showing their names in a standard system font.

6. Control the jobs as necessary:

- To delete a job, select it and click **Delete**.
- To put a job on hold so that other jobs can print, select the job and click **Hold**.
- To resume a job you've put on hold, select it and click **Resume**.
- To stop all jobs (for example, so that you can change the printer's cartridge), click **Stop Jobs**.
- To restart all jobs after stopping them, click **Start Jobs**.

7. Close the printer utility by opening its application menu and clicking the **Quit** command.

8. Open the **Printer Setup Utility** menu, and click **Quit Printer Setup Utility** to close Printer Setup Utility.

Fax Documents and Pictures

Mac OS X includes the capability to send and receive faxes as part of the printing function and allows an application, such as Microsoft Word, to "print" to a remote fax by specifying the fax function as a printer. This service requires that you have a phone line connected to the fax modem in your Mac.

Set Up Faxing

To set up faxing:

1. Open and click **System Preferences**. The System Preferences window will be displayed.
2. Click **Print & Fax**. The Print & Fax sheet will be displayed.
3. Click the **Faxing** tab to display it (see Figure 6-15).
4. If you plan to send faxes from this Mac, enter your fax number in the **My Fax Number** text box.

NOTE

If you've configured your Mac to go to sleep (see "Set Energy Saver Options" in Chapter 5), select the **Wake When The Modem Detects A Ring** check box on the Options tab of Energy Saver if you want your Mac to be able to wake from sleep to receive faxes.

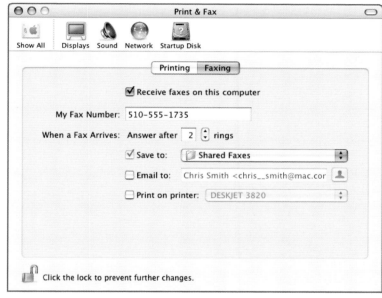

Figure 6-15: Set up your fax configuration on the Faxing tab of the Print & Fax sheet in System Preferences.

5. To receive faxes on this Mac:

- Select the **Receive Faxes On This Computer** check box. Mac OS X enables the When A Fax Arrives group of controls.

- Specify the number of rings in the **Answer After** text box.

- To save the faxes you receive to a folder, select the **Save To** check box and specify the folder in the drop-down list box. The default location is the Shared Faxes folder—the Faxes folder in the /Users/Shared folder.

  - To have Mac OS X automatically e-mail the faxes to an e-mail address, select the **Email To** check box and specify the address in the text box. Mac OS X saves the faxes as PDF files, which helps to keep them relatively compact.

  - To have Mac OS X automatically print each fax received, select the **Print On Printer** check box and specify the printer in the drop-down list box. This setting makes your Mac behave like a fax machine for incoming faxes.

6. Click **System Preferences | Quit System Preferences** to close System Preferences.

Send a Fax

To send a fax:

1. Open the document you want to send. For example, open a word processing document in Microsoft Word.

2. Open **File** and click **Print** to display the Print dialog box.

3. Click **Fax** in the bottom toolbar. Mac OS X displays the Print dialog box for faxing (see Figure 6-16).

4. In the **To** box, type either the fax number to use or the name of a person in your address book. If there's a match in your address book, Mac OS X completes the name and enters the fax number automatically.

5. Enter the subject in the **Subject** text box.

6. If you have multiple modems, make sure the right modem is selected in the **Modem** drop-down list box.

7. To add a cover page, select the **Cover Page** check box and type the message in the text box. Don't press RETURN, because doing so will "click" the Fax button rather than create a new paragraph.

8. Click the **Fax** button. Mac OS X removes the Print dialog box from the display and starts the fax job in the background.

9. To see what's happening, click the **Internal Modem** button on the Dock. Mac OS X displays the Internal Modem window, which shows the progress of the fax. If necessary, you can use the buttons on the toolbar to hold, resume, stop, and restart your faxes.

10. After the fax has been sent, open **Internal Modem** and click **Quit Internal Modem** to close Internal Modem.

Receive a Fax

When you've set up your Mac to receive faxes for you, it handles the process automatically, answering the phone after the number of rings you've specified, receiving the fax, and saving it, e-mailing it, or printing it, depending on your choices on the Print & Fax sheet in System Preferences.

After receiving a fax, you can view it as follows:

1. Activate the **Finder**.

2. Open the folder in which you chose to save faxes.

3. Double-click the fax file. Mac OS X will open the file in Preview.

4. If the fax has multiple pages, click **Page Up** or **Page Down** on the toolbar to navigate from page to page.

5. Open the **Preview** menu and click **Quit Preview** to close Preview.

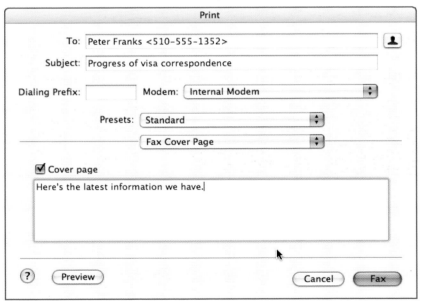

Figure 6-16: Specify the recipient of the fax in this Print dialog box.

Chapter 7

Working with Multimedia

Multimedia is the combination of audio and video. Mac OS X, as an operating system, has to be able to handle audio and video and accept their input from various different devices. In addition, the iLife suite included with Mac OS X has major applications that enable you to work with multimedia and write these files onto CDs or DVDs. This chapter looks first at sound by itself and then at video with sound.

Work with Audio

Audio is sound. Mac OS X works with and uses sound in several ways, the simplest being to alert you to various events, such as when you dump an object into the Trash, receive an e-mail message, or try to take an action that isn't possible. "Change Sounds," in Chapter 2, shows you how to customize the use of sound for these purposes.

QUICKSTEPS

CONFIGURING ACTIONS FOR CDS AND DVDS

To choose what Mac OS X does when you insert a CD or DVD:

1. Open  and click **System Preferences**. The System Preferences window will be displayed.

2. Click **CDs & DVDs**. The CDs & DVDs sheet will be displayed (see Figure 7-2).

3. Use the five drop-down lists to choose what Mac OS X should do when you insert a blank CD, a blank DVD, a music (audio) CD, a picture CD, or a video DVD.

4. Click **System Preferences | Quit System Preferences** to close System Preferences.

The When You Insert A Blank CD and the When You Insert A Blank DVD drop-down lists offer an Ask What To Do choice that makes Mac OS X display a dialog box asking you what to do (as in the example here). From this dialog box, you can choose which action to take with the CD or DVD.

The second use of sound is to entertain or inform you—allowing you to listen to music or lectures from CDs, Internet radio, or another Internet site. This use of sound is the subject of this section, together with the third use of sound—to express yourself audibly.

Play CDs

Playing an audio CD is as easy as inserting the CD in an optical drive. When you insert an audio CD, Mac OS X takes the default action for CDs, which is to launch iTunes (or activate iTunes if it's already running) so that you can play the CD or copy it to your Mac's hard disk. You can change Mac OS X's default actions for optical discs; see the "Configuring Actions for CDs and DVDs" QuickSteps on this page.

How you insert a CD depends on the optical drive in your Mac:

- In a slot-loading optical drive (such as those used on PowerBooks, iBooks, and some desktop Macs), you simply slide the CD into the slot until the mechanism grabs the CD and pulls it in the rest of the way.

- In a tray-style drive (such as those used on iMacs and eMacs), press the **EJECT** button on your keyboard or (in some Macs) the **Eject** button on or near the drive itself to make the tray appear, put the CD in the tray, and then press the same button to close the drive.

After you insert the CD, iTunes will automatically look it up in the Gracenote CDDB (CD Database) if your Mac is connected to the Internet. If the CD is widely distributed, iTunes will display a listing of tracks on the CD along with their titles and artists. iTunes will select all tracks to play (the check marks on the left). Click the **Play** button in the upper-left and the first track will begin to play. On your screen iTunes should look like Figure 7-1, shown with a CD inserted and playing.

You can easily control iTunes:

- Click the **Play/Pause** button to start the selected song playing and to pause play (Play becomes Pause after you start playing a track).

- Click the **Previous/Rewind** button to move to the previous song. Click **Previous/Rewind** and hold down the mouse button to rewind through the current song.

- Click the **Next/Fast Forward** button to move to the next song. Click **Next/Fast Forward** and hold down the mouse button to fast forward through the current song.

- The **Scrubber bar** displays a diamond that you can drag to move quickly through the current song.

- The **Volume slider** is dragged to change the volume iTunes is outputting. (The volume control on your Mac controls the overall volume output.)

- The **Search** box allows you to type the criterion for selecting just the songs that you want to play.

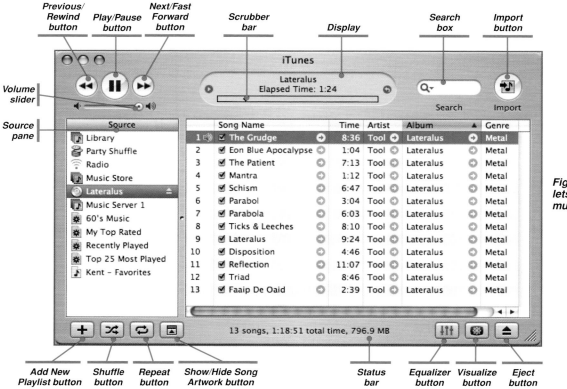

Figure 7-1: iTunes lets you easily play music CDs.

- The **Source** pane allows you to switch among different music sources: your Music Library (the Library item), Party Shuffle (which selects music automatically for you), Internet radio (see "Listen to Radio Stations," later in this chapter), any CD that's loaded, any music libraries other iTunes users are sharing, and the playlists you've created. Click **Add New Playlist** to create a new playlist.

- Click the **Import** button to copy the CD in your optical drive to your Mac. (See "Copy CDs to Your Mac," later in this chapter.)

- Click the **Shuffle** button to randomize the order of the songs. Click it again to restore the normal order.

- Click the **Repeat** button once to repeat all the songs in the current CD or playlist. Click it again to repeat just the current song. Click it a third time to turn off repeating.

- Click the **Show/Hide Song Artwork** button to toggle the display of the picture or pictures associated with the current song. Songs you download from the iTunes Music Store typically have artwork. For other songs, you can add your own pictures manually.

- Click the **Equalizer** button to display the Equalizer window (shown here), in which you can apply both preset equalizations and custom equalizations to change the sound of the songs. Click the **Close** button (the red button) to close the Equalizer window when you've finished using it.

- Click the **Visualizer** button to display visualizations, automatically generated graphics to accompany the music. To control the size of the visualizations, open the **Visualizer** menu and choose how you would like the visualizations displayed—Small, Medium, or Large. Open the **Visualizer** menu and choose **Full Screen** to display your chosen size of visualizations full screen; press **ESC** to cancel full-screen visualizations.

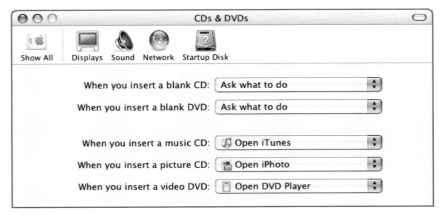

Figure 7-2: Use the CDs & DVDs sheet in System Preferences to tell Mac OS X how to handle CDs and DVDs you insert.

Control the Volume

You can control your Mac's audio volume in several ways:

- Turn the physical volume control on your receiver or speakers.

- If your Mac's keyboard includes volume keys, press them to change your Mac's overall output volume. For example, on most PowerBooks and iBooks, you can press **F3** (without pressing the **FN** key) to mute the sound, press **F4** to reduce the volume, and press **F5** to increase the volume. These same keys are across the top of the numeric keys on the right of the many Apple desktop keyboards.

- Click the **Volume** icon on the menu bar and drag the **slider** to set the volume.

- Drag the **Volume** slider in iTunes itself. Changing the volume in iTunes changes iTunes' output volume but doesn't change your Mac's overall output volume. So if, for example, you turn the volume in iTunes up to its maximum setting but your Mac's overall output volume is set very low, the music output will be low.

- Drag the **Output Volume** slider on the Sound sheet in System Preferences (open and click **System Preferences**, and then click **Sound**). This is the least convenient method of changing the volume unless System Preferences is already open.

Listen to Radio Stations

iTunes's Radio feature lets you listen to radio stations around the world that broadcast their programs across the Internet, either in addition to conventional broadcasting or instead of it. Internet radio works best over a broadband connection that delivers at least 128 Kbps (see Chapter 4 for details of Internet connections), but you can also listen to lower-quality radio broadcasts over a dial-up connection.

To use the radio:

1. If iTunes isn't running, open it by clicking the **iTunes** icon on the Dock.

2. Click **Radio** in the Source pane. iTunes will display the available categories of radio stations.

TIP

Click the **Bit Rate** column heading to sort the stations in ascending order by bitrate. Sorting this way can help you identify the stations using the bitrates you prefer (or that your Internet connection can handle). If the radio frequently stops and iTunes displays the Network Stalled dialog box (shown here), you need to switch to a lower-bitrate station.

Network Stalled

Rebuffering stream...

▭▭▭▭▭▭ (Stop)

3. Click the **right-pointing gray triangle** on a category to expand it (see Figure 7-3). Click the resulting **down-pointing gray triangle** to collapse the category again.

4. Double-click a radio station to start it playing.

5. Click the **Stop** button to stop the radio.

You can also open MP3 audio streams that iTunes doesn't list. To do so, open **Advanced** and click **Open Stream**, type or paste the stream address in the Open Stream dialog box (shown here), and click **OK**. Add the stream to a playlist so that you can access it more easily next time.

Open Stream

URL:

http://aud-one.kpfa.org:8000

(Cancel) (OK)

Figure 7-3: iTunes' Radio feature allows you to listen to Internet radio stations.

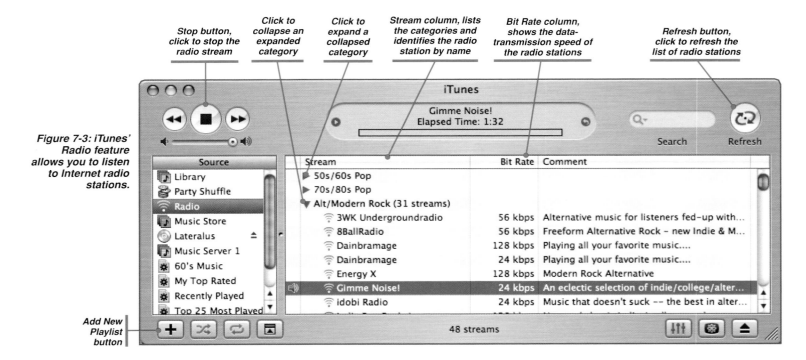

Stop button, click to stop the radio stream

Click to collapse an expanded category

Click to expand a collapsed category

Stream column, lists the categories and identifies the radio station by name

Bit Rate column, shows the data-transmission speed of the radio stations

Refresh button, click to refresh the list of radio stations

iTunes

Gimme Noise! Elapsed Time: 1:32

Search   Refresh

Add New Playlist button

Source		Stream	Bit Rate	Comment
♪ Library		▸ 50s/60s Pop		
Party Shuffle		▸ 70s/80s Pop		
⩗ Radio		▾ Alt/Modern Rock (31 streams)		
♪ Music Store		3WK Undergroundradio	56 kbps	Alternative music for listeners fed-up with...
Lateralus	⏏	8BallRadio	56 kbps	Freeform Alternative Rock – new Indie & M...
♪ Music Server 1		Dainbramage	128 kbps	Playing all your favorite music....
⚙ 60's Music		Dainbramage	24 kbps	Playing all your favorite music....
⚙ My Top Rated		Energy X	128 kbps	Modern Rock Alternative
⚙ Recently Played		Gimme Noise!	24 kbps	An eclectic selection of indie/college/alter...
⚙ Top 25 Most Played		idobi Radio	24 kbps	Music that doesn't suck -- the best in alter...

48 streams

3 4 5 6 7 8 9 10

Buy Music Online

If you're planning to buy music online for use with the Mac, your first stop should be Apple's iTunes Music Store, which is tightly integrated with iTunes. The iTunes Music Store offers a wide selection of music—more than 700,000 songs at this writing—for around $0.99 a song.

To use the iTunes Music Store, click **Music Store** in the Source pane. iTunes will access the iTunes Music Store and display its home page (see Figure 7-4). From here, you can browse or search to find songs that interest you. Double-click a song to play a 30-second preview of it and help you decide whether you want to buy it.

Before buying a song, you'll need to create an Apple account and specify the details of the credit card with which you want to pay. When you click a Buy Song link, the iTunes Music Store walks you through the process of creating an account.

Figure 7-4: The iTunes Music Store offers more than 700,000 songs for purchase.

NOTE

iTunes 4.5 and later versions enable you to import files in the Windows Media Audio (WMA) format and convert them to the AAC format. This feature works only with unprotected WMA files, not with the protected WMA files that most of the major online music stores other than the iTunes Music Store sell.

TIP

Copying songs from a CD to digital files on your computer is usually much quicker than playing the CD in real time. Although iTunes stores the songs in a compressed format, the song files take up a lot of space on your hard disk if you create a large music library. You can adjust the settings by opening the **iTunes** menu, clicking **Preferences**, and then clicking the **Importing** button to display the Importing tab. iTunes' default settings are to use the AAC (Advanced Audio Coding) format and the 128 Kbps bitrate, which delivers high audio quality at an acceptably compact file size. For higher audio quality, choose a higher bitrate; for smaller files, choose a lower bitrate. For the highest quality audio in compressed files, use the Apple Lossless Encoder format.

Locate Music on the Internet

Apart from Internet radio and the iTunes Music Store, there are many other sources of music on the Internet. Some locations, such as the Internet Underground Musical Archive (IUMA; www.iuma.com), provide legal audio files for free download; others provide illegal audio files for free download; and an ever-increasing number of online music stores sell legal audio files for download.

At this writing, major online music stores include BuyMusic.com (www.buymusic.com), Walmart.com (www.walmart.com), MusicMatch Downloads (www.musicmatch.com), RealPlayer Music Store (www.real.com/musicstore), and Listen.com RHAPSODY (www.listen.com). These stores provide an increasing variety of music—but all are aimed at users of Windows computers and do not work with the Mac. Smaller online music stores, such as Wippit (www.wippit.com), offer some music in the widely used MP3 format, which you can use with iTunes on the Mac.

Copy CDs to Your Mac

iTunes gives you the ability to copy songs from your CDs to your hard disk, to build and manage a library of music, and to copy this material to recordable CDs or recordable DVDs. To copy from a CD:

1. Insert the CD from which you want to copy songs. Mac OS X will automatically open iTunes. If iTunes doesn't automatically display the CD's contents, click the CD's entry in the Source pane.

2. If you have an Internet connection, iTunes will automatically connect to the Gracenote CDDB (CD Database) music server and download the CD's details.

3. iTunes will automatically select the check boxes for each song on the CD. Clear the check boxes for any songs you don't want to copy.

NOTE

The material on most CDs and DVDs is owned and copyrighted by some combination of the composer, the artist, the producer, and/or the publisher. Copyright law prohibits using the copyrighted material in ways that are not beneficial to the copyright holders, including giving or selling the content without giving or selling the original CD or DVD itself. iTunes provides the ability to copy copyrighted material to your hard disk and then to a recordable optical disc or a portable player (such as an iPod) with the understanding that the copy is solely for your own personal use and that you will not sell or give away copies.

CAUTION

To prevent people from violating copyright law, some CDs (and most DVDs) are protected to make copying difficult. Such CDs typically carry a warning, such as "Copy Protected," or a notice such as "Will *not* play on PC or Mac." Don't put such CDs in your Mac, because it may be unable to eject them. Even if the copy protection doesn't work and your Mac can copy the CD, it's illegal to do so because of provisions in the Digital Millennium Copyright Act (DMCA).

4. Click **Import** in the upper-right corner. iTunes will start copying the audio from the CD (see Figure 7-5) and storing it in compressed audio files on your hard disk.

5. When the copying is finished, click the **Eject** button to eject the CD.

6. If you've finished using iTunes, open the **iTunes** menu and click **Quit iTunes** to close it.

Figure 7-5: iTunes enables you to copy songs from CDs to compressed files on your hard disk so that you can build a music library.

Organize Music

Once you have copied several CDs and have, perhaps, downloaded other songs to your hard disk, you will want to organize them. iTunes' Music Library feature helps by automatically indexing the songs you add to your Music Library. To view your Music Library, click **Library** in the Source pane.

The easiest way to browse through your Music Library is to use the Browser panes at the top of the window (see Figure 7-6). You can toggle the display of the Browser panes by clicking the **Browse** button (shown here) in the upper-right corner when the Library is displayed.

You can also combine songs into a new playlist so that you can play songs from different CDs in your preferred order. To create a new playlist:

1. Click the **Add New Playlist** button. iTunes will add a new entry in the Source pane and display an edit box around it.

2. Type the name for the playlist and press RETURN.

3. Browse to each desired song in turn, and then drag it to the playlist.

4. Click the playlist to display its contents.

5. If you want, drag the songs into a different order.

6. Click the first song, and then click the **Play** button to start playing the playlist.

Browser panes, click the artist or album you want to display

Add New Playlist button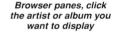

Figure 7-6: The Music Library provides a way to manage the songs on your Mac.

Make an Audio CD

Once you have created a playlist (see the previous section), you can burn it to a writable or rewritable CD or to a DVD. You can create either an audio CD—one that you can play in most CD players—or an MP3 CD, a CD that contains only MP3 files and that will play only in a computer CD drive or an MP3 CD player. You can also create a data CD or data DVD to back up your music in case your Mac's hard drive gets corrupted or stops working.

To create an audio CD:

1. In the Source pane, click the playlist you want to burn to CD.

2. Click **Burn Disc** (it may be gray, but it is active). iTunes will prompt you to insert a disc.

3. Insert a blank CD. iTunes will prompt you to click Burn Disc.

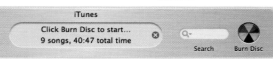

4. Click **Burn Disc**. iTunes will burn the CD and will select it in the Source pane.

5. Click **Eject** to eject the CD.

The resulting CD should be playable in most music CD players and all computer CD drives.

Copy Music to an iPod

If you have an iPod or iPod mini, you can synchronize its contents automatically with those of your Music Library. By doing so, you can put your entire Music Library on your iPod so that you can listen to it anywhere.

The first time you connect your iPod to your Mac via the supplied FireWire cable, the iPod Setup Assistant will be displayed. Type the name for your iPod in the The Name Of My iPod Is text box, select the **Automatically Update My iPod** check box if you want to use automatic updating, and then click **Done**.

TIP

For full coverage of the iPod and iPod mini, see *How to Do Everything with Your iPod & iPod mini*, also published by Osborne McGraw-Hill.

Mac OS X will then launch iTunes and will update your iPod automatically (see Figure 7-7). When iTunes displays the message, "iPod Update Is Complete," click the **Eject iPod** button to "eject" the iPod. You can then unplug the iPod from your Mac and start using it.

Compose with GarageBand

If you have iLife '04, you can use the GarageBand application (see Figure 7-8) to compose your own original music. You can:

- Use prerecorded loops to build tracks quickly
- Play software instruments by using a MIDI (musical) keyboard that you attach to your Mac via USB
- Record physical instruments that you plug into your Mac or that you record via microphones plugged into your Mac
- Mix your music to professional standards and export it to iTunes

NOTE

GarageBand is a powerful application with a steep learning curve. For detailed treatment of this and the other iLife '04 applications (iTunes, iPhoto, iMovie, and iDVD), see *How to Do Everything with iLife '04*, also published by McGraw-Hill/Osborne.

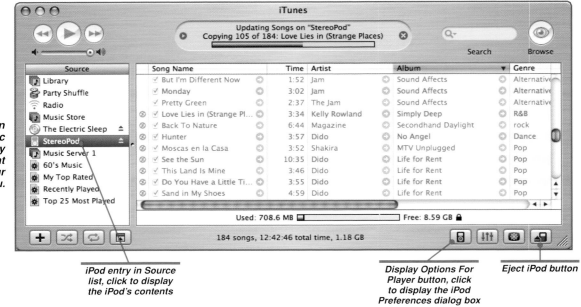

Figure 7-7: You can copy your Music Library automatically to an iPod so that you can take your music with you.

iPod entry in Source list, click to display the iPod's contents

Display Options For Player button, click to display the iPod Preferences dialog box

Eject iPod button

Work with Video

Mac OS X lets you play video from a DVD using the DVD Player application. It also allows you to capture and edit videos from a DV camcorder using iMovie.

Play DVDs

Playing DVDs is as easy as playing CDs: simply insert a DVD in your Mac's DVD drive, and Mac OS X will open DVD Player and start the DVD playing automatically. Use the Controller (shown here) to control the playback as you would use a remote control. To change the size of the video window, open the **Video** menu and click **Half Size**, **Normal Size**, **Maximum Size**, or **Enter Full Screen**.

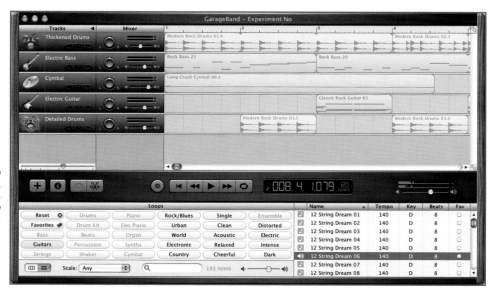

Figure 7-8: GarageBand lets you compose original music by using prerecorded loops and recording your own performances.

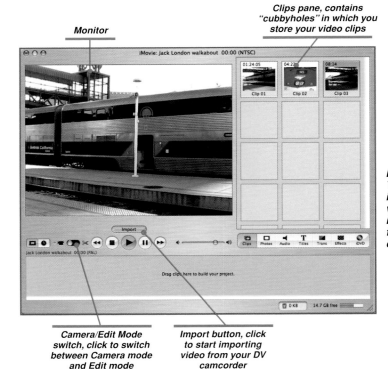

iMovie automatically opens the last movie project you worked with. The first time you run iMovie, there's no last project, so iMovie displays the Welcome To iMovie dialog box to enable you to create a new movie. Click **Create Project**. iMovie will display a Save As dialog box. Type the name for your new movie, select a folder (the default folder is your ~/Movies folder), and click **Save**. iMovie will create the project folder and files, and then display its main window in Edit mode, the mode used for editing video clips.

There can be some copyright issues involved in using music from professionally recorded CDs and tapes. If you are making a movie solely for your own use and are not going to put it on the Internet, sell it, or otherwise distribute it, you should have no problem. If you are going to use your movie in any of the prohibited ways and it contains someone else's copyrighted material (either audio or video), you must get permission from the copyright holder.

Record Video

iMovie lets you record video directly from your DV camcorder to your hard disk. To record video:

1. Click the **iMovie** icon on the Dock. (If your Dock doesn't contain an iMovie icon, activate the **Finder**, open **Go**, click **Applications**, and then double-click the **iMovie** icon). iMovie will open (see the Note).

2. Connect your DV camcorder to your Mac via the FireWire cable.

3. Turn your DV camcorder on. iMovie will automatically detect it and will switch from Edit mode to Camera mode. You will see a blue screen saying "Camera Connected."

4. Click **Import**. iMovie will start importing the video, playing it on the Monitor and breaking the video into separate clips at the breaks in the timecode on the tape (see Figure 7-9).

Clips pane, contains "cubbyholes" in which you store your video clips

Monitor

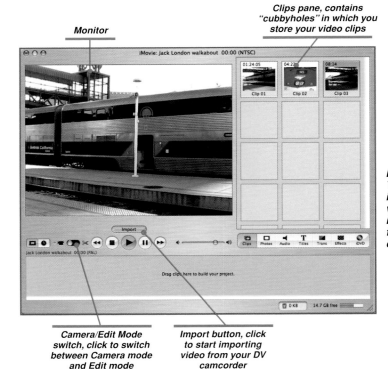

*Figure 7-9:
You can
import digital
video directly
into iMovie
from a DV
camcorder.*

*Camera/Edit Mode
switch, click to switch
between Camera mode
and Edit mode*

*Import button, click
to start importing
video from your DV
camcorder*

NOTE

If iMovie doesn't automatically switch to Camera mode, click to the left of the blue dot in the Camera/Edit Mode switch to switch to Camera mode manually.

TIP

You can import many formats of existing video files into iMovie by clicking **File | Import**, selecting the file in the Import dialog box, and clicking **Open**.

NOTE

A *clip* is a small segment of video, generally one episode of starting the camcorder recording and then stopping it. A clip is made up of a series of frames, where each *frame* is a still image that when viewed in rapid succession with other frames creates the illusion of motion. While you're creating your movie, iMovie considers it a "movie project," or simply "project," rather than a "movie," which is what is created when you export your finished project from iMovie to a movie file (for example, as a QuickTime movie).

5. To stop importing, click **Import** again. Alternatively, wait until iMovie has imported all the video footage from your DV camcorder, at which point it will stop importing automatically.

6. Click the right side of the **Camera/Edit Mode switch** to put iMovie into Edit mode.

Use iMovie

Creating a movie out of the clips you've imported involves editing the clips to show the footage you want; assembling them into a suitable order; and applying such transitions, effects, audio, and titles as are needed. To create your movie, you use Edit mode in iMovie. Figure 7-10 shows the iMovie window in Edit mode with a movie being created.

Controls area

Monitor, displays the clip selected in the Clips pane or the Clip Viewer

Clips pane, select a clip and drag it to the Clip Viewer to add it to the movie

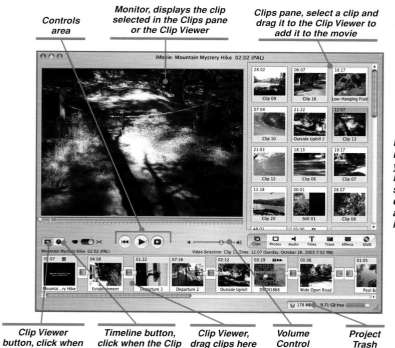

Figure 7-10: To make a movie, you use iMovie's Edit mode to select and edit clips and to add audio and still images.

Clip Viewer button, click when the Timeline is displayed to switch to the Clip Viewer

Timeline button, click when the Clip Viewer is displayed to switch to the Timeline

Clip Viewer, drag clips here to add them to your movie

Volume Control

Project Trash

The main sections of the iMovie window are:

- The **Monitor** displays the clip you've selected in the Clips pane or the Clip Viewer. When you play one or more clips, iMovie displays them on the Monitor.

- The **Clips pane** consists of a large number of "cubbyholes," small boxes that can contain one movie clip each. You can rearrange the clips by dragging them from one cubbyhole to another. To add a clip to your movie, you drag it from the Clips pane to the Clip Viewer.

- The space across the bottom of the window is shared by two views of your movie project. The **Clip Viewer** is the default view and allows you to sequence your clips and rearrange them by dragging. The **Timeline** gives you a precise time measurement of your clips and allows you to trim them and add music and narration. You switch between the Clip Viewer and the Timeline by clicking the **Clip Viewer** button or the **Timeline** button, as appropriate.

Select Video Clips

Selecting and organizing the clips for your movie is a laborious phase, but it provides the foundation for your project and determines what you have to work with in the editing phase. The process of selecting which parts of which video clips to use has four steps:

1. Double-click the first clip to play it. Decide whether you want to use it and whether (and where) it needs to be trimmed.

2. Edit the clip if you plan to use it.

3. Drag the edited clip to the Clip Viewer and position it where you want it in the string of existing clips.

4. To judge how your movie is coming along, play it by clicking the **Beginning** button and then the **Play** button.

5. If necessary, rearrange the clips by dragging them to different locations in the string and/or by removing a clip that you no longer want to use in the movie project.

While working in this phase, the Clip Viewer is usually the best view to use, as it offers the easiest means of seeing the progression of clips and of dragging the clips to change their order.

Beginning button   *Play button*   *Play Full Screen button*

TIP

Alternatively, click the **Play Full Screen** button to play the movie full screen. The video will be grainy, because iMovie doesn't give you full quality until you export your movie, but it will have more effect than on the Monitor because of its larger size.

EDITING VIDEO CLIPS

Editing consists of splitting and trimming clips to get the sequence of frames you want. To edit clips, you can work in either the Clip Viewer or in the Timeline. Most people find the Clip Viewer easier for editing.

SPLIT A CLIP

To split a clip into two parts:

1. Click the desired clip in the Clips pane or in the Clip Viewer. iMovie will display the clip on the Monitor.

2. Move the Playhead (see Figure 7-11) to the exact frame at which you want to split the clip. Drag the Playhead for large movements, press **LEFT AR-ROW** or **RIGHT ARROW** to move the Playhead one frame at a time, or press **SHIFT+ LEFT ARROW** or **SHIFT+RIGHT ARROW** to move the Playhead ten frames at a time.

3. Open **Edit** and click **Split Video Clip At Play-head**.

TRIM A CLIP

You can remove unwanted frames from a clip's beginning or end, or from both ends, by trimming them off:

1. Click the desired clip in the Clips pane or in the Clip Viewer. iMovie will display the clip on the Monitor.

2. Click in the tick marks under the Scrubber bar at the point where you want the start or finish of the trimmed clip to be, and then drag the **triangular crop mark** to the point at which you want the opposite end (see Figure 7-11). You can drag from start to finish or from finish to start. iMovie will display the Start Crop Marker and End Crop Marker and will turn the segment of the Scrubber bar between them yellow. You can also move the mouse pointer over the **tick marks** to display the crop markers, and then drag each in turn.

3. If necessary, move the Start Crop Marker and the End Crop Market to different frames. Click the

Continued...

Add Transitions to Clips

To make your movie flow from one clip to another, you can apply transitions—for example, fading out one clip and fading in the next. To apply a transition:

1. If the Timeline is displayed, click the **Clip Viewer** button.

2. Click the **Trans** button in the toolbar in the lower-right corner to display the Trans pane.

3. In the Clip Viewer, click the clip you want to affect.

4. Select the transition in the list box. iMovie displays a preview.

5. Adjust the speed and any other available parameters.

6. Click **Apply**. iMovie applies the transition to the clip.

Figure 7-11: Drag the Start Crop Marker and End Crop Marker to the frames at which you want to trim the clip.

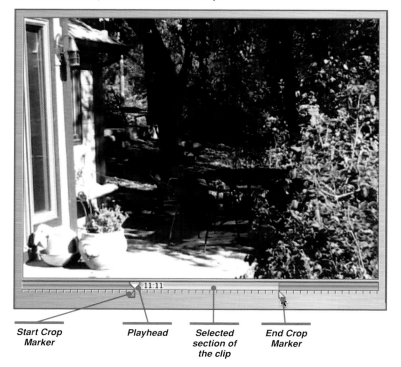

Start Crop Marker   Playhead   Selected section of the clip   End Crop Marker

EDITING VIDEO CLIPS (Continued)

marker you want to move, and then press **LEFT ARROW** or **RIGHT ARROW** to move the marker one frame at a time, or press **SHIFT+ LEFT AR-ROW** or **SHIFT+RIGHT ARROW** to move the marker ten frames at a time.

4. Open **Edit** and click **Crop**.

HIDE THE END OF A CLIP

Instead of trimming off the ends of a clip, you can simply hide them. This technique is most useful when you've placed the clip in the timeline and find that you need to shorten it a little in order to make your movie fit together as you want it. To hide the end of a clip:

1. Display the **Timeline** (for example, click the **Timeline** button).

2. Move the mouse pointer over the end of the clip you want to hide. The pointer turns into a double-headed arrow pointing sideways.

3. Drag the arrow to hide the end of the clip. The Monitor displays the current frame.

RESTORE THE ORIGINAL VERSION OF A CLIP

If you make a mistake splitting or trimming a clip, you can restore the original version—as long as you haven't emptied the Project Trash. To restore a clip:

1. Click the clip in the Clips pane, the Clip Viewer, or in the Timeline.

Restore Clip Media

This will restore the underlying media that was trimmed or split from this clip. (00:06 available at the beginning of the clip). Okay to Restore?

Cancel   OK

2. Open **Advanced** and click **Restore Clip**. iMovie will display the Restore Clip Media dialog box.

3. Click **OK**.

Add Effects to Clips

To make your clips convey a particular impression, you can add effects to them, from applying soft focus to mirroring the picture. To apply an effect:

1. If the Timeline is displayed, click the **Clip Viewer** button.

2. Click the **Effects** button to display the Effects pane.

3. In the Clip Viewer, click the clip you want to affect.

4. Select the effect in the list box. iMovie displays a preview.

5. Drag the **Effect In** and **Effect Out** sliders to change the length of the effect.

6. Use any other controls to change the effect. Click **Preview** to watch a preview again.

7. Click **Apply**. iMovie applies the effect to the clip.

Add Sound to a Movie

If your DV camcorder has a microphone (as most do), your video clips will already contain the sound recorded when you shot the video. When you place your clips in the movie timeline, iMovie puts this sound in the video track so that it plays along with the footage. You can mute the sound in the video track, or you can use other audio to supplement it by using the two audio-only tracks that iMovie also provides.

You can add sound to a project by either inserting a song or sound effect or by recording narration. For either, display the **Timeline**, place the **Playhead**, and display the **Audio** pane:

1. Click the **Timeline** button to display the Timeline (see Figure 7-12).

2. Move the **Playhead** to the exact frame where you want to start recording.

Video Track   Audio Track 1   Audio Track 2   Zoom slider, drag to zoom the Timeline in or out

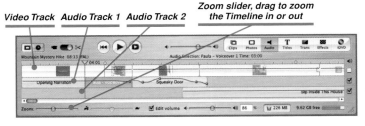

Figure 7-12: Use the Timeline to adjust the positioning of your audio clips.

3. Click the **Audio** button to display the Audio pane (see Figure 7-13).

ADD A SONG OR SOUND EFFECT

To insert a song or sound effect:

1. From the drop-down list in the Audio pane, choose iTunes Library, a playlist, iMovie Sound Effects, or Audio CD, as appropriate.

2. Select the song or sound effect in the resulting list.

3. Click **Place At Playhead**. iMovie will place the audio in the audio track starting at the position of the Playhead.

RECORD NARRATION

To record narration into your movie:

1. Click the **Record** button, and then speak into the microphone.

2. Click the **Record** button again to stop recording. iMovie will place the clip in the audio track starting at the position of the Playhead.

3. To rename the clip from its default name, double-click the clip, type the name in the Clip Info dialog box, and click **Set**.

Figure 7-13: Use the Audio pane to add songs, sound effects, or narration to your movie.

ADJUST THE VOLUME LEVEL

After adding sound clips to the two audio tracks, you can adjust their volume and that of the audio in the video track:

1. To turn off the audio on a track, clear the check box beside Video Track, Audio Track 1, or Audio Track 2, as appropriate.

2. Click the clip whose volume you want to change, select the **Edit Volume** check box, and drag the **Clip Volume** slider to change the volume. iMovie displays a line across the clip indicating its volume. For greater control, click the **line** to create a control point, and then drag it up or down (see Figure 7-14) to create a custom volume curve.

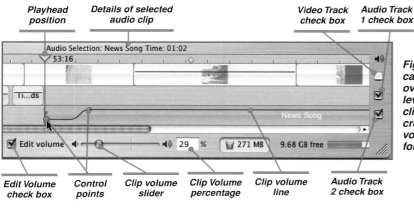

Figure 7-14: You can adjust the overall volume level of each clip or even create a custom volume curve for each clip.

Playhead position | Details of selected audio clip | Video Track check box | Audio Track 1 check box

Edit Volume check box | Control points | Clip volume slider | Clip Volume percentage | Clip volume line | Audio Track 2 check box

NOTE

Once you've added a sound clip to the timeline, you can select it, shorten it, or drag it anywhere in the timeline by using the same techniques used for video clips.

Zoom slider

Duration slider

Choose the iPhoto Photo Library or album here

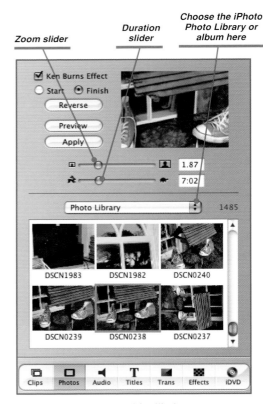

Figure 7-15: You can add still pictures to a movie and spice them up by using the Ken Burns Effect.

Add Still Pictures to a Movie

To add still pictures from your iPhoto Photo Library to a movie:

1. Click the **Photos** button. iMovie will display the Photos pane (see Figure 7-15).
2. In the drop-down list, select your Photo Library or the album that contains the picture. iMovie will display previews of the pictures.
3. Select the picture in the list box.
4. Drag the **Duration** slider to specify how long iMovie should display the picture.
5. Select the **Ken Burns Effect** check box if you want to use the Ken Burns Effect—panning and zooming over the picture. (Otherwise, clear this check box.) Click the **Start** option button and specify the starting position by dragging the **Zoom** slider and then dragging the image in the preview box to the position in which you want it to appear. Then click the **Finish** option button and use the same techniques to specify the zoom and ending positions.
6. Drag the picture to the appropriate position in the Clip Viewer.

Add Titles to a Movie

To add any text to a movie, you add a title:

1. Click the **Titles** button. iMovie will display the Titles pane (see Figure 7-16).
2. Select the type of title in the list box. For example, choose **Centered Multiple** to create multiple lines of centered titles.
3. Type the text in the text boxes. If you chose a Multiple type, you can click the **+** button to add further pairs of text boxes.
4. Drag the **Speed** slider to control the speed of the title effect.
5. Drag the **Pause** slider (if it's available) to control how long the text remains fully displayed on the screen.
6. Use the Font drop-down list, the Size slider, and the Color button to choose the font, size, and color.
7. Select the **Over Black** check box if you want to display the title on a black screen rather than over a clip.
8. Select the **QT Margins** check box if you plan to export this movie to QuickTime.
9. Drag the title to where you want it in the movie track.

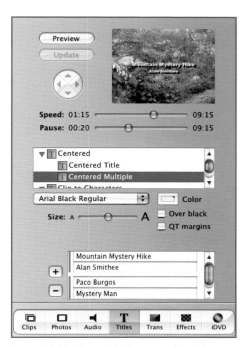

Figure 7-16: Use the Titles pane to add titles or other text to your movie.

Export a Movie

After you've finished creating your movie project, you export it to the appropriate type of video file to create a movie that you can share with other people. iMovie lets you share your movie via e-mail, by putting it on your home page on Apple's .Mac online service, by exporting it to your camcorder, by burning it to a DVD, by using Bluetooth, and by creating a QuickTime movie—the option discussed here.

1. Open **File** and click **Save Project** to save any unsaved changes.

2. Open **File** and click **Share**. iMovie will display the Share dialog box.

3. Click the **QuickTime** button. iMovie will display the QuickTime sheet (see Figure 7-17).

Figure 7-17: iMovie's Share dialog box lets you export your movie in a variety of formats.

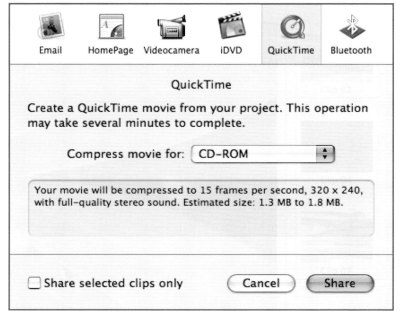

NOTE

If you selected one or more clips before displaying the Share dialog box, you can select the **Share Selected Clips Only** check box to share only the clips you selected. Otherwise, this check box is unavailable.

4. Click the **Compress Movie For** drop-down list and choose the appropriate setting: Email, Web, Web Streaming, CD-ROM, Full Quality DV (digital video), or Expert Settings. iMovie will display details of the frame rate, the size, the sound, and the estimated file size below the drop-down list.

5. Click **Share**. iMovie displays a Save dialog box.

6. Specify the file name and folder and click **Save**.

Chapter 8

Controlling Security

Controlling computer security is a complex subject because of the many different aspects that need protection. In this chapter you'll see how to control who can use a particular Mac, control what a user can do, protect data stored on the Mac, and protect your Mac from Internet attack.

Control Who Is a User

Controlling who is a user of a Mac means to identify the users to the Mac, giving users a secure way of logging in to the Mac while preventing others from using it. This is the process of adding and managing users and passwords.

Set Up a User

If you have multiple people using a single Mac, the best protection is to set up separate user accounts that require each user to sign on. To set up a user account:

NOTE

Most sets of steps in this chapter require that you be logged on as an administrator—a user who has the authority to make major configuration changes to your Mac. If you're not sure whether you're an administrator, open the Accounts sheet of System Preferences using the steps under "Set Up a User" and see whether your account is labeled "Admin" (administrator), "Standard," "Managed," or "Simplified."

TIP

Never enter a password hint for an account. The only point in using passwords is to ensure that your user accounts are secure from intrusion. Even an oblique password hint compromises a password. If you don't need to secure the accounts on your Mac (for example, because it is never connected to the Internet and nobody uses it but you), don't use passwords.

Figure 8-1: The first step in setting up a user is to assign his or her account name, short name, and password.

1. While logged on as an administrator, open and click **System Preferences**. The System Preferences window will be displayed.

2. Click **Accounts**. The Accounts sheet will be displayed

3. Click the **+** button in the lower-left corner. Mac OS X will add a new Standard user and will display the Password tab (see Figure 8-1).

4. Type the user's full name in the Name text box and press **TAB**. Mac OS X will enter a lowercased version of the name, without spaces or punctuation, in the Short Name text box.

5. Change the short name as needed, but leave it lowercase and without spaces or punctuation, and then press **TAB**.

6. Type the password in the **Password** and **Verify** text boxes.

UNDERSTANDING USER ACCOUNTS

To help you control security on your Mac, Mac OS X offers four kinds of user accounts: Administrator, Standard, Managed, and Simplified.

ADMINISTRATOR ACCOUNTS

Administrator accounts are for users who manage a Mac. Administrators can:

- Install new applications in the Applications folder (so that they're available to all users)
- Create, delete, and modify user accounts
- Access, change, or even delete other users' files
- Unlock other users' files encrypted with File Vault (discussed in Chapter 3)
- Change all settings in System Preferences (Standard users can change only some settings)

Every Mac must have at least one Administrator account. Mac OS X automatically makes the account used to install the OS an Administrator account—so if you installed Mac OS X, you will have an Administrator account.

STANDARD ACCOUNTS

Standard accounts are the next grade down after Administrator accounts. A Standard user can:

- Create and manipulate files and folders in his or her Home folder and its subfolders, but not in other folders
- Change some settings in System Preferences, but not major settings such as Startup Disk (which controls the disk your Mac starts from), Network, or Energy Saver

Continued...

7. If the user will need a password hint, type one in the **Password Hint** text box (but see the Tip on page 160 first).

8. If you want to change the account from a Standard user to an Administrator user, click the **Security** tab and select the **Allow User To Administer The Computer** check box. (See the "Understanding User Accounts" QuickSteps for a discussion of the different types of users.) Mac OS X then makes the Limitations tab unavailable, because Administrator users have no limitations (in this sense).

9. If you want to change the Standard account to a Managed account or a Simplified account, follow the procedure described in "Control What a User Can Do," later in this chapter.

10. Click **System Preferences** | **Quit System Preferences** to close System Preferences.

Customize a User Account

Each user account can be unique, with the user's own Dock, desktop, color scheme, and screen saver.

CHANGE THE PICTURE

Most users like to choose a custom picture to represent their account instead of the default picture that Mac OS X assigns when you create the account. The user's picture appears on the login screen (providing your Mac is using the login screen that lists user names), as the default picture in iChat, and on the My Card entry in Address Book.

To change the picture:

1. Open and click **System Preferences**. The System Preferences window will be displayed.

2. Click **Accounts**. The Accounts sheet will be displayed.

3. In the list box on the left, click your account.

UNDERSTANDING USER ACCOUNTS (Continued)

MANAGED AND SIMPLIFIED ACCOUNTS

If a Standard account gives a user too much freedom, you can give the user a Managed account or a Simplified account instead. In a Managed account, you can specify the applications a user can run or the actions he or she can take. In a Simplified account, Mac OS X displays a stripped-down version of the Finder and allows the user to use only the applications that you've specified. See "Control What a User Can Do," later in this chapter, for details on Managed accounts and Simplified accounts.

MATCH ACCOUNT TYPE TO USER

Before creating a user account, consider what the user will need to be able to do:

- If the user will manage the computer, create an Administrator account.
- If the user must be restricted from taking particular actions, create a Managed account.
- If the user (for example, a child) will benefit from having fewer choices available, create a Simplified account.
- Otherwise, create a Standard account.

If in doubt, err on the side of caution when creating accounts. You can change an account from one type to another if you need to.

NOTE

For Simplified users to be able to choose startup items, they must be allowed to run System Preferences.

4. Click the **Picture** tab (see Figure 8-2).

5. Specify the picture to use:

- Click the desired picture in the list box.
- Drag a picture from a Finder window or your desktop to the picture well.
- Click **Edit** to display the Images window (shown in Figure 8-2), which shows the current picture. Change the picture by dragging another picture to the window or clicking **Choose** and using the resulting dialog box to select the picture, or click the **Take Video Snapshot** button to take a picture using your FireWire-connected iSight or camcorder. Drag the slider to change the size of the picture as needed, and drag in the central square to make it display the part of the picture you want. Then click **Set**.

6. Click **System Preferences** | **Quit System Preferences** to close System Preferences.

Picture well

Take Video Snapshot button

Figure 8-2: Choose a picture for the user on the Picture tab.

RESETTING A LOST PASSWORD

If you forget the password for an Administrator account, you can reset it by using the Reset Password utility on the first Mac OS X CD:

1. Insert the first Mac OS X CD in your Mac's optical drive.

2. Restart your Mac. Press **C** at the startup sound to boot from the CD. Mac OS X will start the installation process automatically.

3. Open **Installer** and click **Reset Password**.

4. In the Select The Mac OS X Disk Which Contains A Password To Reset list, click the drive Mac OS X is installed on—for example, **Macintosh HD**.

5. Click the **Select A User Of This Volume To Reset Their Password** drop-down list, and then click the user's name.

6. Type the new password for the user in the two text boxes.

7. Click **Save**. Mac OS X will display the Password Saved dialog box.

8. Click **OK**.

9. Open the **Reset Password** menu and click **Quit Reset** Password.

10. Open the **Installer** menu and click **Quit Installer**. Mac OS X will display the Are You Sure You Want To Quit The Installer? dialog box.

11. Click **Quit**. Mac OS X will restart from the hard disk.

12. Log in using your new password.

13. Drag the Mac OS X installation CD to the **Trash** to eject it.

If your Mac restarts from the CD and displays the Installer again, open the **Installer** menu and click **Quit Installer**. In the Are You Sure You Want To Quit The Installer? dialog box, click **Startup Disk**. In the Choose Startup Disk dialog box, click the entry for your hard disk (for example, **Mac OS X, 10.3.3 On Macintosh HD**), and then click **Restart**.

CHOOSE STARTUP ITEMS

All users can choose applications, files, and folders to open automatically on login by using the Startup Items tab of the Accounts sheet in System Preferences. See "Start Applications Automatically When You Log In" in Chapter 5 for details.

CHANGE USER TYPE

Sometimes you may need to change a user's account type to give that user further privileges or to reduce the scope of actions permitted. To change user type:

1. Open and click **System Preferences**. The System Preferences window will be displayed.

2. Click **Accounts**. The Accounts sheet will be displayed.

3. In the list box on the left, click the user's name.

4. To change a Standard user to an Administrator user, click the **Security** tab and select the **Allow User To Administer The Computer** check box. To change an Administrator user to a Standard user, clear this check box.

5. To change a Standard user to a Managed or Simplified user, click the **Limitations** tab, and then work on the **Some Limits** sub-tab or the **Simple Finder** sub-tab. See "Control What a User Can Do," later in this chapter, for details.

6. To change a Managed user or Simplified user to a Standard user, click the **Limitations** tab, and then click the **No Limits** sub-tab.

7. Click **System Preferences | Quit System Preferences** to close System Preferences.

Change Mac OS X's Login Procedure

To change Mac OS X's login procedure:

1. Open and click **System Preferences**. The System Preferences window will be displayed.

2. Click **Accounts**. The Accounts sheet will be displayed.

3. Click **Login Options** at the bottom of the left list box. The login options are displayed (see Figure 8-3).

4. Choose options (discussed next) and then click **System Preferences | Quit System Preferences** to close System Preferences.

The login options are:

- Choose how to display the login screen by selecting the **List of Users** option button or the **Name And Password** option button in the Display Login Window As area. Prompting for the user name is better for security, but is usually less convenient.

- Choose whether to log in a specified user account automatically (select the **Automatically Log In As** check box and select the desired user in the drop-down list). Automatic login is useful when you're the only person who uses your Mac, but it makes security experts turn pale with horror.

- Select the **Hide The Sleep, Restart, And Shut Down Buttons** check box if you want to remove these controls from the login screen. Security is the usual reason for removing these controls: with default settings, a malefactor can restart your Mac from the login screen, reboot from a FireWire hard disk he or she plugs in, and circumvent your security.

- Turn Fast User Switching on or off by selecting or clearing the **Enable Fast User Switching** check box. (See the next section.)

Figure 8-3: Use the login options to control how Mac OS X handles login.

Turn On Fast User Switching

Fast User Switching enables two or more users to be logged into the same Mac at the same time. Only one user's session (windows and applications utilized by that user) is displayed at a time; any other user's session is hidden until he or she switches to it.

Fast User Switching enables you to let someone else to use your Mac for a while without shutting down all your applications and logging out. In a family or small-office situation, Fast User Switching can save a lot of logging on and off and reduce aggravation. Fast User Switching also has several disadvantages:

- Fast User Switching increases demands on your Mac, particularly its RAM. If your Mac is short of RAM, using Fast User Switching will probably make applications run more slowly.

- While most applications run happily in separate user sessions at the same time, others have problems. Audio players (such as iTunes) and video players tend to be the worst offenders.

- If a user shuts down your Mac, you can lose unsaved changes in your applications. Mac OS X reduces the chance of loss by warning the user that other user sessions are active and providing the choice of either canceling the shutdown or supplying an administrator name and password before effecting the shutdown, as shown here:

To turn on Fast User Switching, select the **Enable Fast User Switching** check box on the Login Options screen (shown earlier in Figure 8-3). You can then use Fast User Switching to switch quickly from one user account to another by clicking the user name at the right end of the menu bar, clicking the name of the desired user, and entering the password if prompted for one.

Control What a User Can Do

In Mac OS X, the main way of controlling what a user can do is by assigning the user the appropriate type of account. As explained earlier in this chapter, Administrator users can take any action on a Mac, and Standard users essentially have freedom within their own user accounts.

For a user who might be irresponsible, you may need to implement more restrictions. You can do so by setting up a Managed account. For a user who finds the standard Mac OS X interface too complex, you can set up a Simplified account that uses a stripped-down version of the Finder.

TIP

To add an application that's not listed, click **Locate** and use the resulting dialog box to select the application.

Set Limits for a Managed Account

To create a Managed user account and set limits:

1. Open and click **System Preferences**. The System Preferences window will be displayed.

2. Click **Accounts**. The Accounts sheet will be displayed.

3. In the list box on the left, click the account you want to manage.

4. Click the **Limitations** tab, and then click the **Some Limits** sub-tab (see Figure 8-4).

5. In the This User Can area, select or clear the **Open All System Preferences** check box, the **Modify The Dock** check box, the **Change Password** check box (available only when the Open All System Preferences check box is selected), and the **Burn CDs And DVDs** check box.

6. To restrict the user to only some applications, select the **This User Can Only Use These Applications** check box, then select the **Allow** check box for each permitted application in the list box.

7. Click **System Preferences | Quit System Preferences** to close System Preferences.

Figure 8-4: Set limits for a Managed user on the Some Limits sub-tab of the Limitations tab on the Accounts sheet.

Set Up a Simplified Account

A Simplified account uses the Simple Finder and lets the user run only applications you've specified. To set up a Simplified account:

1. Open and click **System Preferences**. The System Preferences window will be displayed.

2. Click **Accounts**. The Accounts sheet will be displayed.

3. In the list box on the left, click the account you want to manage.

4. Click the **Limitations** tab, and then click the **Simple Finder** sub-tab.

5. Select the **Allow** check box for each application you want the user to be able to run.

6. Click **System Preferences | Quit System Preferences** to close System Preferences.

Figure 8-5 shows the Simple Finder. These are the main differences from the regular Finder:

Figure 8-5: The Simple Finder provides the user with a reduced set of windows and applications.

- The Dock contains a minimal set of icons: a Finder icon, a My Applications icon for displaying a window of applications, a My Documents for displaying the user's documents, a Shared icon for displaying the contents of the /Users/Shared/ folder, and a Trash icon. Icons for applications the user opens also appear.

- The user can open only one Finder window at a time and cannot resize that window.

- The menu contains only the Force Quit, Sleep, and Log Out commands.

Share Files and Folders with Other Local Users

Mac OS X provides two easy ways to share files and folders with other users of your Mac:

TIP

To provide quick access to the /Users/Shared/ folder via the Finder, drag the **Shared** folder to the Sidebar to create an entry for it.

- Place the files and folders in your ~/Public folder, the Public folder inside your Home folder. (To display your Home folder, activate the **Finder** and click **Go | Home**.) Others can then view the files and folders but not change them.

- Place the files and folders in the /Users/Shared/ folder, which all users can access and change. Similarly, you can access and change the files that other users have placed in this folder.

To access the /Users/Shared/ folder:

1. Click the **Finder** icon on the Dock. A Finder window will be displayed.
2. Click **Macintosh HD** in the Sidebar. The contents of your Mac's hard disk will be displayed.
3. Double-click the **Users** item. The contents of the Users folder will be displayed.
4. Double-click the **Shared** item.

Set Permissions on Files and Folders

Instead of placing files in the /Users/Shared/ folder, you can also share items by placing them in folders on which you set permissions that allow other users the required level of access. For details on changing permissions on a file or folder, see "Change an Object's Permissions and Ownership" in Chapter 3.

Protect Stored Data

You can protect your stored data by locking files against accidental deletion, by encrypting your Home folder using FileVault, by choosing tight security settings in System Preferences, and by locking your Mac with an open firmware password.

Lock Files Against Accidental Deletion

To protect a file against being accidentally deleted, you can lock it. To do so:

1. Activate the **Finder** and navigate to the folder that contains the file.
2. Click the file to select it.
3. Open **File** and click **Get Info**. The Info window for the file is displayed.
4. Select the **Locked** check box.
5. Click the **Close** button (the red button).

When you've locked a file, Mac OS X displays a lock icon at the lower-left corner of its icon. If you try to delete a locked file, Mac OS X displays an error dialog box (as shown here). Click **OK**.

Controlling
Security.doc

To delete the file, clear the **Locked** check box in the Get Info window, and then drag the file to the Trash.

Encrypt Your Home Folder

To help prevent other people from accessing your files, you can encrypt your entire Home folder using FileVault (see "Encrypt Your Home Folder with FileVault" in Chapter 3). After you set a master password for your Mac to ensure that you can recover your files if you forget your own password, FileVault encrypts all the files and folders in your Home folder.

CAUTION

When you log in, FileVault decrypts your files and folders so that you can use them. This means that if anyone else can access your Mac while you are logged in, your files have no protection. It also means that using Fast User Switching can be dangerous: if you leave your user session open while another user works on the Mac, your files remain decrypted (because you are still logged in, although another user is active) and are vulnerable to attack. For this reason, it's best to turn off Fast User Switching if you use FileVault.

Choose Tight Security Settings

The Security sheet of System Preferences offers four options for tightening security on your Mac:

- Requiring a password when waking the Mac from sleep or when the screen saver is running
- Disabling automatic login
- Requiring a password to unlock secure system preferences
- Automatically logging an inactive account out

To tighten your security settings:

1. Open and click **System Preferences**. The System Preferences window will be displayed.

2. Click **Security**. The Security sheet will be displayed (see Figure 8-6).

3. Select the **Require Password To Wake This Computer From Sleep Or Screen Saver** check box to make Mac OS X prompt for a password when anyone wakes it from sleep or interrupts the screen saver.

4. Select the **Disable Automatic Login** check box if you want to prevent any account from logging in automatically.

5. Select the **Require Password To Unlock Each Secure System Preference** check box if you want to ensure that sensitive system preferences are kept locked.

6. Select the **Log Out After *NN* Minutes Of Inactivity** check box if you want Mac OS X to log each user out automatically after they leave the keyboard and mouse inactive for a specified length of time. The shorter length of time you set, the more security this setting offers.

7. Click **System Preferences | Quit System Preferences** to close System Preferences.

Figure 8-6: Choose tight security settings on the Security sheet in System Preferences.

TIP

If you use a password for waking your computer from sleep or for interrupting the screen saver, configure your Mac to start the screen saver after a short interval of inactivity (or by using a hot corner) as discussed in "Pick a New Screen Saver" in Chapter 2, or configure it to go to sleep quickly (see "Set Energy Saver Options" in Chapter 5).

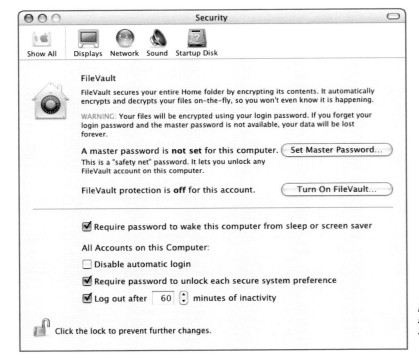

Lock Your Mac with an Open Firmware Password

To prevent other users from using a FireWire disk or a CD to boot your Mac, you can protect it with an "open firmware password"—a password required to start using the firmware (the permanently installed software) on your Mac.

To apply an open firmware password:

1. Insert your first Mac OS X installation CD in your optical drive. A Finder window will open showing the CD's contents.

2. Open **View** and click **As Columns** to switch to Columns view.

3. Click **Applications**, and then click **Utilities**.

4. Double-click **Open Firmware Password**. The first Open Firmware Password window will be displayed.

5. Click **Change**. The Open Firmware Password window shown in Figure 8-7 will be displayed.

6. Select the **Require Password To Change Open Firmware Settings** check box.

7. Type the password in the Password text box and the Verify text box.

8. Click **OK**. Mac OS X displays the Authenticate dialog box.

9. Type your password and click **OK**. The Open Firmware Password application will display a message box telling you that the settings were successfully saved and that they will take effect when you restart your Mac.

10. Open the **Open Firmware Password** menu and click **Quit Open Firmware Password** to close the application.

11. Restart your Mac (for example, click | **Restart**, and then click **Restart**).

Figure 8-7: You can set an open firmware password to prevent anyone else from starting your Mac using a different disk (such as an iPod or other FireWire disk), a CD, or DVD).

After you apply the open firmware password, when anyone tries to start your Mac from a disk other than your regular disk, Mac OS X will prompt for the open firmware password.

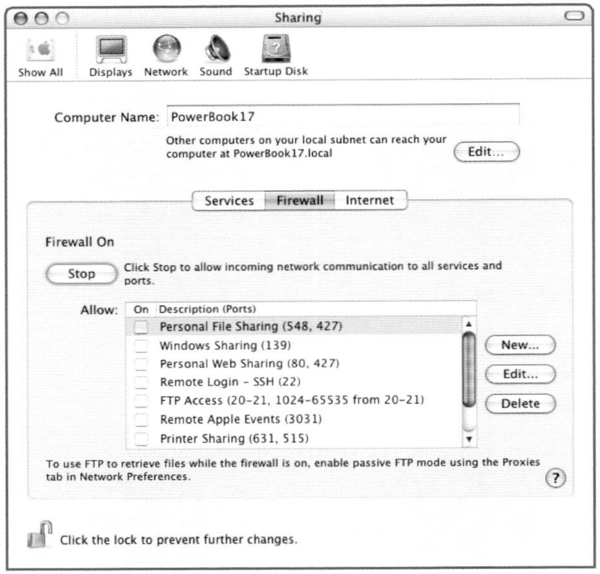

Figure 8-8: On the Firewall tab of the Sharing sheet in System Preferences, turn the firewall on and control the services that can poke holes through the firewall.

TIP

Mac OS X's firewall is usually worthwhile, but it can get in your way both in a local network and with Internet traffic. If, after turning on the firewall, you find that you are having network problems either locally or on the Internet, you may need to turn off the firewall again.

To remove the open firmware password:

1. Insert your first Mac OS X installation CD and run Open Firmware Password.

2. Clear the **Require Password To Change Open Firmware Settings** check box.

3. Authenticate yourself.

4. Open the **Open Firmware Password** menu and click **Quit Open Firmware Password** to close the application.

5. Restart your Mac (for example, click ✿ | **Restart**, and then click **Restart**).

Turn On the Firewall

Mac OS X includes a firewall that you can use to help prevent hackers from getting into your computer while you are online. If your Mac connects directly to the Internet, you should ensure that the firewall is turned on. If your Mac connects to the Internet through a shared Internet connection that already uses a firewall, you probably don't need to turn your firewall on. (For example, many Internet routers and Internet-sharing hardware devices include a firewall.)

1. Open ✿ and click **System Preferences**. The System Preferences window will be displayed.

2. Click the **Sharing** icon. The Sharing sheet will be displayed.

3. Click the **Firewall** tab button (see Figure 8-8).

4. If the readout says "Firewall Off," click the **Start** button to start the firewall.

5. The Allow list box lists the services allowed to open ports in the firewall. You control these services by using the controls on the Services tab (discussed in Chapter 10, "Let Others Access Your Resources"). While you can create new ports by clicking the **New** button, you will seldom need to do so.

6. Click **System Preferences | Quit System Preferences** to close System Preferences.

Chapter 9
Setting Up Networking

Networking is the sharing of resources and information between two or more connected computers—at home, within an organization, or around the world. In this chapter, you will see how to connect to a local area network, or LAN, which is generally confined to a single residence, a building, or a section of a building.

Plan a Network

Mac OS X is a *network operating system* and allows the interconnection of multiple computers for many purposes:

- **Exchanging information**, such as sending a file from one computer to another
- **Communicating**, for example, sending e-mail among network users
- **Sharing information** by having common files accessed by network users
- **Sharing network resources**, such as printers and Internet connections

Networking is a system that includes the connection among computers that facilitates the transfer of information as well as the scheme for controlling that transfer. This is the function of the networking hardware and software in your Mac and the protocols, or standards, they use.

Select a Type of Network

Today the majority of LANs use the *Ethernet* standard, which determines the type of network hardware and software needed by the network, and *TCP/IP* (Transmission Control Protocol/Internet Protocol), which determines how information is exchanged over the network. With this foundation, you can then choose between using a peer-to-peer LAN and a client-server LAN.

PEER-TO-PEER LANS

All computers in a *peer-to-peer LAN* are both servers and clients and, therefore, share in both providing and using resources. Any computer in the network may store information and provide resources, such as a printer, for the use of any other computer in the network. Peer-to-peer networking is an easy first step to networking, accomplished simply by joining computers together, as shown in Figure 9-1. It does not require the purchase of extra computers or significant changes to the way an organization is using computers, yet resources can be shared (as is the printer in Figure 9-1), files and communications can be transferred, and common information can be accessed by all.

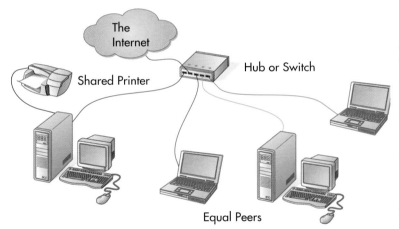

The Internet

Shared Printer

Hub or Switch

Equal Peers

Figure 9-1: In a peer-to-peer LAN, all computers are both servers and clients.

Peer-to-peer LANs tend to be used in smaller organizations that do not need to share a large central resource, such as a database, or to have a high degree of security or central control. Each computer in a peer-to-peer LAN is autonomous and is often networked with other computers simply to transfer files and share expensive equipment or services (such as a fast Internet connection). Putting together a peer-to-peer LAN with Macs is very easy and inexpensive: because all Macs have Ethernet networking built in, you need buy only the cables and the hub or switch.

CLIENT/SERVER LANS

Each computer in a *client/server LAN* performs one of two distinct functions: each is either a server or a client. *Servers* manage the network, centrally store information to be shared on the network, and provide the shared resources to the network. *Clients*, or *workstations*, are the users of the network and are normally desktop or laptop computers. To create a network, the clients and server(s) are connected together, often with additional stand-alone network resources (such as printers), as shown in Figure 9-2.

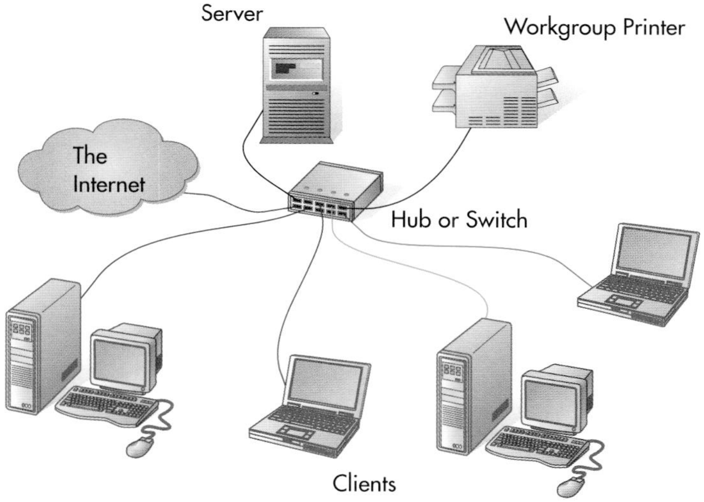

The management functions provided by the server include network security, managing the permissions needed to implement security, communications among network users, and management of shared files on the network. Servers generally are more capable than clients in terms of having more memory, faster (and possibly more) processors, large (and maybe more) disk drives, and special data-storage peripherals, such as high-capacity, high-speed tape drives (for backing up large amounts of data). Servers generally are dedicated to their function and are normally not used for everyday client tasks, such as word processing, spreadsheets, or e-mail. Clients generally are less capable than are servers and, in some cases, may not even have a disk. Clients usually are normal desktop and laptop computers that perform the typical functions of those types of machines, in addition to being part of the network. Clients can also be "mini-servers" by sharing some or all of their disk drives or other resources. The principal difference between peer-to-peer networks and client/server networks is the presence of a dedicated server and the degree to which the network is centrally managed.

Mac OS X is designed to work with Mac OS X Server, Apple's network operating system, to form a client-server network operating environment, with Mac OS X Server performing the server functions and Mac OS X being the client. Mac OS X can also work with other network operating systems, such as Windows Server 2003, Window 2000 Server, UNIX, or Linux.

Figure 9-2: In a client/server LAN, one or more computers are servers and the rest are clients.

Several Mac OS X workstations can operate easily in a peer-to-peer network, either a Mac OS X–only network or one that includes computers running other network operating systems (such as Windows). This arrangement works well for home networks, home-office networks, and the smallest of office networks. Beyond a dozen or more computers, peer-to-peer networks tend to become too complex to perform effectively: the added effort of providing services to multiple computers slows down each peer computer. At this point, a client/server network becomes a better choice, because the server provides the services and centralizes the management functions.

Simple client/server networks, such as those used in many small offices or organizations, may use a single server for all services and management functions. Larger and more complex client/server networks are organized into logical units called *domains* for management purposes, with one or more servers set up as *domain controllers* to run the other servers. In a large organization, a domain-based structure provides many benefits—most importantly, a central registry for all users so that one registration provides access to all the computers and resources in the domain. Domains, however, are very complex and require significant expertise to set up and manage. For that reason, this book focuses on setting up and using a peer-to-peer network and on connecting to shared resources on a client/server network.

Select a Network Standard

Mac OS X supports the two predominant networking standards, wired Ethernet and wireless, additionally offering the option of creating small networks using FireWire. These standards determine the type of hardware you need.

USE WIRED ETHERNET

The wired Ethernet standard comes in several forms based on speed and cable type. These are the three most common standards:

- **10BaseT** provides a network that operates at the regular Ethernet speed of 10 Mbps (megabits, or millions of bits, per second).

NOTE

In the names for the Ethernet standards, 10BaseT and 100BaseT, the "10" or "100" indicates the operating speed in Mbps; the "Base" stands for "baseband," a type of transmission; and the "T" indicates the type of cable required (twisted-pair cable).

TIP

You can connect two Macs directly without a hub or switch by using a *crossover* cable, a special cable that reverses the wires in the cable from their standard arrangement. Some of the most recent Macs are smart enough to be able to use a regular Ethernet cable for a direct connection such as this: the Mac detects that the signal needs to cross over and sends the data to the appropriate wires at its end to implement the crossover.

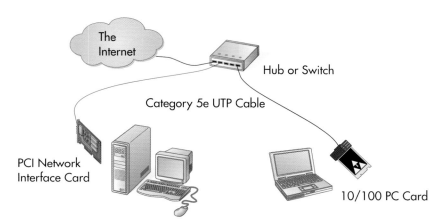

The
Internet

Hub or Switch

Category 5e UTP Cable

PCI Network
Interface Card

10/100 PC Card

Figure 9-3: A wired Ethernet network consists of a network connection on your computer, a hub or switch into which other computers are connected, and a cable connecting the two.

- **100BaseT**, or Fast Ethernet, provides a network that operates at 100 Mbps.
- **Gigabit Ethernet** provides a network that operates at speeds of around 400 Mbps—not the 1 Gbps (gigabit, or billion bits, per second) that its name suggests.

Gigabit Ethernet is used largely in corporate networks that need extremely fast networks. For most home, home-office, and small-office networks, a Fast Ethernet network, or even a regular Ethernet network, is plenty fast enough.

A wired Ethernet or Fast Ethernet network, shown in Figure 9-3, has three major components:

- The **network connection** on your Mac connects it to the network.
- A **hub**, **switch**, or **router** joins several computers together to form the network.
- A **hub**, the simplest and cheapest device, links the computers by using the network equivalent of a telephone party line (everybody can hear everybody else).
- A **switch** is a little more expensive than a hub, but all computers are on the equivalent of a private telephone line. This arrangement allows switches to deliver better network performance than hubs.
- A **router** joins two different networks—for example, joining a LAN to the Internet. Often a router is combined with a hub or a switch, either in a single device or in separate devices, to join several computers to each other and to the Internet.
- An **unshielded twisted pair (UTP)** cable with a simple RJ-45 connector (like a telephone connector, only bigger) joins the network connection to the hub, switch, or router. The most widely used types of UTP cable are Category 5 ("Cat 5") or enhanced Category 5 ("Cat 5e").

Ethernet networks are very easy to set up (see "Set Up a Network," later in this chapter), have become pervasive throughout organizations, and typically cost less than $30 per computer on the network. Because all recent Macs have network connections built in, Macs can be even less expensive to connect to the network than PCs (some of which don't have built-in network connections).

NOTE

Depending on the computer, a network connection may be built into the system board (or motherboard) or installed separately.

WIRELESS LANS

Wireless LANs (WLANs) replace the cable used in a wired network with small radio transceivers (combined transmitters and receivers) at the computer and at the hub or switch. There are several wireless standards at this writing, with further standards being developed to provide faster data transmission and greater security.

The most common standard is 802.11b, which is widely referred to as *Wi-Fi* (wireless fidelity) and provides data transfer of up to 11 Mbps with tolerable security. A newer standard, 801.11g, is quickly gaining popularity because it is five times faster than 802.11b (up to 54 Mbps), is compatible with 802.11b, and is not that much more expensive. Another standard, 802.11a, also offers 54 Mbps speed, but because it's not compatible with 802.11b or 802.11g, it's best avoided.

A WLAN has two components (see Figure 9-4):

- An **access point** is connected to the wired Ethernet network via a hub, a switch, or a router. It uses one or more transceivers to communicate wirelessly with cards installed in or attached to computers using the WLAN.

- An **adapter** is installed in or plugs into your computer and has a transceiver built in to communicate wirelessly to an access point within its range. For laptop computers, built-in adapters are increasingly common (for both Macs and PCs). For desktop computers, adapters are typically either installed in the computer as a PCI card or attached to the computer via USB.

The Internet

Wireless Access Point

Figure 9-4: A wireless network consists of a card in your computer and an access point that is connected to a wired network, the Internet, or both.

Wireless PCI Adapter

Wireless PC Adapter

CAUTION

Lessened security is also a potential downside with wireless networks if they're not configured properly. For example, if you don't turn on encryption and don't force users to use passwords, your neighbor might be able to connect to your network or examine your network traffic. Even with encryption, passwords, and other security turned on, a wireless network is less secure than a wired network. This is because, with a wired network, an attacker must usually have direct access to the physical network to attack it. By contrast, using a high-gain antenna, an attacker can attack a wireless network from a distance—even from several miles away.

NOTE

If your Mac has Bluetooth built in (or added on), you can also use Bluetooth to create a network among Macs. Bluetooth has slow data-transfer rates and limited range, so you probably won't want to use it for networking Macs unless all the other networking options are unavailable—in which case, it will suddenly become much more attractive. Bluetooth is primarily intended for transferring data among personal devices, such as mobile phones and PDAs, or between a personal device and a computer (for example, a Mac).

If the access point is connected to a hub or switch on a wired network, the wireless computers within the range of the access point operate on the network in exactly the same way, except for being a little slower, as they would operate with a cable connection. A WLAN has some significant benefits over a normal wired LAN:

- You do not have the expense of cabling and the even higher expense of installing and maintaining cabling.
- Adding users to and removing them from the network is extremely easy.
- Users can move easily from office to office.
- Users can roam within an area—for example, carrying their laptops to a meeting.
- Visitors can easily connect to the network.

The downside is cost and speed, but both of these considerations are improving rapidly. The cost per computer of a wired network, as noted above, is less than $30; the cost per computer of a wireless network is generally above $40, but this cost is coming down. The speed difference is more significant, not just because of the difference between an 11 Mbps or 54 Mbps access point and a 100 Mbps or faster wired network, but also because of the net rate of dividing the speed of the access point by the number of people trying to use it. Despite these drawbacks, WLANs are enjoying great popularity, with many systems being sold for both homes and offices.

USE FIREWIRE

Instead of wired or wireless Ethernet, you can network Macs quickly and easily by using the FireWire capabilities built into all recent Macs. FireWire allows data transfer at extremely high speeds—up to 400 Mbps for regular FireWire and up to 800 Mbps for FireWire-800, the latest generation of FireWire devices.

The catch is that the maximum length of any FireWire cable is 4.5 meters, or about 15 feet. Even if you use a FireWire hub, all the computers on the network will probably need to be in the same room; and for best results, the number of computers on the network should be small.

SELECTING WIRED ETHERNET HARDWARE

Hardware used in a wired Ethernet network includes a network connection, a hub or switch, and cabling. Many brands are available, with the lower end of the market competing on price. To ensure that your network is reliable and that you can get support when you need it, stick with name-brand products from companies that are likely to be around for a while. Respected brands include Asante (the Apple Store carries various Asante networking products), 3Com, D-Link, Linksys (now a division of networking giant Cisco Systems), and Netgear.

SELECT A NETWORK CONNECTION

All Macs come with an Ethernet network connection built in, so you're unlikely to need to add a network adapter to a Mac. If you haven't identified the jack, look for one that looks like a telephone jack but is wider and is marked with the symbol <...>.

SELECT CONNECTING DEVICES

There are two common connecting devices: hubs, which are like a party-line telephone system; and switches, which are like a private-line telephone system. Switches currently cost almost the same as hubs and run from under $50 for an 8-port switch to under $150 for a 24-port switch. You need a port for each user, but you can plug one switch into another switch to increase the number of ports on your network. If you plan to do this, choose switches that are designed to stack one on top of the other for neatness and for speed (their interconnecting bus is faster than a wire connection).

Continued...

Set Up a Network

When you installed Mac OS X, a full set of networking services was installed and configured using your input (for example, for your Internet connection) and system defaults. These default settings typically provide an operable networking system, enabling you to plug your Mac into an Ethernet network or connect to a wireless network (if your Mac has an AirPort card installed) and start using the network, with a minimum of further configuration.

This section walks you through creating a network using the four means you're most likely to use: wired Ethernet, wireless using an access point, wireless without an access point, and FireWire. It then shows you how to check that your network configuration is working and how to make key changes to it.

Set Up an Ethernet Network

To create an Ethernet network, you need a Cat 5 or Cat 5e Ethernet cable for each computer that will be connected, and a hub or switch with enough ports for each computer or other device that you will connect. Switches deliver faster network throughput than hubs and cost only a little more, so unless you already have a hub or you're squeezing every cent, a switch is a better choice.

If you want, you can leave your Mac running while you connect it to an Ethernet network; if you prefer, you can shut your Mac down first. If you're connecting PCs to the network as well, it's best to shut them down before connecting them.

1. Plug one end of an Ethernet cable into your hub or switch and the other end into your Mac.
2. Repeat the process for each of the other Macs that will be part of the network.
3. Turn on the power for the hub or switch.
4. If you have shut down your Macs or PCs, turn them on.

Set Up a Wireless Network Using an Access Point

To create a wireless network using an access point, you need a wireless adapter in each Mac and an access point. The wireless adapters and the access point must be compatible with each other:

- All Wi-Fi–certified 802.11g products if you want 54 Mbps speeds
- Either a mixture of Wi-Fi–certified 802.11g products and Wi-Fi–certified 802.11b products or all Wi-Fi–certified 802.11b products if 11 Mbps is good enough

INSTALL THE HARDWARE

If the wireless adapters aren't installed in the Macs, install them first. Then set up your access point by following the instructions that come with it. A typical setup process for an access point involves connecting your computer to it using an Ethernet cable so that you can communicate via a wired network in order to configure the wireless network. Configuration typically also includes:

- Specifying the name, or service set identifier (SSID), of the wireless network—often simply a descriptive text name (for example, Wireless1).
- Choosing whether to use encryption. If your access point offers a choice, choose Wi-Fi Protected Access (WPA) over Wired Equivalent Privacy (WEP), an older standard that includes known compromises; but even Wired Equivalent Privacy is better than no encryption at all.
- Choosing whether to restrict the network to a specified list of wireless adapters (identified by their Media Access Control number, or MAC number) or to leave it open to any wireless adapter within range.

QUICKSTEPS

SELECTING WIRELESS HARDWARE

Hardware for a wireless network includes a wireless adapter and a wireless access point.

SELECT A WIRELESS SPEED

For a new wireless network using Macs, you'll typically want to choose the 802.11g standard in order to get the fastest data rate available, 54 Mbps. The faster rate is especially important if you're building a multi-user network, as each computer has to share the capacity with all the other computers on the network at any given time.

If you'll need only to connect to public Wi-Fi networks, such as those in airports and coffee shops, you can get away with the 802.11b standard and its 11 Mbps data rate. However, given that 802.11g equipment can connect to 802.11b networks, 802.11g is usually a better choice—but see the next section for limitations.

SELECT A WIRELESS ADAPTER

Higher-end PowerBooks come with wireless adapters built in. You can install wireless adapters on all other Macs, from iBooks to Power Macs.

Your first choice for a wireless adapter in a Mac should be an Apple AirPort card. There are two types of AirPort cards: standard AirPort cards, which use 802.11b, and AirPort Extreme cards, which use 802.11g. Each Mac can accept either an AirPort Extreme card (in newer Macs) or an AirPort card (in older Macs): You must get the type that fits into your Mac.

Your other option is to install a third-party wireless adapter: a PCI card (in a desktop Mac), a PC Card (in a 'Book), or a USB adapter (on any Mac). Because Apple's AirPort cards have most of the market, the selection of

Continued...

TURN YOUR AIRPORT ON

If your AirPort is off, you can turn it on in either of two ways:

- If the AirPort icon is displayed on the menu bar, click it to open the menu, and click **Turn AirPort On**.

  —Or—

- Open **Internet Connect** (click the **Finder** icon on the Dock, click **Applications** in the Sidebar, and double-click **Internet Connect**). Click the **AirPort** tab, and then click **Turn AirPort On**. Leave Internet Connect open so that you can specify which wireless network to connect to.

CONNECT TO THE WIRELESS NETWORK

When you turn your Mac's AirPort on, Mac OS X will automatically identify wireless networks that it can connect to. To choose a wireless network:

1. If the AirPort icon is displayed on the menu bar, click it to open the menu, and then click the network on the menu.

2. Choose the network in the Network drop-down list on the AirPort tab of Internet Connect. Then open **Internet Connect** and click **Quit Internet Connect** to close Internet Connect.

If Mac OS X prompts you to enter the password for the network, enter it in the Password text box. Select the **Add To Keychain** check box if you want to add the password to your Keychain. Then click **OK**.

SELECTING WIRELESS HARDWARE

(Continued)

third-party wireless adapters with Mac drivers is relatively thin. (By comparison, the selection of third-party wireless adapters with Windows XP drivers is huge.) Generally, an AirPort card is the best choice, especially if you also choose an AirPort as your access point.

SELECT A WIRELESS ACCESS POINT

Wireless access points come in simple versions that plug into a wired Ethernet network and in more sophisticated versions, called "wireless broadband routers," that terminate a DSL or cable Internet connection. When choosing a wireless access point, you can choose between these two types. You can also choose the speed of the access point.

Apple's AirPort and AirPort Extreme cards work with any wireless access point. (You must use an 802.11g access point to get 54 Mbps with AirPort Extreme cards.) But if you're selecting a wireless access point for a Mac network, an AirPort or AirPort Extreme access point is likely to be your best choice, as it is designed to work seamlessly with Mac OS X and with AirPort cards.

TIP

To check the signal strength of a wireless network, see how many black curved bars the AirPort menu icon is displaying: from four bars (for a strong signal, as shown here) down to one bar (for a very weak signal). For a more precise indication, open **Internet Connect**, click the **AirPort** tab, and check the **Signal Level** readout.

The Keychain is a Mac OS X feature that helps you consolidate all the passwords you need for networks and services when you're logged in. After you've proved your identity to your Mac by logging in, Mac OS X automatically stores the passwords you enter so that it can supply them for you the next time they're required. In some cases, such as connecting to a network, Mac OS X lets you decide explicitly whether to add the password to your Keychain. You can manage your Keychain by activating the **Finder**, clicking **Go | Utilities**, and double-clicking **Keychain Access**. This utility lets you lock and unlock your Keychain, change your password, delete items from the Keychain, or specify whether Mac OS X should use an item automatically or prompt you to decide.

CONNECT TO A CLOSED NETWORK

If the wireless network's access point is configured not to broadcast its SSID (for security), the network won't appear in the AirPort menu or in the Network drop-down list box in Internet Connect. Such a network is called a *closed* network. You'll need to know the network's name, security type, and password before you can access it.

1. Click **Other** in the AirPort menu or in the Network drop-down list in Internet Connect. Mac OS X will display the Closed Network dialog box.

2. Choose the type of security (for example, **WEP Password**) in the Wireless Security drop-down list box.

3. Type the network name and the password. (If you've connected to this closed network before, you can select the network in the Network Name drop-down list box. Otherwise, you'll need to type it.)

4. Click **OK**.

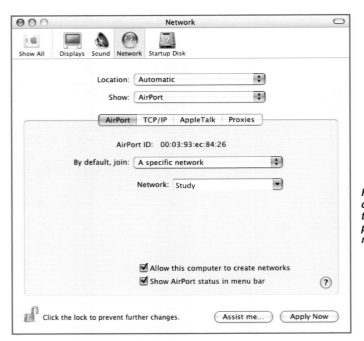

UICKSTEPS

UNDERSTANDING TCP/IP ESSENTIALS

Networking protocols are sets of standards used to package and transmit data over a network. The protocol determines how the information is divided into packets (units) for transmission, how it is addressed, and what is done to ensure it is transferred reliably.

To transmit data between your Mac and another computer, Mac OS X uses TCP/IP, the networking protocol used on the Internet. TCP/IP is a powerful protocol and very complex. Mac OS X makes TCP/IP configuration as straightforward as possible, masking most of the ugly details from your sight. Yet it helps if you understand a few essentials about TCP/IP.

IP ADDRESSES

TCP/IP identifies the different computers (actually, the different network interfaces—more on this in a moment) on a network by using addresses called *IP addresses*. An IP address takes the form of four groups of three decimal numbers separated by periods—for example, 192.168.0.1. The first group (here, 192) defines the largest unit; the second group defines the unit within that unit; the third, another unit within the second unit; and the fourth, another unit within the third. In layperson's terms, each of the numbers can go up to 255. (This is a generalization and ignores some exceptions.)

For identification, each IP address must be unique on the network it's being used on, so each network interface on a network is assigned a different IP address. Most Macs come with several ways to connect to another computer or network: the network connection, the FireWire port, the internal modem, and maybe an AirPort card.

Continued...

SPECIFY A DEFAULT WIRELESS NETWORK

To set your Mac to connect to a particular wireless network by default:

1. Open and click **System Preferences** to open the System Preferences window.
2. Click **Network**. The Network sheet will be displayed.
3. Select **AirPort** in the Show drop-down list box.
4. Click the **AirPort** tab if it isn't already displayed (see Figure 9-5).
5. In the By Default, Join drop-down list box, select **A Specific Network**.
6. In the Network drop-down list box, select the network by name.
7. Click **System Preferences | Quit System Preferences** to close System Preferences.

Near the bottom of the AirPort tab, you can also choose whether to allow this Mac to create networks (see "Set Up an Ad-Hoc Wireless Network," later in this chapter) and whether to display the AirPort status in the menu bar.

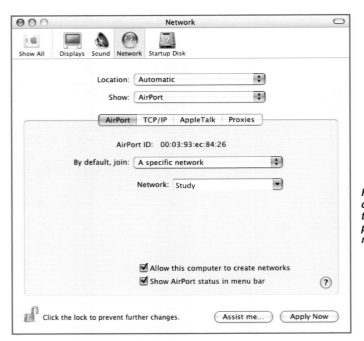

Figure 9-5: You can tell your Mac to connect to a particular wireless network by default.

UNDERSTANDING TCP/IP ESSENTIALS *(Continued)*

You can use two or more connections at the same time, so one Mac can have two or more IP addresses at once. These IP addresses can be on the same network, but they'll typically be on different networks. For example, when your Mac is connected directly to the Internet, it has one IP address on the Internet and another IP address on your local network.

The Internet functions as a single huge TCP/IP network, so each computer on the Internet has to have a unique IP address. When you connect your Mac to the Internet, your ISP assigns it an IP address from the block of IP addresses allocated to the ISP. For a typical dial-up connection, the IP address is *dynamic*, meaning that it is likely to be different each time you establish the connection: the ISP allocates one of the addresses assigned to its modem pool. For a typical broadband connection, the IP address is *static*, meaning that you keep the same IP address all the time (your ISP reserves the IP address for you).

NETWORK ADDRESS TRANSLATION

To reduce the number of computers directly connected to the Internet, many networks use a process called Network Address Translation (NAT). In NAT, one computer (or a special-purpose device, such as a router) is connected to the Internet and has an IP address on the Internet. The NAT computer shares the Internet connection with the other computers on the internal network as required, funneling Internet requests and replies through its IP address. This process is often compared to the mailroom in a

Continued...

DISCONNECT FROM A WIRELESS NETWORK

To disconnect from a wireless network, turn your Mac's AirPort off:

- If the AirPort icon is displayed on the menu bar, click it to open the menu, and click **Turn AirPort Off**.

  –Or–

- Open **Internet Connect** (click the **Finder** icon on the Dock, click **Applications** in the Sidebar, and double-click **Internet Connect**). Click the **AirPort** tab button, and then click **Turn AirPort Off**. Click **Internet Connect | Quit Internet Connect** to close Internet Connect.

Set Up an Ad-Hoc Wireless Network

If you don't have an access point, you can set up an *ad-hoc* or *computer-to-computer* wireless network by using a Mac as a "software access point." This capability means that one Mac starts broadcasting a SSID and other Macs can join the network. Ad-hoc computer networks work well for small numbers of computers, but if you plan to add more than a half-dozen computers to your wireless network, an access point will give you better results.

To set up an ad-hoc wireless network:

1. Turn on your Mac's **AirPort** (as described in the previous section).

2. Select the **Allow This Computer To Create Networks** check box on the AirPort tab of the Network sheet in System Preferences (as shown in Figure 9-5).

3. Display the **Computer To Computer** dialog box or sheet:
   - If the AirPort icon is displayed on the menu bar, click it to open the menu, and then click **Create Network**. Mac OS X displays the Computer To Computer dialog box, which is shown in Figure 9-6 with all its options displayed.
   - Otherwise, open **Internet Connect**, click the **AirPort** tab, and choose **Create Network** in the Network drop-down list box. Internet Connect displays the Computer To Computer dialog box.

4. Type the name for the network in the Name text box.

UNDERSTANDING TCP/IP ESSENTIALS *(Continued)*

building, through which all incoming and outgoing mail is directed.

GETTING AN IP ADDRESS

IP addresses can be allocated either manually or automatically. Manual allocation is handy for some situations, but automatic allocation is the norm for most networks because it is more efficient. Most automatic allocation is performed by a DHCP (Dynamic Host Configuration Protocol) server, either at your ISP (for an Internet connection) or on your local network.

When your Mac detects that no DHCP server is available, it falls back on Automatic Private IP Addressing (APIPA). APIPA assigns an IP address in the address range 169.254.0.0 through 169.254.255.255 and checks that no other computer on the network is using that IP address (and if one is, changes the IP address until it is unique on the network).

NOTE

Mac OS X can't use WPA on an ad-hoc wireless network at this writing, so 128-bit WEP is the best choice for security.

NOTE

You can also enter the password in hexadecimal notation (HEX) if you want to do so. ASCII is easier.

5. Choose the wireless network channel in the Channel drop-down list box. In most cases, the best choice is Automatic (11) unless you know you need to use another channel to avoid conflicts with an existing wireless network.

6. If you want to use encryption (which is usually a good idea), click **Show Options** to display the lower part of the Computer To Computer dialog box.

7. In the WEP Key drop-down list, choose the length of password to use for the WEP key. Choose 128-Bit over 40-Bit (More Compatible) unless a wireless adapter that you'll use on another computer on the network is limited to 40-bit WEP.

8. In the Password and Confirm text boxes, type a password of the length specified by the readout at the bottom of the dialog box: 13 ASCII (regular text) characters for 128-bit WEP, 5 ASCII characters for 40-bit WEP.

9. Click **OK**. Mac OS X creates the AirPort network. If the AirPort icon is displayed in the menu bar, you will see the symbol for an ad-hoc network, as shown here:

You can now join other Macs to the network as described in "Connect to the Network," earlier in this chapter. To tear down your ad-hoc network, click **Turn AirPort Off** on either the AirPort menu or the AirPort tab of Internet Connect on the Mac that created the network.

Computer to Computer

Please enter the following information to create a Computer to Computer Network:

Name: PowerBook17

Channel: Automatic (11)

☑ Enable encryption (using WEP)

Password: ••••••••••••

Confirm: ••••••••••••

WEP key: 128–bit

The WEP key must be entered as exactly 13 ASCII characters or 26 HEX digits.

Hide Options   Cancel   OK

Figure 9-6: Create an ad-hoc wireless network in the Computer To Computer dialog box.

Set Up a FireWire Network

As explained earlier in this chapter, FireWire offers you the option of setting up a small but very fast network among Macs. Because each FireWire cable is limited to 4.5 meters (15 feet), the computers must be physically close to each other, even if you use a FireWire hub to connect two cables and so double the cable length.

If you need to connect only two Macs, all you need is a six-pin to six-pin FireWire cable. To connect three or more Macs, you need a FireWire hub with enough ports and a cable to connect each Mac to the FireWire hub.

CREATE THE FIREWIRE NETWORK

With the Macs running, connect them to each other using FireWire cables. Use a FireWire hub if necessary. If the hub requires power (rather than drawing it from one of the Macs), connect its power adapter.

Then perform the following steps on each Mac in turn:

1. Open and click **System Preferences**. The System Preferences window will be displayed.

2. Click **Network**. The Network sheet will be displayed.

3. Choose **Network Port Configurations** in the Show drop-down list box. Mac OS X will display a list like that shown in Figure 9-7.

Figure 9-7: From the Network Port Configurations list on the Network sheet in System Preferences, you can create a new networking connection using FireWire.

4. Click **New**. Mac OS X will display a sheet for creating a new connection.

5. In the Name text box, type the name you want to use for the network—for example, <u>FireWire Network</u>. In the Port drop-down list box, select **Built-in FireWire**.

A new configuration is for a specific port. You must name your configuration and choose a port.

Name: FireWire Network

Port: Built-in FireWire

Cancel   OK

6. Click **OK**. Mac OS X will add the new network item to the bottom of the list in the list box.

7. Drag the new network item to the top of the list.

8. Click **Apply Now**. Mac OS X applies the changes to your network configuration.

9. Click **System Preferences | Quit System Preferences** to close System Preferences.

Figure 9-8: The Network Status screen on the Network sheet in System Preferences gives you a quick overview of your Mac's network connections.

Change Your Network Configuration

The Network sheet of System Preferences lets you change your network configuration. The previous sections have shown you specific examples of the changes you'll typically need to make in order to implement a particular network (for example, a FireWire network). This section shows you how to get an overview of your network connections, change the order of your network connections, and how to specify which method Mac OS X should use to get an IP address.

Start by displaying the Network sheet of System Preferences:

1. Open **** and click **System Preferences**. The System Preferences window will be displayed.

2. Click **Network**. The Network sheet will be displayed.

GET AN OVERVIEW OF YOUR MAC'S NETWORK CONNECTIONS

To get an overview of your Mac's network connections, open the **Show** drop-down list on the Network sheet and click **Network Status**. Figure 9-8 shows the Network Status screen.

From here, you can:

- Configure one of the connections by either double-clicking it in the list box or by clicking it and then clicking **Configure**
- Disconnect a connection by clicking it and clicking **Disconnect**
- Access a different area of the Network sheet by using the **Show** drop-down list box

CHANGE THE ORDER OF NETWORK CONNECTIONS

If your Mac has established multiple network connections via different network interfaces, you must tell Mac OS X the order in which to use the interfaces.

1. On the Network sheet of System Preferences, click the **Show** drop-down list, and then click **Network Port Configurations**. The Network Port Configurations sheet is displayed. (See Figure 9-7, earlier in this chapter, for an example of this sheet.)

2. Select the check box for each interface you want to make active. Clear the check box for each interface you don't want to use.

3. Drag the items in the list box into the order you want to use them for connecting to a network.

4. Click **Apply Now** to apply your changes.

SPECIFY HOW MAC OS X SHOULD GET AN IP ADDRESS

To specify how Mac OS X should get an IP address:

1. On the Network sheet of System Preferences, click the **Show** drop-down list, and then click **Built-In Ethernet**, **AirPort**, or **FireWire** as appropriate. This example uses Built-In Ethernet.

2. Click the **TCP/IP** tab button (see Figure 9-9) to display the TCP/IP tab.

NOTE

AirPort appears in the Show drop-down list only if your Mac has an AirPort card. FireWire appears only if you've created a configuration for FireWire networking, as described in "Set Up a FireWire Network," earlier in this chapter.

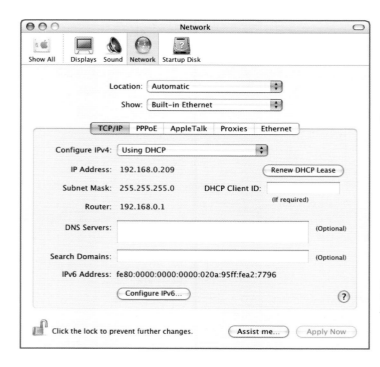

Figure 9-9: Use the Configure IPv4 drop-down list to specify how Mac OS X should get an IP address.

CAUTION

Remember that private ranges of IP addresses work only with computers on their own subnets and with IP addresses from the same range. You can tell what the subnet is from the subnet mask. For example, with a subnet mask of 255.255.255.0, all computers in the network must have IP addresses with the same first three numbers, varying only in the last number. For example, computers with the IP addresses 192.168.104.001 and 192.168.104.002 are on the same subnet.

3. Click the **Configure IPv4** drop-down list and click the appropriate item:

● Click **Using DHCP** to have Mac OS X request an IP address automatically from a DHCP server (possibly your DSL router).

● Click **Manually** to specify an IP address manually. Type the IP address, the subnet mask, and the router details in the text boxes that Mac OS X displays.

Configure IPv4:	Manually
IP Address:	192.168.0.11
Subnet Mask:	255.255.255.0
Router:	192.168.0.1

4. Click **Apply Now**.

After you've finished working on the Network sheet, click **System Preferences | Quit System Preferences** to close System Preferences.

Check Network Interface Status and Connections

To check the status of a network interface or find out if a network connection is working, launch Network Utility.

1. Activate the **Finder**.

2. Open **Go** and click **Utilities**. The Utilities folder will be displayed.

3. Double-click **Network Utility**. Network Utility will open.

You can then use Network Utility as discussed in the following sections.

CHECK THE STATUS OF A NETWORK INTERFACE

To check the status of a network interface:

1. Click the **Info** tab button in Network Utility to display the Info tab (see Figure 9-10).

Figure 9-10: The Info tab of Network Utility lets you check the IP address, link speed, and status for a network interface.

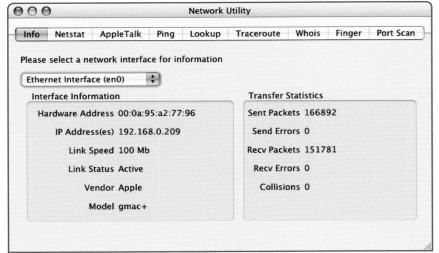

NOTE

Computers start counting with 0 rather than with 1, so your Mac considers en0 its "first" Ethernet network interface and en1 its "second."

NOTE

The link speed shown in Network Utility is the maximum speed of the link. The actual speed you get for data transfer will often be lower.

2. Select the network interface in the Please Select A Network Interface For Information drop-down list box:

- **Ethernet Interface (en0)** is the Ethernet adapter.
- **Ethernet Interface (en1)** is the AirPort card (and will only appear if your Mac has an AirPort card).
- **Ethernet Interface (fw0)** is your Mac's FireWire connection.

3. The Interface Information area displays the following information:

- The **Hardware Address** (also called the MAC, or Media Access Control, address) is an address encoded into the physical network adapter—for example, 00:0a:95:a2:77:96. This address doesn't change.
- The **IP Address** is the IP address currently assigned to the network interface—for example, 192.168.0.209.
- The **Link Speed** is the speed of the network connection in megabits (Mb) per second: 400 Mb for FireWire, 100 Mb for Fast Ethernet, 54 Mb for 802.11g, 11 Mb for 802.11b, and 10 Mb for regular Ethernet (10BaseT).

CHECK A CONNECTION TO ANOTHER COMPUTER

To check a connection to another computer:

1. Find out the computer's IP address. (If the computer is a Mac, you can use the technique described in the previous section).

2. Click the **Ping** tab button in Network Utility to display the Ping tab (see Figure 9-11).

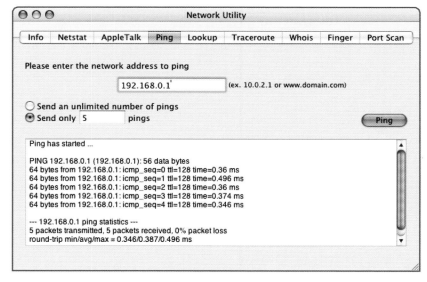

Figure 9-11: Use the Ping tab of Network Utility to test the TCP/IP connection to another computer.

GETTING A BLOCK OF IP ADDRESSES

The block of IP addresses you use with the Internet Protocol depends on whether the computers to be assigned the addresses will be private or public.

GET PRIVATE IP ADDRESSES

If the computers will be operating only on an internal network, they are *private* and need be unique only on the internal network. Four blocks of IP addresses have been set aside and can be used by any organization for its private, internal needs:

1. 10.0.0.0 through 10.255.255.255 (typically used for large networks)

2. 169.254.0.0 through 169.254.255.255 (used for the Automatic Private IP Addressing protocol, or APIPA)

3. 172.16.0.0 through 172.31.255.255 (typically used for medium-sized networks)

4. 192.168.0.0 through 192.168.255.255 (widely used for small networks)

GET PUBLIC IP ADDRESSES

Computers that are connected directly to the Internet are *public* and thus need a globally unique IP number. Your ISP will probably provide the IP addresses you need. For a larger block, you may have to go to one of the three Internet registries:

- American Registry for Internet Numbers (ARIN), at www.arin.net/, which covers North and South America, the Caribbean, and sub-Saharan Africa

- Réseaux IP Européens (RIPE), at www.ripe.net/, which covers Europe, the Middle East, and northern Africa

- Asia Pacific Network Information Center (APNIC), at www.apnic.net/, which covers Asia and the Pacific

3. Type the other computer's IP address in the Please Enter The Network Address To Ping text box.

4. Select the **Send Only *NN* Pings** option button and type a low number (such as 3 or 5) in the text box.

5. Click **Ping**. The Ping utility sends data packets to the specified address and displays its results. The example in Figure 9-11 shows responses from the address that was pinged, with the Statistics section showing that 5 packets were sent and 5 packets received, indicating that the connection is working. If Ping gets no response and the Statistics section indicates a "100% packet loss," you know the connection isn't working.

After you've finished using Network Utility, click **Network Utility** | **Quit Network Utility** to close it.

Chapter 10

Using Networking

Networking brings a vastly enlarged world of computing to your Mac, giving you access to all the computers, printers, and other devices to which you are connected and have permission to access.

Using a network and its resources is no harder than accessing the hard disk, printer, or Internet connection that is directly connected to your Mac. Your network connection can be either wired or wireless. You'll seldom notice the difference between the two, other than that the hardware is different and that a wireless network may perform more slowly than a wired network.

In this chapter, you'll see how to access other computers and printers over a LAN, how to let others access your Mac and its resources, and how to access your Mac remotely, either across a LAN or over the Internet.

10

Access Network Resources

To access files and folders on a network, you typically connect to shared folders, mounting them on your Mac so that you can use them as if they were local folders. You can print on network printers in the same way as you can print on local printers, and you can access the Internet via the network.

Connect to a Shared Folder

To connect to a shared folder:

1. Activate the **Finder**.

2. Open **Go** and click **Connect To Server**. Mac OS X will display the Connect To Server dialog box.

3. Specify the server you want to connect to:

   - The **Server Address** text box contains the address of the last server you used. You can type another server's address over this address.

   - To select a server you've designated as a favorite, click it in the Favorite Servers list. (You can add the server in the Server Address text box to the Favorite Servers list by clicking the **Add Server To Favorites** button.)

   - Click **Recent Servers** and choose a recent server from the drop-down list.

   - If you don't know the exact name of the server, click **Browse** to display a Finder window listing the servers on the network. Double-click the server you want, and supply your user name and password as described in the next two sections.

4. Click **Connect**. Supply your name and password as described in the next two sections. (The procedure is different depending on the type of server sharing the folder you're connecting to.)

CONNECT TO AN AFP SHARE

Follow these steps when connecting to a folder being shared by another Mac. AFP, or Apple File Protocol, is the protocol used by Macs for sharing files with each other.

1. When you attempt to connect to an AFP share, Mac OS X will display the untitled dialog box shown in Figure 10-1. This dialog box offers you the choice of connecting as a guest or as a registered user.

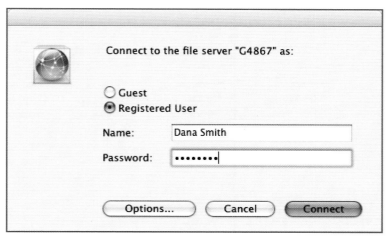

2. If you have a user account with this computer, select the **Registered User** option button and enter your name and password. Otherwise, select the **Guest** option button.

3. If you're connecting as a registered user, click **Options**. The options dialog box shown in Figure 10-2 will be displayed.

4. If you want to add the password for this share to your Keychain so that you don't have to enter it when you connect to the share in the future, select the **Add Password To Keychain** check box. Click **Save Preferences** if you want to save these settings as your defaults. Click **OK** to close the options dialog box and return to the previous dialog box.

Figure 10-1: When connecting to an AFP share, enter your user name and password, and then click Options.

Figure 10-2: Choose options for connecting to the AFP share.

5. Click **Connect**. Mac OS X displays a dialog box listing the volumes you can mount.

6. Choose the volumes you want to mount:

- To select a volume, click it.

- To select a contiguous range of volumes, click the first volume and then **SHIFT**+click the last.

- To select noncontiguous volumes, click the first volume and then ⌘+click each of the other volumes.

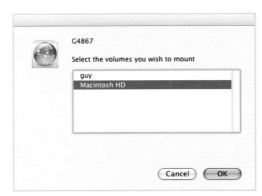

G4867

Select the volumes you wish to mount

guy
Macintosh HD

Cancel   OK

7. Click **OK**. Mac OS X will close the dialog boxes, mount the specified volume or volumes on your desktop, and will open a Finder window showing the contents of the last volume.

Figure 10-3: Mac OS X displays the SMB/CIFS Filesystem Authentication dialog box when you're connecting to a Windows, Linux, or UNIX share.

SMB/CIFS Filesystem Authentication

Enter username and password for ACCELERATED:

Workgroup/Domain
LAUREL

Username
Chris Smith

Password
••••••••

☑ Add to Keychain

Cancel   OK

CONNECT TO A SMB/CIFS SHARE

Follow these steps when connecting to a folder being shared by a Windows computer or a computer running UNIX or Linux. SMB is the abbreviation for Server Message Block and is sometimes called "Samba." CIFS, or Common Internet File System, is a networking protocol for sharing files among computers.

1. When you attempt to connect to a SMB/CIFS share, Mac OS X will display the dialog box shown in Figure 10-3.

2. Change the workgroup or domain in the Workgroup/Domain text box if necessary.

3. Change your user name in the Username text box if necessary. (Mac OS X enters your Mac OS X user name the first time you connect.)

4. Type your password in the Password text box.

QUICKSTEPS

CONNECTING AUTOMATICALLY TO A SHARED FOLDER AT LOGIN

If you always need to connect to the same shared folders, you may want to make Mac OS X connect to them automatically when you log in. To do this:

1. Connect to the shared folder as described in "Connect to a Shared Folder." Save the password for the connection in your Keychain.

2. Open and click **System Preferences**. The System Preferences window will be displayed.

3. Click **Accounts**. The Accounts sheet will be displayed.

4. Click your account in the left list box.

5. Click the **Startup Items** tab.

6. Drag each shared folder from the desktop to the These Items Will Open Automatically When You Log In list box.

7. Select the **Hide** check box for each shared folder you add if you want to prevent Mac OS X from displaying a Finder window showing the folder's contents when it connects.

8. Click **System Preferences | Quit System Preferences** to close System Preferences.

If you find that the above method doesn't make Mac OS X connect automatically to the shared folders, try creating a URL file to connect to the shared folder.

1. Activate the **Finder**, click **Go | Applications**, and double-click **TextEdit** to open TextEdit.

2. Type the URL for the shared folder using this format: *protocol://username:password@server/volume*, where *protocol* is afp or smb (depending on the server type), *username* is your user name, *password* your password for the server, *server* is the server, and *volume* is the shared folder. For example, you would use smb://csmith:secur1ty@accelerated.mshome.net/resource to connect to the shared folder "resource" on the SMB server named

Continued...

5. Select the **Add To Keychain** check box if you want to add the password to your Keychain.

6. Click **OK**. Mac OS X displays the SMB Mount dialog box.

7. Click the **Select A Share** drop-down list and click the name of the share.

8. Click **OK**.

Disconnect Your Mac from a Shared Folder

To disconnect your Mac from a shared folder:

- Drag the shared folder's icon on your desktop to the Trash.

  –Or–

- Click the shared folder's icon on your desktop, open **File**, and click **Eject**. (The Eject command shows the shared folder's name—for example, Eject Public for a shared folder named Public.)

Mac OS X disconnects your Mac from the folder and removes the folder's icon from the desktop.

Copy Network Files and Information

After connecting to a network share, you can access its files and folders in the same ways you access the files and folders on your Mac's hard disk:

- To open a Finder window showing the folders and files on the network share, double-click the icon for the network share on your desktop.

- Drag a file or folder from the network share to your hard disk to copy it there. For example, drag a file to an entry in the Sidebar, and then use the Spring-Loaded Folders feature (see the note under "Customize Finder Preferences" in Chapter 3) to navigate to where you want to store the copy of the file.

- Drag a file or folder from your hard disk to the network share to copy it there. Again, you can use the Spring-Loaded Folders feature to open the folder in which you want to store the copy.

- Double-click a file on the network share to open it using your Mac's default application for that file type. For example, double-click a document file with a .doc extension to open the file for editing in Microsoft Word (assuming Microsoft Word is installed on your Mac).

Print on Network Printers

After connecting to a network printer, as discussed in "Install a Network Printer" in Chapter 6, you can print using the same techniques as for a local printer (see the "Printing" QuickSteps, also in Chapter 6).

Access a Network Internet Connection

If the network your Mac is connected to has an Internet connection, your Mac is automatically connected to it and can use it directly unless it requires a user name and password. In most cases, you can access the Internet by simply opening your browser (click the **Safari** icon on the Dock) or your e-mail application (click the **Mail** icon on the Dock). See Chapter 4 for more information.

Let Others Access Your Resources

The other side of the networking equation is sharing the resources on your Mac so that others can use them. This includes sharing your files, folders, and disks, as well as sharing your printers and other resources, such as an Internet connection.

Share Your Folders

Mac OS X makes sharing your folders with other users as straightforward as possible. The procedure for sharing with Mac users differs from sharing with Windows users. You start both sharing processes, however, from the Sharing sheet in System Preferences:

QUICKSTEPS

CONNECTING TO A WINDOWS COMPUTER

To connect to a folder that a Windows computer is sharing, use the procedure for connecting to a SMB/CIFS shared folder. Before you can connect, however, you must set up sharing on the Windows computer. To make sharing easier, you should also use the Directory Access Utility to tell Mac OS X which workgroup your Mac belongs to.

SHARE A FOLDER ON WINDOWS

1. On the Windows computer, click **Start | My Computer**. A Windows Explorer window will be displayed showing the My Computer view.

2. Navigate to the folder you want to share.

3. Right-click the folder and click **Sharing And Security** on the shortcut menu. The Properties dialog box for the folder will be displayed, with the Sharing tab foremost.

4. Select the **Share This Folder On The Network** check box.

5. If necessary, change the default name in the **Share Name** text box to describe the shared folder more clearly. You must keep the name to 12 characters or fewer; otherwise, Mac OS X will not be able to access it.

6. Select the **Allow Network Users To Change My Files** check box if you want network users to be able to change the files rather than just read them.

7. Click **OK**. Windows will close the Properties dialog box and apply the changes.

8. Open **File** and click **Close** to close the Windows Explorer window.

Continued...

1. Open and click **System Preferences**. The System Preferences window will be displayed.

2. Click **Sharing**. The Sharing sheet will be displayed.

3. Click the **Services** tab if it isn't displayed (see Figure 10-4).

4. Check the name displayed in the Computer Name text box. If you want your Mac to appear on the network under a different name, click **Edit**, type the new name, and click **OK**.

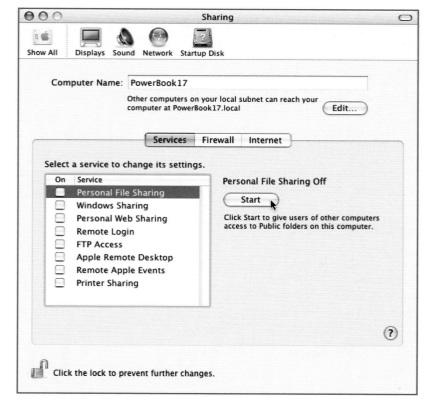

Figure 10-4: The Sharing sheet in System Preferences lets you specify what to share on the network.

SPECIFY YOUR WINDOWS WORKGROUP

To tell Mac OS X which workgroup to connect to:

1. Activate the **Finder**.

2. Open **Go** and click **Utilities**. A Finder window showing the Utilities folder will be displayed.

3. Double-click **Directory Access**. Directory Access will open.

4. Click the **Services** tab if it isn't displayed (Figure 10-5).

5. If the controls are grayed out, click the **Lock** icon, enter your password in the Authenticate dialog box, and click **OK**.

6. Double-click the **SMB** item to display the dialog box shown here:

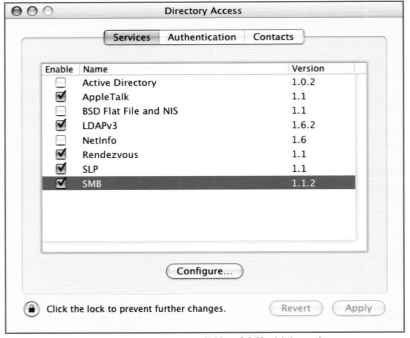

7. Choose or type the workgroup in the Workgroup drop-down list.

8. Click **OK**.

9. Click the **Lock** icon if you want to lock Directory Access again.

10. Click **Directory Access | Quit Directory Access** to close Directory Access.

SHARING FOLDERS WITH OTHER MACS

Mac OS X provides folders specifically for sharing files with other users securely. In each user account that you set up, Mac OS X creates a Public folder that's accessible to other users but that can't be changed by them. By putting files in this folder, which you'll find in your Home folder (~/Public, where ~ is UNIX shorthand for your Home folder) and turning on Personal File Sharing (see the following section), you can provide them to other network users. Each Public folder also contains a Drop Box folder (~/Public/Drop Box) that other users can drop files in, even though they're not allowed to see the contents of the folder (let alone access them).

Figure 10-5: Use Directory Access to tell Mac OS X which workgroup your Mac belongs to.

TURN ON PERSONAL FILE SHARING

To turn on Personal File Sharing:

1. Click **Personal File Sharing** in the Select A Service To Change Its Settings list. (Just click the entry, not its check box. Selecting the check box starts or stops the service.)
2. Click **Start**. Mac OS X makes the contents of your Mac's Public folders available on the network.

Users of other Macs can see your Public folder when they:

1. Activate the **Finder**.
2. Click **Network**. Aliases for the servers on the network will be displayed.
3. Double-click the alias that represents your Mac.
4. In the resulting dialog box, double-click the volume with your name. Mac OS X displays a Finder window showing the contents of your Public folder, including the Drop Box folder (to which users can drag files to make them available to you).

SHARE YOUR FOLDERS AND PRINTERS WITH WINDOWS USERS

To share your folders and printers with Windows users, click the **Windows Sharing** entry (not the check box) in the Select A Service To Change Its Settings list, and then click **Start**. Windows XP users can then access your Mac when they:

1. Open **Start** and click **My Network Places**.
2. Click **View Workgroup Computers** in the Network Tasks pane.
3. Double-click the entry for your Mac.
4. Enter the name and password in the Connect To dialog box, and then click **OK**. The Explorer window lists the shared folders and printers available on your Mac.

Share Your Printers

You can share the printers attached to your Mac with other users of your network. To share the printers with other Mac users:

1. Open and click **System Preferences**. The System Preferences window will be displayed.

TIP

Remember to turn off sharing (click the **Stop** button that replaces the Start button on the Sharing sheet) when you want to stop sharing your folders on the network.

2. Click **Sharing**. The Sharing sheet will be displayed.

3. Click the **Services** tab if it isn't displayed.

4. Click **Printer Sharing** in the Select a Service To Change Its Settings list box, and then click **Start**.

To share your printers with Windows users, follow the procedure described in "Share Your Folders and Printers with Windows Users," earlier in this chapter.

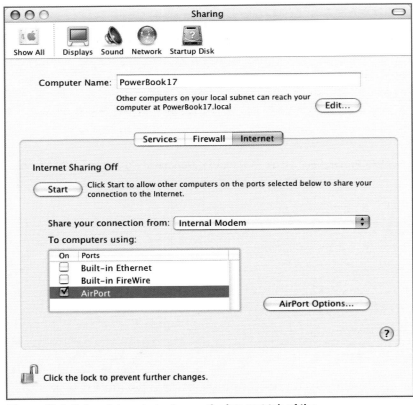

Figure 10-6: Set up Internet sharing on the Internet tab of the Sharing sheet in System Preferences.

Share Your Internet Connection

Chapter 4 describes how to set up a dial-up Internet connection. Once you've made such a connection, you can share it with other computers on the network by using Mac OS X's Internet Sharing feature. You can also use Internet Sharing to share a broadband connection that connects directly to your Mac rather than connecting to the hub, switch, or router on your network. The Mac that runs the Internet connection is called the "host," and the other computers that use the connection are "clients." Both the host and the clients need to be set up independently.

CONFIGURE THE HOST

To configure the host for sharing the Internet connection:

1. Open and click **System Preferences**. The System Preferences window will be displayed.

2. Click **Sharing**. The Sharing sheet will be displayed.

3. Click the **Internet** tab (see Figure 10-6).

4. In the Share Your Connection From drop-down list, select the network connection that you're using to connect to the Internet:

   - Select **Internal Modem** for a dial-up connection.

   - Select **Built-In Ethernet** for a broadband connection connected to your Mac via Ethernet.

10

NOTE

You can select multiple connections in the To Computers Using list box. For example, if you have a combination wired and unwired network, you might select both Built-In Ethernet and AirPort. You can't use the same connection as you're using to connect to the Internet.

NOTE

To stop sharing your Internet connection, click **Stop** on the Internet tab of the Sharing sheet in System Preferences.

5. In the To Computers Using list box, select the check box for each network interface you'll use for sharing your Internet connection with your other computers. For example, select **AirPort** if you'll use an AirPort connection to share the Internet connection.

6. If you're sharing over an AirPort, click **AirPort Options** and set options in the resulting dialog box (see Figure 10-7). You'll recognize these options (for naming the network, choosing the channel, and applying encryption) from the Computer To Computer dialog box (discussed in "Set Up an Ad-Hoc Wireless Network" in Chapter 9). Click **OK** to close this dialog box and return to the previous dialog box.

7. Click **Start**. Mac OS X will display a message box warning you that sharing your Internet connection may disrupt your network settings.

> **Are you sure you want to turn on Internet sharing?**
>
> If your computer is connected to a network, turning on Internet sharing may affect the network settings of other computers and disrupt the network. Contact your system administrator before turning on Internet sharing.
>
> Start Cancel

8. Click **Start**. Mac OS X starts the sharing.

9. If your Mac is configured to go to sleep, click **Energy Saver** and configure it to not go to sleep. (If your Mac goes to sleep, the other computers will not be able to access the Internet through the shared connection.)

10. Click **System Preferences | Quit System Preferences** to close System Preferences.

Figure 10-7: Choose wireless network options if you're sharing your Internet connection via AirPort.

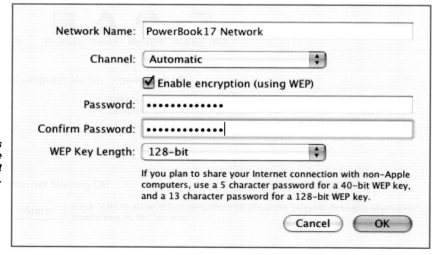

Network Name: PowerBook17 Network

Channel: Automatic

☑ Enable encryption (using WEP)

Password: ••••••••••••

Confirm Password: ••••••••••••

WEP Key Length: 128-bit

If you plan to share your Internet connection with non-Apple computers, use a 5 character password for a 40-bit WEP key, and a 13 character password for a 128-bit WEP key.

Cancel   OK

CONFIGURE THE CLIENTS

To configure each client Mac to use the shared Internet connection:

1. Open and click **System Preferences**. The System Preferences window will be displayed.

2. Click **Network**. The Network sheet will be displayed.

3. In the Show drop-down list, select the item for the connection you're using to share the Internet connection. This example uses AirPort.

4. Click the **TCP/IP** tab button.

5. Click the **Configure IPv4** drop-down list and click **Using DHCP**. This setting will make your Mac request its IP address from the Mac that's sharing the Internet connection.

6. Click **Apply Now**.

7. Click **System Preferences** | **Quit System Preferences** to close System Preferences.

Access Your Mac Remotely

If your Mac is a PowerBook or iBook, chances are that you'll take it with you wherever you might need to use it. But if you have a desktop Mac, you may need to be able to access it when you're somewhere else. Mac OS X provides three ways for you to access your Mac remotely: file sharing, remote login and secure shell (SSH), and virtual private networking (VPN).

Connect via File Sharing

If you've already set up your home Mac to use Personal File Sharing (as described in "Turn On Personal File Sharing," earlier in this chapter), and your home Mac is connected to the Internet, you can access your home Mac remotely by using this feature. Personal File Sharing lets you copy files to and from your home Mac, but you can't run applications or control your home Mac directly.

You'll need to know the IP address assigned to your home Mac's Internet interface, so check this before you leave home. This assumes that your home Mac is connected to the Internet via a broadband connection that remains

---

TIP

Remote access to your Mac is a wonderful tool for getting you out of a jam when you discover, on the road, that you don't have the files you need with you. But remote access often requires you to use slow dial-up connections, the command line, or virtual private networking. If your computing setup that requires remote access consists of a desktop Mac and a PowerBook or iBook, consider storing your documents on the 'Book rather than on the desktop Mac. Network the 'Book to the desktop Mac using FireWire, and you will be able to access the documents at high speeds using the desktop Mac while you're at home. When you take your 'Book on the road, you will have all your documents with you and won't need remote access to your desktop Mac.

connected and that provides a static IP address (one that doesn't change from one session to another).

1. On the remote Mac you're using, activate the **Finder**, open **Go**, and click **Connect To Server**. Mac OS X displays the Connect To Server dialog box.

2. Type your home Mac's IP address in the Server Address text box.

3. Click **Connect**. Proceed as described in "Connect to an AFP Share," earlier in this chapter. Bear in mind that the connection across the Internet will be much slower than a connection over a LAN.

Connect via Remote Login and Secure Shell

If you need to take actions on your home Mac when you're somewhere else, you can do so—but there's a learning curve, as you must use the command-line interface of the Terminal. To connect, you turn on Remote Login on your home Mac, and then use Secure Shell (SSH) from a computer at your remote location.

TURN ON REMOTE LOGIN

1. Open and click **System Preferences**. The System Preferences window will be displayed.

2. Click **Sharing**. The Sharing sheet will be displayed.

3. Click **Remote Login** in the Select A Service To Change Its Settings list.

4. Click **Start**. Mac OS X starts the Remote Login service.

5. Click **System Preferences** | **Quit System Preferences** to close System Preferences.

CONNECT VIA SECURE SHELL

To connect via Secure Shell (SSH):

1. Activate the **Finder**, click **Go** | **Utilities**, and double-click **Terminal**. A Terminal window will open.

2. Type _ssh_ _username@hostname_, where _user name_ is your user name and _hostname_ is your home Mac's IP address or network address ("powerbook.mshome.net"), and press **RETURN**. For example, type _ssh chris@192.168.0.44_ and press **RETURN**. Terminal will display a message telling you that the authenticity of the host can't be established and asking if you want to continue.

NOTE

If your home Mac uses a dial-up connection, connecting remotely via File Sharing will probably require a helper at the home Mac to ensure that it is connected to the Internet at the required time and to tell you the dynamic IP address that your ISP has assigned to it.

TIP

You can connect via SSH using computers that run operating systems other than Mac OS X. For example, you can connect from a Windows, Linux, or UNIX computer.

3. Type <u>yes</u> and press **RETURN**. Terminal will first display a warning that it has added the host Mac to the list of known hosts and will then prompt you for your password.

4. Type your password and press **RETURN**. Terminal will display a login message and a prompt for the remote Mac.

5. Type commands for the Terminal (such as the following), pressing **RETURN** after each command:

   - Use the ls command to list the contents of the current directories.

   - Use the cd command to change directories.

   - Use the scp (Secure Copy) command to copy files from one computer to the other.

6. When you've finished, type <u>exit</u> to end your SSH session.

7. Open the **Terminal** menu and click **Quit Terminal** to close Terminal.

Connect via VPN

Virtual private networking (VPN) uses an insecure public network to handle secure private networking. Most commonly, VPN means using the Internet to connect to a LAN. You can think of VPN as a secure pipe through the Internet connecting computers on either end. VPN replaces both leased lines between facilities and the need for long-distance direct dial-up connections, thus saving considerable amounts of money.

Mac OS X includes the capability to connect to another network by using VPN, but it does not have the capability to host a VPN itself. Your use of VPN is likely to be restricted to calling in to a network that hosts a VPN—for example, a corporate network running Windows. Accordingly, this example uses a Windows computer as the VPN host.

To set up your Mac to connect to a VPN:

1. Activate the **Finder**.

2. Open **Go** and click **Applications**. A Finder window showing your Applications folder will be displayed.

3. Double-click **Internet Connect**.

4. Click **VPN**. The dialog box shown next will be displayed.

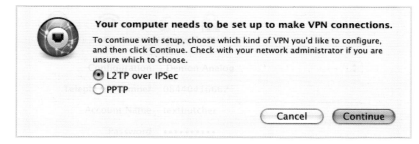

5. Select the appropriate option button, L2TP Over IPSec or PPTP.

6. Click **Continue**. Mac OS X displays the configuration sheet for the connection.

7. Enter the address of the VPN server as a registered host name (such as osborne.com) or an IP address (such as 123.10.78.100).

8. Type your account name and your password.

9. Select the **Show VPN Status In Menu Bar** check box if you want to be able to monitor the VPN's status from a menu-bar icon.

10. Click **Connect**. Internet Connect connects to the VPN server.

NOTE

VPN typically uses either the Point-to-Point Tunneling Protocol (PPTP) or Layer 2 Tunneling Protocol (L2TP). Network administrators prefer L2TP because it's considerably more secure than PPTP. Mac OS X can make VPN connections using either PPTP or L2TP. Ask the administrator of the network you're connecting to which VPN protocol you should use.

11. You should now be able to work on the VPN as if you were connected to its network locally, except that your Internet connection will probably act as a bottleneck, making the use of network resources much slower.

12. After you finish working with the VPN connection, click **Disconnect** in Internet Connect to disconnect the connection.

13. Click **Internet Connect** | **Quit Internet Connect** to quit Internet Connect.

TIP

After you choose L2TP Over IPSec or PPTP, Mac OS X assumes that you'll stick with that choice for future connections. To switch to the other protocol, open **File** and click **New VPN Connection** in Internet Connect.

mouse
   customizing the, 38-39
   keys, 36
   pointer. *See* pointer
   using the, 6
movies. *See* iMovie
moving objects. *See* dragging
multimedia, 81, 143
music
   buying, 149
   composing, 154
   locating Internet, 147
   organizing, 152
   playing, 144-146, 147-148

N

Network Address Translation (NAT), 189
networks
   changing the configuration of, 192-194
   checking the status of, 194-196
   configuring Internet connections on, 208-210
   copying files on, 203-204
   drives for, 4, 56
   FireWire, 182, 191-192
   passwords for, 183, 186-187, 190
   printers on, 133-134
   transferring documents across, 121
   wired, 46, 178, 180
   wireless, 46, 182-183
network share. *See* shared folders

O

operating system, 1, 177
option button, 12, 13, 15
ownership, 59-61

P

passwords
   consolidating with Keychain, 186-187
   e-mail, 4, 82
   firmware, 171-172
   hints for, 160
   iChat, 89
   Master, 62
   network, 183, 186-187
   resetting lost, 163
permissions, 59-61
Personal File Sharing, 207, 210
pictures
   adding to a movie, 162
   copying from the Internet, 80
   creating, 120
   editing, 128-129, 130
   grouping into albums, 129-130
   importing from a camera, 124-126
   sorting, 126-127
ping, 192, 195-196
playlists, 145
   adding radio stations to, 148
   creating, 146
   smart, 152
Plug and Play, 117
plug-ins, 80, 81
pointer, 2, 6
pop-up windows, 79, 80-81
power failure, 112-113
PPP (Point-to-Point Protocol), 70
PPPoE, 34-35
printers
   installing, 131-134
   sharing, 204, 207-208
printing, 136

   changing the order of, 138
   jobs, 138-139
   queue, 138
   specific pages, 136
   to a PDF file, 136
   web pages, 137
processor performance, 112, 115

R

radio, Internet, 147-148
radio button. *See* option button
RealOne Player, 149
Recent Items, 9
recovering files and folders, 48
refresh rate, 28
regional settings, 41-42
registering Mac OS X, 2
remote access, 211-214
removing
   icons, 21, 33
   software applications, 117
renaming desktop icons, 31
resolution, 27-28
Restart, 9, 17
restoring data, 66-67
right-clicking, 6, 7
router, 181, 182

S

Safari, 13, 74-76
   bookmarks, 76-78
   downloading documents with, 122
   History, 79-80
   printing from, 138-140
   setting a home page on, 78
   SnapBack, 80
   starting, 75
   using multiple windows and tabs in, 77